@the entry level

WITHDRAWN

on survival, success,
& your calling as a

the

entry

young professional

level

> michael ball

pure.play.press
los angeles

Published by Pure Play Press, Los Angeles, California.
A Career Freshman Company
www.careerfreshman.com

Pure Play Press books are available at special quantity discounts for bulk purchases. Custom books or book excerpts can also be created to fit specific needs. For details, direct inquiries to pureplay@careerfreshman.com.

First Edition

Publisher's Cataloging-in-Publication Data

Ball, Michael.
        @ the entry level: on survival, success, & your calling as a young professional / Michael Ball.
                p.   cm.
        Includes index.
        ISBN 0-9721566-0-7
        1.   Vocational guidance—United States.   2. Career development.   3. Work—Psychological aspects.   4. Young adults—Conduct of life.   I. Title.
HF5382.5.U5 B35   2003
650.14—dc21   2002092498 CIP

Printed in the United States of America

10 9 8 7 6 5 4 3 2 1

for evie,

look what all that unconditional love and encouragement did.

@cknowledgements

Writing is a solitary business; downright lonely in certain spots. But if I weren't doing this, I sometimes think, I'd probably be playing sycophant to some self-aggrandizing corporate twinkie. Instead I'm kickboxing at the gym in the middle of the afternoon. So this is, gratefully, how I make a living.

Although I don't think you could've really called it that until just recently. For as much as I've sacrificed and as holed-up as I've been to write this book, there's a close group of others in my life who've selflessly carried me through the frustration, the poverty, the rejection, and also those couple of breakdowns. For starters, my amazing grandparents Joseph and Dolores Latzer, who've offered me everything from compassion and support to room and board. No two people, in fact, deserve more credit (or blame, as you might decide) than they do, and even as a wordsmith I strain to convey my gratitude deeply enough. Perhaps I might just leave it at saying I love you, and that you've been true parents to me.

Responsible for just about everything else is my mom (the stuff she'd want to claim, anyway). Had her voice not been on the other end of the phone some days, I honestly doubt I'd have managed to stay clean of all major psychoses, antidepressants, cheating girlfriends, and, um, gainful employment. She even proofread my manuscript. So at the risk of sounding like a mama's boy—and rest assured all proper and healthy boundaries remain—I say that the least of her gifts to me were those 14 excruciating hours of labor; by far, it's been her friendship since.

Speaking of which, there are a couple of guys from college who, for all of my reclusive ways, haven't given up on me. One of them I call my best friend, Raymond Muñoz, and the other I call to do my taxes, Roshan Sonthalia. A people-magnet and a JD / MBA / CPA whiz kid, respectively, they've spent the past year and a half backing my dreams through a merciless salvo of digs, knocks, taunts, and general abuse. Also the occasional meal on the house. I'm forever thankful for their continued friendship, and look forward to our kids beating each other up one day. (Don't think it's all about the 1040's, buddy; there are plenty of ex-Andersen folks who need the work).

Insofar as the actual rendering of this book goes, I first owe a debt of thanks to Ms. Angela Rinaldi, my agent. While I've ultimately started Pure Play Press to bring it to market, she nonetheless got the proposal on all the "right desks" beforehand. Which today, interestingly, don't feel like they would have been very right at all. So here's to retaining all the rights to your writing, and watching New York's elite literati smack themselves on the forehead.

Something I'd be doing myself if I failed to thank both Kalon Gutierrez and Louise Weston for all of their brilliant advice and favors. From her PR strategies and warm words to his insider input and help lining up work, they selflessly stepped in to get me exactly where I needed to be, exactly when I needed to be there. (Why, I still don't know; certainly not for the money, at least, because Kalon even sprung for the coffee).

In addition, I'd like to individually acknowledge several of the authors I lean on so heavily in my discourse, beginning with fellow twentysomething pioneers Alexandra Robbins and Abby Wilner. They're the ones behind *Quarterlife Crisis*, a watershed book toward documenting the after-college condition and supplying some of the credence it so badly deserves. Cheers for priming the pump, and for saving me all that legwork.

Equally influential to my arguments is the labor of Thomas Neff and James Citrin, co-authors of *Lessons From the Top*. This unmatched assemblage of interviews offers a rich brain-picking of business' biggest leaders, from which I, in turn, have plucked here and there to underscore my points and borrow some of the credibility I don't have firsthand access to. As I also did from Lucinda Watson's *How They*

Achieved—a related question-and-answer-style title that skillfully draws on a more eclectic swath of CEOs, entrepreneurs, and visionaries. I'm obliged to all.

I would certainly be remiss, as well, if I didn't extend my appreciation to Joanne Ciulla for her groundbreaking book, *The Working Life*. Not only did this tome serve to inform and guide my discussion, but it even acted as a backdrop against which to understand my own corporate experiences. It's really the most thoughtful, academic treatment I've ever seen of the subject, and I'm floored by its comprehensiveness and honesty.

Still, no author has informed and shaped my beliefs more than Dr. Mark Albion, whose provoking *Making a Life, Making a Living* helped me realize that I could, in fact, do it my way and actually make it work. (Plus that it ought to work for something bigger than just me). I hope I've suitably taken handoff of the baton, and expanded on some of his thoughts with acumen and principle.

Yet no author has helped to fashion my scribblings more than P.J. O'Rourke, my personal deity of the written word. This journalist, of untold genius and wit, is far and away the most wry, fearless, and original penman I've ever had the privilege of reading, equally inspiring awe and respect and the purchase of a really good dictionary. My secret wish is that, after looking this work over, he'll agree to have lunch with me. Oops, secret's out.

Finally, I say thank you to God, as I try to most nights. Without faith, I've learned, it's pretty hard to take the smart risks that make life so worthwhile. Like, say, quitting your job to go write a book. But I don't believe He puts it in us to want anything that's not, in the end, right for our souls—no matter how much it may hurt along the way. So I honor the star over my head, and trust that I've put His gifts to their intended use here. Actually, I'll let you be the judge of that first; God, I imagine, will let me know when He's ready.

contents

introduction

1 wherefore and where to?

2 found & lost

on becoming a professional

3 who moved my life?

4 the last rite of passage

on survival & success

@only what you learn

6 branding the bottom

survival by subject III
dancing the dance

7 all the spinning plates

on to your calling

8 what gets you up in the morning?

I@introduction

wherefore and where to?

caught in the draft

How do you want to be remembered? What do you want to look back on your life and see? It's a heady subject to begin a conversation about entry level work, I know, or to even broach at all. And that's the problem.

Only the most romantic young professionals think in this direction when choosing their first several jobs, with everyone else much more concerned about money, prestige, advancement, designer footwear, and the like. No time for highbrow idealism when there's all that to be had—and some of it on sale. So they leave the wind to contend with the windmills.

Their career paths, too. As long as the draft carries enough stuff along with it, the wide majority is also usually content to let themselves be haphazardly blown about the corporate landscape. Wetted finger to the sky and double-talking recruiter on the phone, if the position looks sexier, pays better, and in general makes for more impressive wordplay among associates and disinterested others, then away they go.

And what's the rationale, anyway, among those purposeful few with their feet defiantly planted in unknown organizations and un-regarded positions? What are they doing allowing the weighty brand names to gust past their résumés, obstinately clutching on to a salary that nearly qualifies as debris? Doesn't the raw satisfaction of "bigger, better, more" hold universal sway? I mean, doesn't everyone eventually want overpriced art and well-educated people to fearfully agree with them?

Not that anyone is seriously listening to the noises coming out of the entry level, of course. As you know only too well—and as this book will finally expose—the life of an early-stage grunt is mindless, laborious, and absent of the "work hard – play hard" glamour that company reps vend at career fairs with an I'm-getting-paid-to-believe-this kind of manufactured verve. Turn left, turn right, turn around, it's inescapable during the first several years in the labor market, which means that even the high-intentioned bunch is pushed down like all of the other misled degree-holders with sore knees and sorer egos. But you'd never know it to look at them.

They stand tall in a work that they enjoy and feel good about doing, even if not everyday. Sure, like all other enterprising entry levelers, the laborers in this clique still look for the loftier title and larger paycheck; there *is* a certain mystique to that supple, over-sized leather chair at the head of the boardroom table, after all. But they'll only slide their way up there when those coups have a meaning beyond their otherwise grubbing roots.

Understanding what is and what isn't sustainable over the long term, they recognize that far sooner than later the money's going to grow old and the corporate demands grow stronger, and sense that they've got to have something to get them out of bed every morning for the rest of their professional lives. If not a work that embodies their hopes and values as a person, then what?

If you close this book with only one message echoing in your head, let it be this: YOU'VE GOT TO LOVE WHAT YOU DO FOR A LIVING. Love the work itself. No amount of cash, realize, will ever finance an intrinsically poor job; no vaunted corporate rank will ever compensate for the debilitating pull of a bottomless vocation; no outside interest or personal relationship will ever act as a found surrogate for a lost career; no over-the-top lifestyle maintained for appearances will ever endure for long before degrading into an over-the-edge existence clung to out of panic and desperation.

Passion for your profession is the only genuine means for continuous growth and lasting fulfillment, and the realization of your complete and true *raison d' etre* hangs in the balance of you reaching your dreams. It is your mission as an early-stage worker, then, to begin the search for your calling, and the mission of this book to help you get there. This is what it's all about. This is what those ridiculed souls have carried inside of them all along, silently pocketing the offhand remarks of the outspoken masses—who they already see glimpsing a mirror one day, and having absolutely no idea what to say to themselves. With no one to pay for an answer.

But, again, there's not much to be said for anyone at the corporate entry level. In this world, you're a freshman once more—a *career freshman* with all the rights and privileges pertaining thereto, including your company's disinterest, disrespect, and sometimes outright disdain. So in order to reach the work you were made to do, you first have to scrap your way through the work they make you do. My goal is to help you fight that good fight in pursuit of your dreams: dispelling the myths, whispering the tricks, and validating your feelings and fears.

The plain and painful fact of the matter, to confirm your hunches, is that your first few positions out of college (spanning any number of years) will in all likelihood be knockdown, drag-out fights with your companies and with yourself; you may not last six months at a job. I hope to give you the tools to make each experience as valuable and worthwhile as possible, and to inspire you to take your next step in line with your heart.

Whether or not this is a message that's personally resonant or even terribly relevant right now, it's critical that you start thinking about it regardless—to use as a touchstone when evaluating whatever else you read, hear, or experience with regard to your work. As we'll discuss throughout the book, the obsessive seekers of professional passion also tend to be the happiest, best-rounded, most successful people (financially and otherwise) living among us, resilient to even the roughest of occupational squalls. And I, personally, would be derelict in my duties as an entry level survivor if I only told you how to beat the game, but I didn't challenge you to think about why you're even playing it to begin with.

on your way

Along the journey of finding your calling as a career freshman, you travel a three-stage path, which this book is designed specifically to guide you through. And it all begins with one of the most difficult and complicated transitions you've ever faced: BECOMING A PROFESSIONAL.

This is the period where you finally confront that long-awaited—but surprisingly poorly considered—departure from college, seek out an understanding of what's shifted in the working world, and then cope with those losses as you firmly reestablish your identity. You'll also grind through the Entry Level Rite of Passage during this phase, requiring you to drag your expectations back down to sea level, swallow your pride (without choking), and pay your dues—but pay them *intelligently*. It's doable, if demeaning, when you walk the line properly, and I give you the rulebook here that they neglected to stuff into your orientation packet. (Which you, naturally, would have mailed back after opening).

Indeed, the workplace for America's corporate young is mostly about servitude and subdued acceptance until you understand things well enough to spin them to your advantage, making SURVIVAL & SUCCESS the second leg after the corporate changeover. In all probability, you'll continue to volley regularly over the two levels of achievement, just as your boss commonly oscillates between being intentionally misleading and doing it without trying.

For the downswings, you will first need a finely tipped understanding of how to manage your manager, cope with your coworkers, and maximize your mentors; those good only at working with numbers, in the end, generally become one. Also the case if you don't see how to demonstrate your initiative with a keen political sensitivity, remain properly accountable for both your wins and losses, and consistently deliver a top quality product before it needs to be. Learning myself by agonizing counterexample, I'm mercifully now in a position to offer you my time-tested SURVIVAL BY SUBJECT layout, showing you tug-by-tug just how to pull your bootstraps up to the next level. Plus how to stitch them back together when they inevitably snap apart.

Once you get the day-to-day down, you'll then be prepared to effectively leverage the upturns: establishing your distinctive professional presence, wresting away the competitive advantage from peers, and in general glittering and sparkling. Specifically, I'll teach you how to construct a strong personal brand, commit to a philosophy of ravenous and endless learning, and carve out a professional and personal balance—not only giving you a taste of triumph, but also showing you where your skill sets best match your heart.

Now stable and humming, it's time to progress to the last and most fundamental stage of the entry level: YOUR CALLING. Here I push you to grow a deep understanding of your values, uncovering the roots beneath your dreams, improving the certainty with which you make your working decisions, and illustrating the smart risks that will define the zigs and zags of your professional path. Tactically, strategically, and psychologically, you'll finally be ready to graduate once again; except this time into a passionate and rewarding career.

As you should have from the start. Because when everything's said and done, meaning is really all you've got left—and waiting until midlife to start looking for it doesn't seem to work very well. At least not for the millions of gray, saggy corporateers who wish they had those 20 years back.

found & lost

a discovery...

College is one of the most fantastic and enduring times of your life. It's a way of living and being that you only get to experience once—and only for a handful of years—but that shapes you as a person and fills your memory for decades to come. Before we really get started, take a moment to think about all of the amazing circumstances and nuances that made up your undergraduate world:

- Familiar, smiling faces abounded, and a host of quick hellos, hugs, hand slaps, and head nods accompanied most any walk to class or the library. You had an instant social network (just add beer).
- Days could be scheduled as you liked, making sure there was a two- or three-hour break in between lectures for a leisurely lunch, and maybe even some past-due reading. Well, definitely lunch.
- Studies were new and challenging, as you began to think about things you had no conception of just a few months before; "ah-has" came in floods.
- Classes were shared with the most colorful assortment of individuals you'd ever seen, who regularly spouted out comments

and opinions that astounded you—often the ones you sus-
pected couldn't claim ownership of a single clarified thought.

- You learned exactly how to work the system, knowing just
  what to study, just when to show up to class, and just what to
  say to tease those two or three midterm questions out of a professor. You were a master of the universe.

- There was a new kind of freedom you experienced when
  you noticed for the first time that absolutely nobody was
  watching you.

- That feeling was matched only by the incredible sense of belonging you felt when you first realized that there *are* other
  people like you in the world.

- You had complete control over your essays and assignments,
  taking whatever stance you felt suited the task at hand.

- And when you participated in project teams, you struggled
  to find agreement on much of anything except that you absolutely couldn't work with each other.

- No friend or acquaintance, even in the briefest passing, escaped inquiry into the easiest electives, because you *had* to
  have that throwaway class each term.

- Meaningless theories were memorized by the stack, as you
  did your best to regurgitate them accurately and with conviction on exam day—after which time you had to look at your
  transcripts to even remember the name of the class.

- You fought valiantly not to doze off during those 8 a.m. lectures; that is, when you actually made it to the battle.

- Time belonged to everyone but you, as there was always
  something to study for or do.

- Still, your future spanned in front of you infinitely, just
  glistening.

- You had almost no money, and were about as happy as you've
  ever been in your entire life.

When else is there always such a purpose and excitement to the
day, where you've barely slept, have a dozen things to juggle, survive

only by virtue of adrenaline and caffeine, and can't possibly imagine slowing down? When else is there such a closely held goal among such a diverse group of people, all of whom share a silent but understood unity? When else does something or someone new tumble into your life practically every time you step outside your door? Indeed, college is an adventure unlike any other you'll ever experience. And not that your body could handle another go-round.

...and a deception

This remarkable escapade crescendos with deceptive subtlety, and your working life easily settles in. In the beginning, the transition is filled with anticipation and novelty: new things to learn, new places to travel, and plenty of new people to meet—all to be financed by your hearty corporate cash flow. There's also a wonderful and unfamiliar freedom from constantly having to study something, and the prospect of just doing nothing with your evenings for a while is provoking. The new responsibilities coming your way further seem to befit your stature as a graduated professional, and a sense of zeal and haste precedes each untaken step. Yes, this is just the next stage in the incredible journey that's become your life.

And then something happens:

- You report to a manager, generally far less intelligent than he supposes, who wields a disproportionate amount of control over your work, your time, and your future.
- That once-limber schedule is now locked firmly into place—a sunless place—during which time you typically stay within a 100-yard radius of your cubicle. Casual absences are anything but.
- A new caution must be exercised with respect to what you say, when you say it, and whom you say it to—as you cultivate a delicate taste for shoe leather.

- There are clear but unspoken political dictums dealing with power and advancement in your company, which you really should've been aware of before walking in. What, nobody told you?
- Your work is unreachably below your level of competence, yet you're jawboned into a numbing patience, trading in challenge and stimulation for gruntwork and migraines.
- Your performance with this menial drivel, nonetheless, is completely dissected, with the only throwaway now being your boss' regard for your opinion.
- Attempts to push for better assignments are met with frowns, and attempts to prove your intelligence met with laughs. The tricks in your college bag turn against you, as the universe looks to have reassumed the mastership role.
- The more effort you invest, the more consistently you feel overlooked and under-appreciated by middle management; top administrators neither know nor care that you breathe within their walls and steal their pens.
- It's expected that you'll fraternize with coworkers after business hours and mingle with company brass at firm-sponsored gatherings, all in hopes of securing your footing on that next rung up.
- While the pocketbook is reasonably stuffed, you take less pleasure in buying things than you thought you would—though that still hasn't slowed you down much.
- Practically every position you come across seems to be more exciting and rewarding than yours, and you even feel a little fraudulent for taking a job completely unrelated to your undergraduate degree.
- You begin to think about the meaning of life—ad nauseaum—wondering how and where you fit into the world.
- You feel lost and scattered as you try to uncover the kind of work you're interested in doing.
- Your career decisions, however, feel like they have in-stone consequences that may forever prevent true happiness.

- All at once pressured by parents and peers to keep pace with the Fortune 500 pack, the temptation to ashamedly bury your dreams underneath your paycheck is overpowering.
- You discover that your vitality for life is slowly draining from you, as it gets more and more difficult to wake up for work each day.

With no warning signs after four or five successful and fulfilling years, the world falls on top of you at the entry level, just when you were sure it was the other way around. Blindsided by frustration, uncertainty, and deep disappointments, most career freshmen are quick to realize they know frighteningly little about achieving success as a hamstrung corporate laborer. And even less about finding fulfillment as an inexperienced adult. And next to nothing about how to not make everything worse. As a result, far too many feel alone and isolated with their worry and confusion, struggling silently through the early years of post-college twentyhood.

I know I did—in a way that I had never come to grips with anything before. So why have I chosen to revisit a period of life that I, myself, barely made it through? My story, I think, will help you better understand why you're reading this book today.

my promise

My chest was constricted. I could hardly breathe. The incessant knocking of the machine was trumped only by the furious pounding of my heart. Here I was, strapped down and locked into a coffin-sized MRI chamber, contemplating my own mortality at the age of 21. Drenched in sweat and dizzied by the surreal experience, I vowed that cancer wasn't going to end it here. I wouldn't let it.

On the car ride home, though, I came unglued. My steadfast strength and resolve had managed to pry itself free just as I was doing the same from the hammering contraption that stole my oxygen. But the tears didn't come because I was scared of the pain, or for fear of any of the other hardships that this type of ordeal brings; I wasn't even really afraid of dying. No, I broke down when I realized that this affliction might take me away before I could start a family.

I wasn't considering what job I may never have, or what kind of car I may never drive, or what size house I may never live in. I was just thinking about what it would mean not to ever be a husband or a father or a grandfather. I'd never before (or since) experienced such a deep and painful sadness, and pledged at that moment I would lead my life with value and richness if I were allowed to survive.

And after another gut-wrenching year of testing, poking, prodding, and medical head-scratching, the doctors finally decided that the then-walnut-sized lump on my neck was benign. I cried again.

I knew that God had heard my promise and not only mercifully endowed me with continued life, but with one of the rarest, most blessed gifts in the world—perspective. The fight I was now facing wasn't biological, but rather philosophical: With the chance that I've been given, how do I craft my life around my values and priorities? How do I lead with my heart, and allow my deepest personal goals and professional dreams to be with me everyday? This was such a momentous realization to have been given at such a young age that I knew I had to do something important with it; the question was *what*.

Several months afterward—now comfortably into my senior year of college—corporate recruiters descended like locusts upon the UCLA campus, and I began brushing over the options I was pelted with. The intensity of my trial and urgency of my calling had faded quietly into the details of life over that time (as those types of experiences tend to do), and I was once again seduced by the allure of Big Business, just as dumb-facedly as prior to noticing that fateful protrusion while smoothing out my day-old stubble. After all of the sobbing and heartache and pious vowing, I was ready—eager—to take ranks doing work that resembled little of what I had dreamed, but instead what I had been sold. And sold hard.

I secured interviews with most every company I was interested in, and was strongly leaning toward going into consulting for one of the Big Five (now Four). Even then had you cornered me and really pushed for a compelling reason why, I probably wouldn't have been able to give you one. The work seemed fairly interesting, the money was good, and the organizations offered solid nameplates. In spite of everything, what else could I really expect? Besides, it's what I *should* want—you're not supposed to ask why.

But something inside of me disobediently was. Adamant to make its point, my body pushed a familiar queasiness further through its passageways with each successive round of interviews I made it through; it was all I could do, in fact, to hold down my final $200 in-house luncheon, compliments of my first-choice company. Forcibly convincing myself it was my nerve-riddled stomach protesting the lightly brazed salmon rather than my heart protesting its heavy-handed mistreatment, I choked down their eventual offer and excused myself from the job-hunt table as the envy of my friends.

Perhaps they wouldn't have been quite as enamored, though, if they enjoyed the same kind of sleep I did in the months leading up to my office debut: I was haunted by regret and doubt, both of which visited me bedside just about every evening with true Dickens flair. What had happened to the promise I made to myself—and to God—such a short time ago? What about finding a true way to pursue my real passions and goals in life? Was this really it? Was this what I was hyperventilating about in that claustrophobic MRI machine?

Shortly before I started with the firm, I met one of my group's managers for dinner at a local brewing-company restaurant, looking for an early inroad and desperate for some validation of my decision. It was uncommonly bad timing, however, as I had just gone in for routine blood work that day (which I'm yet to find anything routine about), and it left me feeling even more frazzled and exhausted than what had become my norm. Being in the hospital environment again also brought back some dark and intrusive memories, which were enjoying themselves thoroughly playing darts with my attention on shoptalk.

And after a while it all built up—fatigue, frustration, disorientation, whatever other sensations I can't put a name to—and abruptly gave way, as I cut off this captain of industry mid-sentence in what became a compelling need to share my deeply personal story with a near stranger. I never really spoke about it much to anyone, so my choice of candidates was intriguing; in retrospect, I can see that it was a classic test. Notwithstanding, I meticulously unloaded my cancer scare experience onto this entirely unprepared audience, surprising even myself by the detail with which I revealed the emotional and physical rigors I had gone through, and the life-changing realizations that had arisen out of the ashes.

When I finished, I sat back in silence to watch his reaction. How would the Big Five, as personified by this neatly kempt and potbellied man, relate to its newest employee on such a personal level? I was clearly plunging my shovel into unbroken ground here, as you well know this type of thing just isn't done in the stoic, unfeeling corporate world—especially by someone who hadn't yet set foot in the door, and who was still liable to get his offer rescinded.

With pursed lips, this waylaid manager first ran his finger uneasily along the inside of his blue and white striped Ralph Lauren shirt collar, stretching it out an inch or so to let in some extra air (which seemed to elude everyone when it came to this matter). Beginning with a fractured smile—and an immediate order of another drink from the hostess fortuitously ambling by—he did his best to string together a hopeful collection of encouraging words. Which, of course, was right before he retreated into the particulars of an upcoming engagement just as soon as he saw the opening.

It was exactly what I expected. Whereas a fellow collegian or professor would have surely offered their wisdom and heartfelt encouragement, my new associate couldn't close the topic fast enough. In all fairness, it was a jump-in-the-alleyway approach; still, his response was characteristic of the distant, uncommitted attitude shared by most business professionals, and I frankly saw nothing professional in it. If I'm going to commit myself to working with this guy for 10 or 12 hours a day, I thought, isn't this the least I can expect? It was all part of my expansive naïveté, of course, and we parted uncomfortably not long thereafter. I was certain I had sabotaged any chance of keeping my job. Which, I suppose, is what I was subconsciously trying to do.

But I was mistaken. For a long, defeating time. In fact, I couldn't seem to get anything right until the do-no-wrong dot-com boom finally lured me to a promising-looking Silicon Valley startup company. Hungry for some excitement, fulfillment, and most importantly an escape from the humiliating and hellish grind that had become my daily life, I believed that playing for a smaller team would provide me with a bigger role, and perhaps even allow me to do some of the work I was only allowed to make photocopies of as a prestigious consultant. Just as significantly, I also believed that I understood the founders, and so badly wanted to clutch onto a mission that I could feel good about—even if it extended only as far as improving Internet usability. I obviously wasn't going to change the world there, and I knew that the job, at best, only weakly resounded with my beaten and neglected self-promise; but it did feel like a step in the right direction. Frankly, it was that or wait for the threat of another disease, which no doubt was already well on its way.

So I piled my things into my car and began the 400-mile journey north, without even an apartment to dump them in once I got there. Taking Pacific Coast Highway at over 90, I felt the blood course through my veins again, as if for the very first time. And as I tasted the salt from the foaming ocean spray and reddened under the rejuvenating burn of the sun, I remembered what it was to be alive and decided to stay there. Reflecting on the unrecognizable person I had become since leaving UCLA—the place that defined me when I first realized I needed defining—I understood that I alone now owned my identity, and what became of it couldn't be left to a company.

Which, of course, is exactly what I did. Not six months later was I grappling with nearly the identical issues I faced back home: suffering through brainless drudgery (except now of the unprofitable upstart variety), regularly spending umpteen hours a day at the office, and completely neglecting my own physical and social health. Further frustrated by my failed attempts to uniquely position myself in the organization—completely at a loss for how management confused ambition with distraction—I began to feel intense loneliness and confusion. What did I just uproot my life, however barren and insupportable, to do? Had I actually only made a long-distance jump from the frying pan?

Even worse, my aging promise to myself was now all but dead, and thoughts of being trapped doing this kind of empty work for the next 30 years plagued me. It wasn't long before I scarcely had the energy or will to pull myself out of bed in the morning—exhausted like once before, but now by the intense self-scrutiny I put myself under. Wondering if I wasn't too *young* for all of this, I nonetheless wrestled violently to find some rhyme or reason as to why I couldn't find success, much less happiness, in this overwhelming post-college life. I had lost myself. Again.

In the midst of this profound disappointment, though, my survival instincts were still strong, and I knew that I had to make another change to keep going. But my outlook was scalded—not unlike a burned tongue that makes even the sweetest foods taste dull and uninteresting—and it left me unsure of where to turn. Doomed to repeat history it looked like, I again decided to open up to a senior colleague, but this time who I at least already shared a decent rapport with.

Supported by a far more welcoming atmosphere than my first confession, I expressed to her everything I'd been thinking and feeling, musing how even with the slimmed down company (I was one of only four layoff survivors from a department of 20), I still couldn't carve out a good niche for myself. I admitted how my earlier plans to go back to business school didn't feel like the light at the end of this black tunnel I was in, and how I simply didn't know what to do to shake the general dissatisfaction and uncertainty that had settled over me. And what she proceeded to say—in the calmest and most measured of tones—changed me forever:

"Well, Michael, welcome to the entry level."

It was uttered with such a disarming matter-of-factness that it left me speechless, as if I'd just been socked in the gut. Reeling, I was at first indignant; how dare she be so dismissive! But then, slowly, my righteous offense unveiled to reveal something else... An epiphany:

Of course, this happens to everyone!

In a blinding flash of the obvious, I realized that what I was going through is exactly what so many people at this stage of life experience. While this may have been my own special version of it, there were themes to my life that pervade the existences of almost all young professionals: my disillusionment, my indecision, my search for a calling and passion—it was all so natural!

The question, then, became how could a condition so common be so poorly communicated to and understood by those going through it? Not once did somebody breathe a straightforward word of warning to me about this transition from college to work (none that I found worthwhile enough to pay any consideration, at least), to say anything of credible advice about what to actually do to make it successful. Had it not been for the blunt and unwitting candor of a coworker, chillingly, I may have floated for years longer in coming to many of the realizations I've since arrived at. So what about the millions of early-stage workers who sink even faster than I did, wanting for the sharp tongue of truth to explain what it is that they actually see in front of—or, more accurately, underneath—them?

This is why the clandestine life of the career freshman can remain a secret no longer. Bruised and scraped and having waited too long, I finally present this tribal knowledge to everyone, giving the unsteady days of early gruntwork the credence they deserve and the clarity they call for. There's information being wrongly held from the ears and messages being blindly kept from the hearts of young professionals; I write this book to share these untold perspectives. I write this book to present entry levelers with tangible and meaningful insights that will engender a real sense of personal control. I write this book to offer a powerful, expositive, and dissenting voice in the dominant social dialogue. But most of all, I write this book to now fulfill my overdue promise. And all the while it's been to you.

II @on becoming a professional

who moved my life?

where *am* I?

I dentity is a funny thing. It rests so precariously on what we do, where we are, and whom we have in our world at any given point, yet it's the bedrock for how we see ourselves over a lifetime. So, assuming Darwin's ideas are worth their salt, you'd think evolution would have handed us down a pretty flexible sense of self, right? It turns out, actually, that "adaptable identity" is way behind "good looking" and "a lot of money" when it comes to natural selection these days. I guess that's why we find so many middle-aged men at hair clubs and European sports car dealerships when their self-concepts are in flux.

But it doesn't take a half-century of living to lose yourself (and I didn't pay enough attention in my lower-division anthropology lectures to know much else about Darwin). Although the story does begin in school, where young university academicians are all shakily supported by their studies, the campus environment, the college student lifestyle, and the classmates they share these things with. Pulling out even one plank offers the potential to send their educationally-based identities plummeting, though the luminous horizon of graduation doesn't give much incentive to look down, and doing so would teeter on sacrilege anyway.

Yet when the corporate entry level generously yanks all four away and disinterestedly watches fledgling professionals flail with feelings of immobility and isolation on the way down, there's a distinct sense that the glimmer of what lay ahead was somehow done up as a distraction from what lay below.

Duped and now clutching for a new personal definition outside of the comforting auspices of college, most recent grads unsurprisingly turn to their careers for direction—there seems to be a natural progression from "What's your major?" to "What do you do?" Yet this move typically only intensifies the angst, as so many career freshmen are disappointed with their first couple of entry level positions; to think their jobs define them as people opens up that cold, gaping chasm still wider. College, it seems, really did a number with this one.

In an attempt to buy themselves some time to figure things out, many nonetheless escape back to the familiar by going to graduate school, quickly forgiving the mean and undeserved deception out of dependence on the academic system. The retreat, however, is usually just a two- to four-year band-aid, with most coming out equally as confused—if not more so—than when they went in, but now five or six figures deeper into debt and dealing with the working world that much later. It's no wonder, then, that frustration, apathy, and doubt commonly plague workers throughout their twenties, and that depression appears to be a seriously under-diagnosed condition for this browbeaten group (I certainly fell victim, if not clinically than pretty close).

Though the phenomenon is far from new, it wasn't until Alexandra Robbins and Abby Wilner threw some weight behind it in their 2001 twentysomething treatise, *Quarterlife Crisis*, that an elder-focused society so much as batted an eyelash about the problems welcoming recent college migrants into their postgraduate toils. "It can throw someone's life into chaotic disarray or paralyze it completely," they begin. "It may be the single most concentrated period during which individuals relentlessly question their future and how it will follow the events of their past. It covers the interval that encompasses the transition from the academic world to the 'real' world...[and] is usually most intense in twentysomethings." Predictably, most experienced professionals still dismissed the idea as ungrateful complaint, accusing young laborers of an underdeveloped work ethic and overdeveloped self-worth, and sloppily lumping them under the much-maligned "Generation X" label. (They haven't reached a consensus about how to disparage "Y" yet).

Coupled with what you now know to be the bitter truths masked by the sugarcoating that recruiters slap on their pitches, it's bluntly evident that the responsibility is yours alone to understand and own the changeover to the world of work. Your knowledge about the shift is what will empower you to make it through the continued mental and emotional challenges, and the resultant sense of control is what will buoy you up amidst all of the heartwarming solidarity and forthright candor.

But even then, I'm sorry to say, you'll probably never fully recapture that light, carefree school feeling as you push further into the unsmiling reality of corporate life; there's good reason, remember, that everyone is always so buttery and nostalgic about college. What you will develop, however, is a deeper, more sophisticated sense of fulfillment and happiness as you grow and evolve as a working adult. (Unless, of course, you continue to go to frat parties).

Over time, the simple pleasures of studenthood—which probably still maintain their pull in large measure—will seem, well, just too simple, and you'll conveniently romanticize those years in your memory as have those before you (myself included). But honor for now that this transition represents a departure from everything you've grown to love during the most developmental years of your adult life, and that you have every cause to be unsettled and upset.

Move forward from here knowing that the only constant you can count on in life is change like this—with the most dramatic stuff still en route—and that the only way to love something new is to put out an old flame. So here's to new beginnings that don't begin very well, but that do have the potential to burn brighter than any fire before.

expected turbulence

Your life to date has been a well-defined series of "nexts," practically from birth to the time you read this book. Until now, you have always been able to say with reasonable certainty where the upcoming few years of your life would take place, and what exactly you would do with them—school.

For the first 17 years or so you were either told where to go or it was a natural progression, which worked just fine until you reached that fateful decision every hopeful high school senior faces: where to continue your procrastinating. I mean learning. But between tuition, location, and actual acceptance letters, your university alma mater probably picked you more than the other way around. And even then the differences break primarily down to clout, weather, sports teams, and how far away you can get from the parents.

Instead, your original directional choice came when your under-grad academic advisor finally insisted that you select a subject to major in. Given the popularity of "undeclared" among coeds up to that crossroads—right behind its closest substitute, psychology, in which I'm a proud bachelor—and noting how this fickle bunch tends to change majors between one and three times even after picking a route, odds are that you had a rocky start on the path of big-time decision-making.

Sadistically, the choice you faced after that was what to do with the rest of your life after graduation. As an incubated college senior, you were expected to make one of the most difficult directional decisions you'll ever encounter—to clairvoyantly determine which "next" was the right one for you—with practically no experience in making significant life judgments, and with little honest exposure to the so-called real world or meaningful guidance about how to operate in it. It's a cruel and unusual demand to be placed upon a group of people who at most have an internship or two and perhaps some part-time experience, neither of which are much of a guiding light. Hell, they're not even a flashlight.

Know, then, that as a career freshman facing an open-ended 30-year block of time when you're used to only dealing in scripted four-year chunks, it's almost inevitable to be hit by massive fluctuations in your thoughts, feelings, and desires about where you want your future to lead—regardless of where you've landed now. You're pretty well prone to waking up a different person on any given day: What excites you one week can quickly fade the next, and a string of good months can be unexpectedly and dramatically followed by an extended period of deep confusion and introspection. Which is all unexpectedly and dramatically normal.

In the search for oneself, it's incredibly common to clutch at straws and vacillate wildly, particularly during the first several years as a young professional. Chalk it up to the standard and customary process of growth and development that career freshmen have to endure to root themselves in their post-college lives—which is unfortunately compounded by the pressures of adaptation to a new environment.

"No matter how well this process of starting one's own career and finding one's professional identity goes, the individual will suffer from considerable tension and stress," conclude Fernando Bartolomé and Paul Lee Evans in their *Harvard Business Review* study, "Must Success Cost So Much?" (Leave it to the pros to state the obvious and make it sound official). Still, it's a point aptly considered for grads sailing through on-campus interviews, thinking the swells are going to stay small and easy.

Even for those who get an offer from their top company and are ushered in with warm smiles and interesting assignments (all three of them), the basic—but very new—stresses of office life naturally give rise to questions and doubts about goodness of fit in the organization, and even in the world of work altogether. In fact, more Harvard-published research suggests (this time estimably) that a year-long depression is practically preordained when making a significant career shift—and the first-time transition from student to worker is arguably as significant as the things get.

Findings show that people don't necessarily exhibit the classic signs of despondence and melancholy (although many do), but that they undergo strong feelings of ambivalence, loss, and apprehension that the job may not work out. The actual disappointments that entry levelers encounter at the office, further, only feed this looming idea that they didn't make the right occupational choice.

And to tie a bow on it all, early-stage grunts commonly believe that their initial career decisions may be their last. With an overstated sense of finality, they ask, "What if I want to move in a different direction?" "How can I get the experience I need to make the switch?" "Could I even get hired by another company at this point?" "Are they going to find out I was never really in that honor society?"

These fears (except maybe for the last one) are shared by practically every young laborer at one point or another, and I'm glad to report that almost any job flop, working error, or professional misjudgment you make at this stage of the game has next to no lasting negative impact on the rest of your vocational life. (More often than not, in fact, it tends to have a very *positive* long-term impact, as we'll explore later in the book).

Your underdeveloped perspective at this stage, quite frankly, throws the situation out of proportion, because how can you as a squeaky new member of the workforce know what the right proportion is to begin with? Still, this doesn't stop the majority of unsullied corporate youths from beating themselves up and worrying themselves ill over choices that they made to the best of their abilities and knowledge at the time. It's really all that anyone can expect, and probably the only good explanation for most politicians getting elected. Plus I have some ideas I'll share on how to better go about it. (Making decisions, that is; I have absolutely no idea how to keep moral no-shows out of office).

Appreciate and accept the fact that your "next" suddenly becomes a very individual thing at the entry level, and that the wealth of choices you face can be overwhelming—downright crippling—if you aren't at terms with your goals and values. I'll do my best to help get you there, but consent right here that it's going to be a winding, tricky search to find your way in the workforce, and that you're going to hit your head on all manner of obstructions, roadblocks, and superiors. Uncertainty is the career freshman way of life, calling on you to embrace your exceedingly difficult, yet entirely survivable circumstances. As master Taoist philosopher Lao Tzu said, "Yield and overcome." (Advice good enough, incidentally, to start a religion).

you want me to do what?

and they're off and running

Turning your college tassel truly marked the bittersweet end of an era, spanning almost 18 book-congested, lecture-heavy, sleep-deprived years. All of which took place in a highly controlled, esoteric environment that deeply shaped your attitudes, behaviors, expectations—pretty much your entire view of, more or less, everything. So even with a couple summers of practice under your belt and a chameleon-like ability to adapt to your surroundings, it's still pretty unreasonable to expect to understand the workplace well enough to perform at even a fraction of the level you're accustomed to.

It begins with recognizing that your first years in the workforce are a distinct transitional or limbo stage, where you're no longer a student, but also not quite yet a matured professional. (In a way it's like being 13-years-old again, but not quite as gawky looking and with better skin). In fact, studies show that during the bumpy acclimation period, career freshmen instinctively react to the office environment as if it were an educational institution, with 80 to 90 percent of first-year on-the-job difficulties arising from them stubbornly trying to apply their inapplicable university ways.

Most companies spotted the schoolish pattern some time ago, and know full well the gamble they're taking whenever they saddle up a fresh graduate. That's why an offer letter to a new laborer is much more a racetrack ticket than it is a sales receipt: Even after a firm has put down their money, they still don't know exactly what they've bought. Just as there's no telling what will happen from race to race with a prize-winning horse, good university records all too often don't translate into good entry level records; a grad may have swept the College Triple Crown, but finish a disappointing also-ran in the working world. So organizations play the odds and bet the favorites, more heavily handicapping those without undergraduate exposure to the business environment.

Internships and even early post-grad experience notwithstanding, as an entry leveler you're still untested and untrusted (a concept we'll discuss exhaustively next chapter), which means the company is going to start off by putting you where you can do the least amount of harm and let you earn your way up from there. That, as you've distressingly figured out by now, typically takes the form of mind-numbing—and still absolutely scrutinized—gruntwork, which at times is probably so far below you that you have trouble believing the firm is paying you as much as they are to do it. Which still isn't saying much. About either of you.

Yes, big multinational organizations pride themselves on hiring smart people for stupid jobs, and you're the ideal target: young, educated, enthusiastic, teachable, willing to put in long hours—basically a prime candidate for exploitation. (Come to think of it, you should probably reconsider any decision you might have made to go to work for one of those mis-voted congressmen). But know that it's not complete corporate cruelty, as the broader intention is to bring the level of work up to the fuller extent of entry level abilities, and companies couldn't do that if they didn't grab the good ones and put them through their paces first. Plus fresh grads and early-stage refugees are a cost effective, low profile, and relatively safe way for the firm to accomplish the tasks that have to get done, but that it doesn't pay for anyone else to do (and not that they would). As things move forward, career freshmen gain experience, learn new skills, and eventually grow into—and then out of—the position.

The Fortune 500 strolls along that low road, however, by selling tomorrow's job today. They're only too aware that smart, ambitious young professionals aren't going to sign up for the real entry level post, and accordingly break out the smoke and mirrors to work their Vegas-style magic: Instead of a frank and candid dialogue about the true career path, they set up hors d' oeuvre-laden information sessions with flashy multimedia presentations and enthusiastic employee representatives—and typically at fire-sale prices. This is where recruiters get to use all the right buzzwords and glossy brochures to hype (read: lie about) the exciting and challenging work you'll do with diverse colleagues and key clients, and explain (read: make up) how you will receive world-class training and mentoring from the top people in the company. They sometimes even offer sweeping promises of travel to exotic destinations and abounding opportunities for personal growth and professional advancement (read: after you quit).

That sends most young workers into a firm with guns blazing, ready to burn their brand into its side. After a few months at the bottom, however, they're usually ready to turn the guns on themselves and put the hot pokers in their eyes. Without the pledged "mission critical" and "value added" work, most corporate grunts have difficulty understanding why they were recruited so heavily for the job, and begin to choke loudly on their pride. With expectations wined and dined to such ridiculous heights, though, who can fault the career freshmen?

The companies can. And do. In their minds, the dog-and-pony show they put on isn't supposed to rile impatience in entry levelers—just enthusiasm. About the gruntwork? Well, no. The pay? Not really. How about the pressure and late-night travel and political infighting? We don't have to bring that up. Fine, so what *should* they be all hot and bothered about?

Okay, maybe Corporate America hasn't thought this completely through. But the fact remains that they're upset with the pushy requests and right-now attitude, and it's up to you to fix that. Happily, it ends up working in your personal interest when you do so, which is something we'll talk about later. Firms, after all, shouldn't be the only ones doing the clever marketing.

mental mush

This move by Big Business to stash their greenbeans in the basement, however, has deeper-reaching consequences for career freshmen: Little or no responsibility, influence, or intellectual stimulation at work commonly throw entry level psyches into the downward spiral described earlier. The persistent challenge provided by school—if grueling and overwhelming at times—keeps life feeling purposeful and complete, and only with its absence comes the emptiness. The real enemy, interestingly, is no enemy at all.

Elemental to college was an excitement – relief dyad, where the inherent yin and yang of that system kept you motivated and in balance. The challenge of your curriculum, campus organizations, and commingling relationships was diverse and intense, and energized you to keep pushing forward and stretching yourself. At the end of an onerous academic term, close-run election, or agonizing group project, for example, you could let out an exultant sigh and ready yourself for the next set of wide-ranging contests ahead. It was a natural back and forth, and it worked.

At the entry level, however, it all grinds to an "exacting" halt, as you now get to wake up every morning at the *exact* same time, go to the *exact* same place, sit at the *exact* same desk, interact with the *exact* same people, and do the *exact* same IQ-threatening work for hours on end. It's boring to the point of calculus, and most young professionals just want some "hard" back.

When they first discover it missing, most find themselves seeking it out wherever they can—often taking on an excess of assignments and enjoying nightfall by office window every other evening, scrambling to finish things ahead of schedule. This way they can slip behind again with some style. But it's obviously not the same (or sane), and the drive weakens over time.

As muscle turns to fat when it's not exercised, so it goes with the desire for that challenge: If you're not being worked-out in significant and concrete ways, then after a while you just stop showing up. And once you get flabby, ironically, the challenge to get back into shape half becomes a burden you languidly want to be rid of, and half becomes an ache you want to rip and tear your way through. (Which is also why so many people are overweight and yet so many gyms still in business). This struggle to stay mentally fit is highly fatiguing, and contributes to the deflation so many young professionals feel when hitting the entry level with that characteristic walloping thud.

So make no mistake, you'll have to continue fighting to keep yourself fresh and engaged as an early-stage worker. Slowing in your drive to outmatch your circumstances can have irreparable effects carried throughout your early corporate life, including failure to position yourself for the next job on the road to your calling. Also failure to keep the one you've got.

There are, of course, certain self-driven, neurotransmitter-awakening initiatives to be taken, and we'll get to those; but know that more than three-quarters of what you will do during your stint as a grunt is, amazingly, gruntwork. This means that the development of some head-down-and-grind discipline will be one of the most important areas for your personal growth as a career freshman. Right behind restraint from slugging company employees in the mouth.

sit...stay...good boy!

Compounding the frustration is a new lack of reward and acknowledgement in the office arena. If you're like most young laborers, you've grown quite cavalier over the years with the wealth of recognition school provided you with for a job well done, pushing your pride and defiance ever higher with each successive victory. In fact, our entire educational system is built around formalized praise (meaded out with those big, defining A's and B's), which sends most undergraduates off to shamelessly indulge in that college-patented drunken revelry—casting doubt on the very basics of their socialization, much less their ability to score a 92 on a university exam. Indeed, life feels good in academia and egos seldom miss a meal. Or a drink.

And at the entry level, of course, pats on the back are sporadic, soft-handed, and often more of a professional courtesy than anything else. Most early-stage efforts, instead, are either taken for granted, harpooned, or better yet, swiped by a manager or senior who collects full credit and compliments. Once-a-year performance reviews also have more to do with opinion and perception than actual work quality. Plus without a curve or fixed percentage of grades, weekend work and predawn projects are required just to hold pace with the pack—to say nothing of shining for the labors. It's a far cry from the patronizing recognition system this country's higher-learned have been weaned on, and most newly appointed entry levelers are crushed when they can't find their congrats again.

You can actually think of yourself as one of Pavlov's dogs who's been conditioned to work hard because of the close challenge – reward pairing in college. You slobbered when the bell rang in school because, even though you knew it was going to be punishing, you could already taste the savory reward that was sure to come from it. But in the workplace, you take on the task pretty much because you know that rent is coming due, and doing the job well is a basic precondition to your continued employment. So you stop salivating after so many unremunerated chimes, to which this Nobel Prize-winning scientist would probably have a remark similar to yours about Corporate America's brilliance.

Thus the entry level skillfully extinguishes one of the few career-applicable behaviors college conditions, calling on you to relearn the system and adjust to the new reward schedule. Big Business' psychological savvy aside, understand that you'll go to bed hungry most nights if you don't appropriately shrink your appetite for hearty gratitude and credit, and learn to subsist on just the basic staples of a well-placed thanks and knowing smile after a tough project. Granted, it doesn't make for great dining as a career freshman, but it does begin to build up the personal sense of satisfaction you derive from doing your work well—which may be all you get. It also demonstrates to your tightlipped superiors that you don't need their commendation to keep you full—which may be all they need to hear.

downs & ups

Alas, it's a lengthy flight of stairs you travel to the entry level cellar, passing by the clear direction and abundant challenges and rewards that you've come to lean on. There's no question that you'll make it back to the top; just looking at some of the managers bumbling around your office should allay that fear in short order. But you will do some measure of tripping and clasping to the handrail on the way up, where you regain your balance only through a commitment to the long and humbling downward journey you first have to take in order to turn yourself back around.

Regardless of how deceptive companies may be in luring you there, it works to your ultimate gain when you open-mindedly strive to understand what's going to help you ascend each successive step. Just because they lied, remember, doesn't make discovering the truth any less useful; and it certainly doesn't make the politics or mechanics of the climb any different. Rather, it's up to you to determinedly figure out where, when, and how you can secure your footing, holding blame-less (and silly) the associates who would have you stuck in between the slats.

Still more regrettably, the descent goes deeper than you probably realize, which is why you need to see it walked before you get any further. The Entry Level Rite of Passage to be negotiated throughout your initial years is both complicated and unforgiving—not unlike the managers responsible for its administration—and the information you take in next chapter will help to set you on the right footing. Even after they trip you.

the last rite of passage

mind the gap

There's no easy way to say this, so I'm just going to come right out with it before anything else is discussed: You probably don't know as much as you think. Not yet, anyway.

Don't get me wrong; I have the deepest faith in, greatest respect for, and most genuine concern about career freshmen. But as a first-rounder, the distance between what you believe you understand today and what you actually do is likely about as wide as the one between what your university syllabuses required, and what you actually read. Plus the suggested books.

I found that out by walking into my inaugural corporate office with the posture that I could hang with the old-timers—now one of the many outlandishly arrogant moves collecting dust in my retrospect. Much as I love UCLA, I was given no reason to believe otherwise, having been sent off summa cum laude, Phi Beta Kappa, with College Honors, and two nose-in-the-air internships. What I lacked in experience, I felt I could certainly make up for in smarts; really, I thought I couldn't be touched. That is, of course, until I was summarily beaten up and had my lunch money stolen.

Vanity and pride commonly swell the heads and chests of new young professionals, and most of that hubris is sorely misplaced. With a haughty, boisterous swagger, far too many tote the triumph of their first couple offer letters all the way to their cubicle, and then expect applause from those who were also not only awarded with one, but who have already done something with it—often half a career's worth of something.

Hatchling workers invariably fail to grasp the fact that the collective knowledge and experience in the workplace—the things that the people there have seen, heard, done, and know—put to shame even the greatest college and entry level feats many times over. And what greenbeans have only read and been told rumors about, company veterans have actually lived, and usually lived hard (if the scars and war stories are any indication). Trying to equate the two is embarrassingly naïve, and the big boys make sure that's well understood.

Career freshmen are also quick to forget—or too self-absorbed to consider—that while their initial employers see enough merit to give them a run, wagers are being hedged and performance is being measured against an established "First 90 Days" set of criteria. Any corporate coddling called for after a university recruit or early-stage refugee has signed their letterheaded trophy signals a bad bet, and even then a company will only stroke an entry level head for so long before they unsympathetically slap it. It can be a surprising sting to the healthy egos of recent diploma-grabbers, most of which are bolstered up by handholding parents and empty collegiate assurances of world domination shortly after recovering from post-graduation hangovers.

It's in this way that the corporate entry level begins to "break" fresh graduates and short-time professionals, prevailing as America's last real rite of passage for its young. The overall technique actually isn't entirely dissimilar to what colleges do with weeder classes, by wearing down and plucking out students who don't fit to make room for those who do. Firms just don't do it with the explicit intention of getting rid of anyone, but instead budget for poor recruiting decisions, normal attrition, headcount reductions, and business fluctuations naturally pulling and pushing grunts in and out. The economics of the deal have historically worked, and much of the rough treatment has endured as a punitive because-I-had-to-live-through-it legacy. Whether or not they really have.

And though I'm certainly not on board with the methodology,

speaking as a "breakee," I'm all for its results. Plus the market may goose companies to rethink their strategy anyway: While career freshmen remain a relatively expendable pool of cheap labor, firms' turnover costs have skyrocketed in recent years as a result of heavily cycling through them in the rough-and-tumble entry level. After recruiting, training, and management fees are figured in, young professionals are a breakeven proposition at best during their first couple years of employment, and corporations have long counted on good tenures for good returns. Now their bottom lines are increasingly getting hit as entry levelers are increasingly getting out—"two and out," as the mantra goes, and often much sooner. Truth be told, the Fortune 500 isn't exactly sure what to do anymore in an economy where early-stage laborers aren't very good at waiting for the work they signed up to do. Imagine that.

We'll discuss career paths in great depth later in the book, but understand for now, however, that hopscotching from one company to another in an effort to avoid paying dues is shortsighted and done in vain. Indeed, you will travel the Entry Level Rite of Passage during your initial years in the workforce no matter where you try to go, no matter how many times you try to go there, and definitely no matter what the hiring firm tries to say.

Moreover, facing the fire is the first step on the path to your calling. In order to reach that work you're passionate about—much less do it well (or build a respectable library of battle narratives)—you first have to earn the learning and growth that come from walking the following seven steps with poise, confidence, and a will of steel. Also with your head on a swivel:

- Understand the company's position.
- Accept your gruntwork.
- Gain your perspective.
- Develop your humility.
- Keep smiling.
- Kick, scream, and cry when you have to.
- Pay your dues, but pay them *intelligently*.

guilty until proven so

In the world of work, others judge you by what you've done, but you continue to judge yourself by what you believe you're capable of doing. As you well should, but that's the rub—that's the crux of the struggle to prove you belong at the entry level.

It hits you squarely between the eyes as a career freshman, where you have nothing tangible to point to other than a college degree that most everyone else has—and that many have failed only with—but where your heart (and a healthy touch of conceit) tells you that you're destined for greatness. When nobody wants to hear it, the distress is equal parts blow to your self-esteem and knock to your confidence, as your abilities have never before stood trial in this way and you've got no defense to back them up.

College certainly never prepped you. The working assumption there is that you're smart enough to hang, and it's expected—required—that you'll prove it straight away. Pressed by both their personal research commitments and very own egos, faculty members have neither the time nor the inclination to water down their material, figuring (correctly or not) that there was plenty good reason behind you beating out all the people you did to get in. True, schools get their tuition money regardless of how you perform, but that's just a fraction of their income—well behind those fat endowments and grants—meaning that they have to keep churning out top graduates under a rigorous curriculum to keep up their national ranking (pronounced "investment rating").

So professors hold you immediately accountable to top standards of execution on their most challenging work, often requiring you to memorize volumes of information about which you're given grueling exams without apology. Your work is unemotionally judged based solely on your performance relative to your peers, and if you screw up you should've known better. Everyone else did.

If you screw up at the entry level, on the other hand, *they* should've known better. As a career freshman, it's much more like our justice system, where you're guilty until proven otherwise; even though everyone—wink, wink, nudge, nudge—likes to make believe it's the other way around. So no matter how smart your diploma suggests you might be, and regardless of how many people your firm shoved aside to pick you, you're hardly trusted to even be in the same room as anything of grand import. Unless, of course, that room also happens to have a Xerox machine.

Companies usually even put an introductory "probation period" in place as an escape clause, giving them a nice, clean out if you can't keep making coffee that tastes this good. It's not that they're looking to prove themselves wrong, but rather the smart firms (forgive the contradiction) are good students of business history, and they know the damage that can be caused by placing too much responsibility into uncalloused hands.

So managers hold you immediately accountable to top standards of execution on their most anesthetizing work, often requiring you to endure near coma-inducing administrative and research projects without apology. In sharp contrast to college, your work is judged with absolute bias based not only on your relative performance, but also on how you look, communicate, work with others, carry yourself, and ultimately how your manager feels about you—which may or may not be influenced by his other staffers, personal leanings, pressure from above, professional agenda, and what he had for breakfast that morning.

As discussed, that's why so many entry levelers wrestle so difficultly with their pride. Accustomed to a steady inflow of challenging work and unqualified praise for doing it well, they generally feel belittled and demeaned by their trivial assignments and unthankful managers. Knowing that they're better than the work landing on their desk and the recognition falling short of there, young workers simply want the opportunity to demonstrate their acumen—dead sure that they could showcase their talents and prove their worth by running with a big assignment. But when their draconian director may not have enough confidence to give them the nod for a matter of months (and in some cases more than a year), many are too disheartened and unmotivated to do anything with it when the time comes. That is, if they even last that long at the firm.

So the first two steps in surviving the Entry Level Rite of Passage are to understand the company's position, and to accept your own. Until you can build their trust in you—a slow and arduous construction project—there's not going to be much mystery or intrigue to your job, and there's little you can do to speed or spice it up. Pushing too hard too early is a lot like getting into a debate about a midterm grade with a professor: Not only are you unlikely to get what you're shopping for, you also run the risk of her deciding to re-score the exam herself, which usually knocks you down another letter grade.

By continuation, it's essential that you restrain yourself from engaging your initial entry level managers about how you set the curve in such-and-such a class, and how that demonstrates you're capable of doing such-and-such. It doesn't. And even if it did, do you really think a midlevel tool with a bonus tied to individual performance goals is going to trust what some ponytailed university lecturer decided to ask you about Keynesian theories?

In a world where failed tests can cost millions—and your boss his job—you're going to be abused to serve his ends until you break. Because as far as the firm is concerned, college is really just an entry level Wal-Mart: a big place to bargain hunt. It's pocket change to flick you into the basket, a hand in the penny jar to train you, and a short ride back to the store to grab a replacement. Keeping in mind, also, that there's no protection behind your formal job description—which is nothing more than a bait-and-switch scheme recruiters use to play hell with their applicants—your position is whatever your manager tells you it is, for as long as he tells you it is. Especially given how the stop-drop-and-roll entry level regularly jettisons gruntwork midstream and whimsically flip-flops projects, yoga-like flexibility is a must.

By faltering in work quality, gusto, or patience after six to 12 months—or just about when you're ready to crack and, incidentally, when your in-charge is finally ready to entrust some important work to your capable hands—you can easily knock down all that you've suffered so valiantly to build. In spite of all this, though, the company's not out to see you fail; as explained earlier, their long-term cost containment rests on the good performance and good endurance of inexpensive frontliners like you. Plus, more immediately, they're not too keen on getting back in the car and spending another $6,000 to $8,000 dollars bringing a replacement home, and another $10,000 to $12,000 training them. Even quick trips and small sums can add up, and nobody wants to spend money they don't absolutely have to.

Yet they'll willingly let you go or forcibly toss you out if you consistently have trouble choking down your entry level work, or are just too apathetic to open up and say "ah" (minus the colorful expletive that generally follows). It's a much cheaper move for your first employers, to whom you're just a commodity—much like any other overqualified recent college grad they can succor and sucker. I'll teach you how to build a strong brand in Chapter Six to de-commoditize yourself, but keep this point in mind whenever you feel slighted and are about to make a stupid vanity-provoked move; Wal-Mart stays open pretty late.

'round the block

The problem with experience, the saying goes, is that you don't get it until *after* you need it. (Same for driver licenses and the truth about most exes). While it's more than happy to grace you with its insight immediately following the debacle you initiate to earn it, experience gets too much of a voyeuristic kick out of watching you trip to ever give you a break. But why should you be so concerned about this omnipresent leg-in-the-aisle anyway? What makes experience so important? Here's what everyone who's tumbled enough times already knows:

- It builds perspective: the greatest predictor of success.
- You can't outwit it—no matter how smart you are.
- If you don't respect it, you'll get beaten every time.
- You can't study for it, and it has no true substitutes.
- It's the most valuable career asset you will ever own.
- The more you have, the less the entry level hurts.

Robert E. Kelley, a professor at Carnegie Mellon University's Graduate School of Industrial Administration—and man duly subjected to the peeping-tom of experience—has filtered it cogently through the eyes of the ER: "I think of perspective as pattern recognition plus experience," he says. "Think of how doctors work: over time, they see hundreds and hundreds of patients, they build up a base of case histories, and they learn to identify symptoms that go together."

To be a star at your job, Kelley analogizes, you have to build up your own personal log and develop your capacity for pattern recognition. Plus it also helps to remember that even top medical school grads do time as low paid, lower regarded residents, and usually can't get a real position practicing medicine before their early 30s. And when you're standing there all cold and vulnerable in your open-backed gown, you don't want them there any sooner. I know I'd take a well-aged physician who's seen whatever I've got dozens of times before over some hotshot rookie with a good MCAT score.

So even with solid internship and early entry level exposure, your perspective of the working world is still spotty and entirely incomplete. The fact is that you don't understand it until you've lived it day-in and day-out for years—until you can know when the train's coming before it starts steaming people over. Adopting this attitude, however, isn't easy because it means conceding how far you have to go before you'll be back in a place of knowledge and control. This admission, in turn, breeds humility, which can be an equally unfamiliar and uncomfortable bedfellow.

Even for top executives. Bankrupted Kmart, as one example among many, ousted their youngish chief in early 2002, favoring a more elder statesman to carry the company out of Chapter 11. "I'm just a little bit older, and maybe slightly wiser," said the discounter's new fifty-something chairman and CEO, James Adamson, upon replacing the 41-year-old demoted and departed Chuck Conaway. Translated from the smoothed-over PR language, that's tantamount to saying the guy turned the place into one giant Bluelight Special because he was too inexperienced to know what he was doing.

I watched the same thing happen firsthand, for that matter, shortly before I left the Silicon Valley. As more and more dots began to bomb, the founder of the company I worked for was asked by the board to step aside as head chief, making room for someone with some gray hair to take the company to the next level. Even though he had a BS from Harvard, an MBA from Stanford, and managed to raise $35 million to start a company, at 29-years-old this unwrinkled exec simply wasn't seasoned enough to keep running the very business he built. Talk about a humbling experience. But he's obviously an incredibly bright individual, and he'll get to where he needs to be—though not a moment before he's put in his time like everyone else.

All the big hitters have been there, and they all share a healthy respect for and keen understanding of the game. That's why they're big hitters. Take Steve Case, Pizza Hut manager turned founder and chairman of America Online (and $104 billion later, AOL Time Warner), who relied heavily on his practiced outlook to make the right decisions when executing his duties atop the largest media company in the world. "Because I've been doing this for so long," he explains in *Lessons From the Top*, "I am able to bring an historical context, and a kind of even-keeled perspective to things, because I've usually seen some version of this movie before." Probably while enjoying a large pepperoni. (Although now it'll be from the couch, as he's stepping down in May 2003).

So has Larry Bossidy, former Honeywell chairman and ex-GE executive, who was among the most respected and modest leaders out there. "Today, being a CEO is a humbling job," he allows, "and the more you learn, the more you recognize every reason that you have to be humble, because the competitive environment is so fierce that there's so much more to do all the time."

It was a message initially lost on John Chen, top chief at software-maker Sybase, who was unusually amorous of his Caltech-pedigreed self when he first started telling people what to do. "In the early days of my management career, I always thought everyone else was an idiot and I was so smart I just couldn't stand myself," he recalls. Probably nobody else could either. Fortunately his brains kept him around long enough to finally smarten up: "The more I achieve," Chen now admits, "the more I know the truth of the old Chinese maxim that says there are always higher mountains. It's absolutely true. There are always better people. There are always better minds."

Perhaps in the head of Lou Noto, vice chairman of Exxon Mobil Corporation (the second largest firm on the globe), who made no wholesale firings and undertook no radical restructuring when he was appointed to his position in 1999. As he explains, "I knew much less about Mobil, as a company, than did many of the people on my management team. I would have to have been a complete jerk if I didn't take the attitude, 'Look, fellows, I just happen to be here. I was chosen for this, but if we don't operate as a team, I don't see how we are going to get anything done.'"

As evidenced, humility and perspective—however late in coming—are simply par for the course of success. Sometimes very big success. And at the very least, approaching your work with the same humbleness found in the best people will help you dodge the backlash that sent me flat on my backside. Indeed, owning your "knowledge gap" (the unread-book-sized one, if you'll recall) demonstrates tested maturity, and will help endear you to your manager and seniors. That's not to say you don't demonstrate appropriate confidence in yourself and in your abilities, but that you maintain a certain quietness and reservation about it, especially when first starting off.

Remember that even if you're walking in the entry level door with a 4.0 college GPA, several top-shelf internships on your résumé, or a brand-name first employer who you couldn't quite see eye-to-eye with (and I've managed to miss every time), you're still playing in an environment where your neighbor can probably boast of similar or even better qualifications. Plus, usually, actual hardened years in the trenches. This admonishment isn't to discount your difficult years of schooling, of course, and it's certainly not to encourage you to be excessively demure or self-deprecating—which will just undermine your credibility—but rather to remind you to keep your braggadocio at bay. And not to break your arm patting yourself on the back.

By patiently earning your perspective and developing good humility, you walk the second two steps of the Entry Level Rite of Passage, and those will ultimately yield the respect and trustworthiness you need to be successful. "It takes time to get to the top, and that's good," notes the Schwarzenegger-taming Maria Shriver in her book, *Ten Things I Wish I'd Known—Before I Went Out into the Real World.* "Because by the time you get there, you'll have learned what you need to know in order to stay there."

The only reason that I, myself, can write this book is because I've first breathed it. Otherwise it would ring hollow, and you would hear it right away; there would be an absence in my words that would strike you as disingenuous and out-of-touch. My credibility comes from my history and so must yours, which is the slowest, but only genuine way to build your name. To quote the great "Bird," Charlie Parker, "Jazz comes from who you are, where you've been, what you've done. If you don't live it, it won't come out of your horn."

all in the attitude

smile up a (desert) storm

Joining a company at the entry level is a lot like signing up for basic training in the armed forces: it's rough, you get dirty, your drill sergeant—er, manager—yells and flings around orders, and the answer to any painful challenge is "Thank you sir, may I have another!" Assuming a boot camp mentality here actually isn't such a bad idea, given that the firm is trying to knock you down in hopes you'll get back up. Resilience is what's going to prove your mettle; rebounding with a smile is what's going to prove you're a soldier.

It serves you well, then, to begin your conditioning by maintaining a positive, upbeat demeanor. Just about every executive and manager ever polled since the beginning of time (or at least since the beginning of polls) has cited "good attitude" as one of the—if not *the*—most important attributes a new employee can have. In addition to the obvious benefits of promoting good client service and maintaining high productivity, there are two other pretty basic reasons that these very same people generally won't cop to, so let me clue you in.

First, and as you've doubtlessly already gathered, enthusiasm is a rare trait in the sober corporate atmosphere, reserved usually for late Friday afternoons, free lunches, project closings, and managerial illnesses. And even then it's kept to a low rumble. Now, what you may not have paid as close attention to is how well it's received when offered out of turn, or how quickly the levity can spread. Corporateers love to be around animated people at the office not only for the entertainment value, but because it legitimizes the allure of their own jobs—which is why good moods are so contagious in the workplace.

If you can get excited about this stuff, the psychology goes, it's hard for others not to respond in kind. And then not only do they start to feel good about the work, but they also feel good about you making them feel good. At some point, of course, they'll come crashing back down to reality and hit their head on the desk, but by then you've already done your part. Notably, this isn't to recommend strolling into the office everyday artificially dressed up with sunshine and rainbows (which you probably couldn't muster even if you tried, and I've seen sad and unfortunate breakdowns as a result), but simply to call out the positive residual effects of a consistently good attitude. It's also the sort of thing, by the way, that managers merrily mention during performance reviews.

Second, if you happily accept your floor-scraping new assignments—albeit through the cacophonous gnashing of your gritted teeth—it'll engender the respect and esteem of your superiors. Your manager isn't (entirely) stupid, and he knows that the work he doles out is pretty mindless, even by his standards. If you smile and take it, he's going to want to funnel better days your way not because you corner him or complain noisily enough (both of which have a near-perfect failure rate at the entry level), but rather because he'll grow to like you and will want to see you do well.

Plus your syrupy performance suggests that you might prove effective in gruntworking his upper-drawer endeavors. Not only more gratifying for you, these types of projects are among the best opportunities for forward motion, as you're interacting with your boss on a higher, more visible plane. (Assuming, of course, that's something you can stomach). Regardless of where you end up standing, however, it's critical never to lose sight of the fact that the company is endlessly kicking your tires and slamming your doors as a young professional to see how you're built. So if you end up becoming a squeaky wheel, for whatever reason, chances are you won't get oiled. Why should they get their hands all greasy when Wal-Mart's so close?

easier said

Sure this sounds great in principle, but swallowing your pride with a grin goes down pretty rough in practice, and this is particularly so for men. "Nothing is more important to a man's pride, self-respect, status, and manhood than work," explains psychiatrist Willard Gaylin in *The Male Ego*. "But...pride is built on work and achievement, and the success that accrues from that work."

Since there's not really any of that in the corporate basement, fragile y-chromosomed psyches tend to suffer harder—especially those attached to academically successful collegians. Personally, a night would scarcely go by at the entry level where I wouldn't find myself swearing out loud in the shower when reflecting on the day. (In the car and at the supermarket, too, which didn't sit well with the checkers). For both sexes, though, symptoms can include deep-seeded feelings of anger and resentment about being overworked, underpaid, and disvalued, as well as a pervading sense of worthlessness and plummeting self-esteem. Sometimes the emotions are even accompanied by physical manifestations, such as headaches, acne, muscle tension, weight gain or loss, and excessive sleep or significant lack thereof. But while feelings of hostility and bitterness are perfectly normal byproducts of injured ego, these emotions have to be kept in careful check at the office, which itself can have an unhealthy accretive effect.

As Joanne Ciulla writes in *The Working Life*, "Organizations, like families and people in general, often bury conflicts and seek to remain pleasant and friendly, even though emotions like anger simmer beneath the surface." This type of control, she notes, is particularly critical for low-ranking employees, who don't have the political clout in the company to validate their stances. Without a proper outlet, then, entry levelers can quickly melt down.

This means it's absolutely essential that you scream, rant, yell, cry, kickbox, or do whatever else you have to do outside of the office to effectively vent your frustrations. Seek continual validation from those whom you're close with, and only pretend to take it all in stride in front of the people who need to see your happy face. To do so at home can make you very sick.

Importantly, if you feel the need to speak with someone or at all sense the onset of depression, which includes feelings of hopelessness and disinterest in things you typically enjoy, then don't wait to visit a professional therapist. Your firm-sponsored health plan should cover all of the costs except for a small copay, and your sessions will be kept completely confidential. But you have nothing to be ashamed of anyway, as scientists unanimously believe that susceptibility to depression has to do with the interaction between personality type and natural body chemistry, as opposed to some falsely stigmatized personal weakness. Trust that far more career freshmen struggle than admit they do—and I freely acknowledge that I did—so don't let your pride or fear compromise your health. Instead, acceptingly walk two very important steps in the Entry Level Rite of Passage by smiling when you have to, but most certainly crying when you need to.

Plus you can round out your support system yourself by mentally turning the situation on its head, thinking of your knocks not as a punishment, but rather as an *entitlement.* That is, you deserve your bumps and cuts at the entry level because you've earned the right to be vulnerable to them. Once again, the best have been there and understand just how it works: "Building EarthLink was a fight—a scratching, clawing, tooth-and-nail battle, and I'm glad for it," reflects founder and chairman Sky Dayton. "Being an entrepreneur is hard, and raising capital is supposed to be an arduous rite of passage."

No question, Corporate America hits with a closed fist at all levels. But by proudly raising your chin like the pros to each new jab in your low-end scuffle, you'll learn just where and how to block the next time the punch is thrown. Building up your experience blow-by-blow, defending becomes less of an issue as you increasingly start to see where you, yourself, can go on the attack. This is how perspective is gained—regardless of the win – loss record you post to get there.

a line in the sand

all hail!

During the early days, sometimes your boss is the pigeon and you're the statue. It's essential to sturdy yourself for that, and it doesn't necessarily make your manager a bad person—or even a bad manager. It can just be his style when under pressure, and perhaps it helps him stay focused and get things accomplished more quickly. Unless, of course, you regularly find yourself needing a shampoo by lunch.

There's only an extent to which you should pay your dues, and it's only so far that you ought to bag your pride. The line in the sand is broken and uneven, however, with the varying degrees of gruntwork existing between companies and managers making it difficult to offer a set rulebook. Moreover, career freshmen have sometimes dramatically different thresholds for tolerating bosses' working personas and managing their frustration about entry level insipidity. So I'll draw on a personal anecdote about my exit from the Big Five consulting sphere—which hails from the furthest reaches of unintelligent dues-paying—and we can work our way in from there.

My story opens with the company signing a $25 million agreement with one of the Big Three automakers to implement a leading enterprise software package. I was in the so-called Change Management practice, which to this day isn't very well understood or appreciated by most clients; this one, naturally, was no exception. Further complicating things was that the project manager on our side, who we'll just call "Bill," didn't understand it either. Bill also happened to be the presiding megalomaniac of the Los Angeles office (he was working on Orange County), and saw his appointment to the head of the project as akin to, for lack of a stronger word, kingship.

He began his reign by rolling my reporting manager off of the engagement after only a few months, primarily on account of her knowing what she was doing. None of that to be had on *his* project. (At least not unless he could assume credit for it). I was sent in as a quick stopgap replacement, and, in spite of my boss' cautions, was sure that I could win his majesty over with my witty charm and good old-fashioned work ethic.

Instead he made me court jester. I was verbally battered for minor errors (e.g., "Michael, do you have an uncle in the firm who got you this job or something?"), was forced to stay at the office until all hours at his caprice (he walked in at 6 p.m. one day, I can recall, and forced me to complete a seven-hour assignment before I was allowed to go home), and my most pressing responsibilities included photocopying, setting up meetings, keeping his files organized, ordering supplies and food, running his errands, and buying playthings for the team to distract themselves with. Picture me in Gucci slacks and a Kenneth Cole lambswool sweater, carefully discriminating between the Koosh Balls and Nerf dart guns amid neon-drenched aisles of Toys "R" Us.

Before I left, two other Change managers were brought in—one of whom was rolled-off again (because she did the impossible by understanding less about Change than Bill), and one who couldn't be removed because she actually outranked Sir William. But she only showed up two days a week anyway, and the extent of her guidance to me was—and I quote—"Just do your best to make him happy." Regrettably, she couldn't be persuaded into a mentoring position.

I begged and pleaded with my reporting partner for months to deliver me from that project, completely at a loss for why he kept dragging his feet. As it turns out, he would've lost some serious face if I became the third Change person to cycle through that project—and maybe even his job. In the end, I was just an entry level commodity to be disposed of (and I was no rookie at that point, mind you). When I finally figured out that the only way I was rolling off of that engagement was to roll right out of the firm, I tucked and turned my way up to the Bay Area within three weeks.

So, in short, they're out there—and usually not far enough away. No matter the company, at one end of the spectrum you've always got head-cases like Bill who take perverse pleasure in the belittlement and privation of their working mates (it's *never* just you), and at the other end you find incompetents who senior management—and usually tech support—have on a watch list. I've been fortunate enough to serve under both. But at the same time, I've had the chance to work for a few bosses who were wonderful teachers and really great people (which, incidentally, also made me wonder what exactly they were doing there). On balance, the mishmash proves that what kind of entry level commanders you receive and what kind of work they give you is more or less a crapshoot. So if your dice have landed anything like mine did, it may be time to consider changing tables.

back from the brink

Pulling ourselves in from the edge, though, let's start by agreeing that you're certainly not out to skirt the donkeywork, but want to be sure it's being put to use properly—for someone who has a method to his madness, and who's making proper use of your efforts and sacrifices. Even if your boss can hardly see past his own reflection, if he's nonetheless got your future on his mind then you've landed yourself a real champion. If he arbitrarily and unthinkingly tosses you assignments, however, or is too preoccupied with his own work to pay much attention to yours, then you've met enemy number one. Regardless of how fun he may be at happy hour.

"By my second day on the job, I saw the unbridled influence my manager had over my career, and therefore my life," reflects Merrill Lynch's exiting (later in 2003) chairman and CEO, David Komansky, about his first entry level guardsman. "I saw immediately that I was on the wrong side of this equation." He's right in a lot of ways, but you don't actually have to *be* a manager right away to succeed; you just need one committed to playing for your team.

Your boss (and mentors, as we'll discuss next chapter) must be

deeply involved in your cause and committed to your growth and success. He may test you, he might pitch ridiculous assignments onto
your desk, and there are even odds that he'll overlook your efforts during busy seasons; but if he's good, you'll be on a precisely directed
track all along the way. If he's not, then you'll have made circles and
had to lick his boots to get there. So walk the last step of the Entry
Level Rite of Passage vigilantly, keeping a sharp and early eye out for
the red flags raised by bullying, abandonment, excessive ignorance,
and other such managerial blights.

Should you get saddled with your own personal "Bill" of sorts, it's
essential to your overall learning, branding, and professional development that you do whatever else you need to do to build your presence
and recognition in the office—which may involve seeking out projects
headed by other managers, or positioning yourself for cross-departmental opportunities that may ultimately result in a transfer. There
are ways to go about all of this, of course, and you'll learn them
throughout the book.

But before calling in the guard, which is very messy politically,
keep in mind that the initial difficulties you experience may largely
be the product of a normal breaking-in process between you and your
boss—kind of like first walking in a stiff new pair of shoes. Rapports
aren't always natural or immediate, and many office relationships
require a basic feeling-each-other-out period before settling into a
comfortable dynamic. Some managers also make you work harder
than others to earn their respect, which requires a strategic mix of
standing up firmly and bending backward like Gumby. It can only
be a situational judgment call, but if you've ever played with one of
those little green pieces of rubber long enough, you know about how
much twisting it takes before the thing just sits there all gnarled for
good. (I found out in Toys "R" Us).

There are plenty of stories about entry levelers first bumping
heads with their in-charges before later becoming strong colleagues
(as also happens with many personal friendships), so don't worry too
much at first about a gap in chemistry or compassion. In fact, de-
manding managers are usually better than the rest, as they challenge

and push you to levels that you may not have otherwise reached. And if it helps keep you grounded, remember that *no* boss lasts forever—especially in the revolving-door, love-'em-and-leave-'em new economy. (Where by "love," of course, I mean to say something else entirely).

Finally, own your half of the relationship and recognize when you, yourself, are being unreasonable. "She can't accept that while the research she's responsible for is very important, there's nothing fantastic or center-stage about it," remarked one fair, but difficult Fortune 500 manager about a talented career freshman during a recent interview. "She wants everything to be meaningful and creative and fun, when a lot of work is simply mundane. She doesn't want to do the time in the trenches."

Coming at it from the other direction, it's useful to consider that trying to keep young professionals happy can actually contribute to managerial burnout—a situation you don't want to be on the receiving end of. Instead, seeing the picture from their perspective and tracing it back to yours is a great way to assess the evenhandedness of your own outlook. And when choreographed with the opening seven steps of entry levelhood, you're perfectly positioned for the rest of the dance that follows. Provided you're still walking.

III

@on survival & success

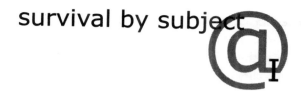

survival by subject

family affairs

it's the entry level, charlie brown!

I n college, it's all about seeing what you can get away with. The world of a student, by and large, revolves around how many times you can skip lecture, how long you can delay studying for an exam, how late in the term you can drop a class without impacting your transcript, and how much language you can possibly plagiarize without the professor catching on. The goal is to push the limits of a system whose design and consequence structure are relatively easy to understand, and playing the game in this kind of milieu is empowering, if somewhat predictable.

And then along comes the entry level with a smirk and a devious snicker. Life in this world is anything but encouraging or obvious, where the limits actually push back and the game is more like *Survivor*. Of course the majority of new grads are never told about it, or at best warned once or twice in hurried speech and hushed tones—and not that it really matters. Endangered as they are, most cautions to career freshmen about life in the labor market seem to be a lot like those to Charlie Brown about what Lucy is going to do with the football: Even if they do find attentive ears, they're still to find receptive feet.

It's not until unsuspecting greenbeans run up to their first couple of companies at a full clip that they find the ball artfully swiped away by managers, working mates, politics, promotions, errors, ethics, initiatives, accountability, and a bewildering array of other colleagues, con-ventions, and customs. With no room to slow down—and no idea what to do with it even if they could—most new workers end up flat on their backs: cheated, contemptuous, cynical, and with strange squiggles over their heads. Good grief.

Perhaps this fate is planned payback for all of that college cocki-ness? Much as that might gratify your old professors, nothing's been purposely plotted out (by a conniving little girl or otherwise). Yet survival does begin by acquiescing that the entry level isn't a system to be tested—a fact probably best evidenced by the bandages you're still enfolded in from an early incident. And which will only continue to bunch and further layer when you don't recognize each major area where your old university MO is a big corporate no-no. Don't worry, everyone sports the "nouveau hurt" look at the beginning; the unravel-ing begins when you finally concede to your betraying wrappings that it's time to choose your eyes over your ego.

Which even then is only the start. As you've also surely realized, the Big Business machine is exceedingly intricate—almost incompara-bly more so than those connect-the-dots colleges—and the only way to fully own it is to take apart the gears and mechanisms to see how everything fits together. This is what the encyclopedia of topics in the three SURVIVAL BY SUBJECT chapters does for you, stripping away the protective covering of misperception and dismantling the major com-ponents to reveal their inner-workings. When used to inform the req-uisite months and years of futzing, tinkering, and cutting up your hands, you'll eventually be able to reassemble the structure on your own terms and confidently seek out the organization that's right for you.

But today you just need to keep from getting caught up in the cogs and wheels, which the knowledge you gain here will help you to do more skillfully and painlessly. I've come close to losing entire limbs in building up my experience, so capitalize on that clumsiness with ava-rice, and use it to balance each consecutive piece of your dreams that you put into place. We'll start with perhaps your biggest surnamed obstacle, and use the remainder of the chapter to work through the rest of the people in your neighborhood.

managers

but, dad!

You can think of managers almost as a third parent: you get whichever one you're given, you're obligated to complete whatever tedious chores they assign you, they reprimand you when you haven't performed, back-talking is done at considerable personal risk, and they're responsible for raising your "allowance." In true guardian figure form, this individual also bears primary responsibility for the quality of the assignments you receive, the level of training you're provided with, your socialization to the company's culture, your access to key employees and clients, your advancement opportunities, the overall tone of your stay with the organization, and in general the air you breathe. I'm sure at some point you've been ready to sacrifice that last one altogether.

In my entry level foray into the working world, I had five reporting managers, all of whom couldn't have been more unique if they were scripted. In fact, when I think about describing them I almost want to go into a rendition of Anthony Michael Hall's explanation of "The Breakfast Club" in his letter to Principal Vernon: a Tasmanian Devil; an absentee; a knuckle-dragger; a lunatic; and a seagull (or a boss who unexpectedly swoops down, makes a lot of noise, craps on everything, and then flies off). And just when I had begun to figure each of them out, we found some way to part company—sometimes through one of us actually parting with the company. And sometimes with the other's blessing.

Until either you or your manager can enjoy the same luck, however, the onus is on you to learn this individual's style, pander to his strengths, cater to his whims, and consistently give him something better than he knew he wanted before he knew he wanted it. But doesn't that make you some biddable toady; aren't you then just this obsequious apple-polisher? Call it what you will, if it gets you out of the entry level with no greater degradation than playing sometimes-lackey or occasional yes-man, you've beaten me by a healthy stretch.

the basics

To begin with, help your manager to look good (as much as can be expected); he's trying to impress his own boss, after all, just as much as you're trying to impress him. Making that happen a little more competently for the guy means you get to better enjoy the results of your otherwise senseless labor. Besides, his bad days usually end up becoming yours.

So when it's going to represent your in-charge—no matter what the assignment—ensure that you research things beyond prescription, vet for accuracy to the last period, add those unusual touches of thought and care, and deliver it well ahead of schedule. In short, make him proud to pass off your work as his own, which he's likely planning on doing anyway. And that's okay: being a methodical and conscientious, well, tool in this way will position you to receive better assignments more quickly (lest he not completely exploit your talents), as well as widen your elbowroom with respect to managerial oversight.

You first have to understand your boss' expectations before you can exceed them, of course, so start by simply stepping up your efforts in noting the marching orders he hands down. Studies show that employees generally retain only about a third of what their managers say (arguably still an excessive amount, but that's another issue), calling out this remarkably easy opportunity to outperform your fellow career freshmen: reliably "out-documenting" them.

It's ridiculous the number of times I've seen (and put) supervisors up-in-arms about projects that suffered no fault other than not being done in the exact quirky way they were asked for. Yet as backward and nonsensical as the orders may seem, there's generally some thin veneer of logic to them, even if only in the client's head. Regardless, business—at its purest, most fundamental roots—is about accommodating the dippy requests of whoever's paying. So, basically, it doesn't have to clear with you so long as the check clears the bank.

Now where you'll begin to really baffle and stun your boss is by equally observing what he only *implies* he wants. Indeed, when you can understand what your manager means just by way of surveying his cues against the backdrop of his habits, you're giving him what he probably can't even get romantically. So start by looking, for example, at things like certain pieces of information he always pays attention to, particular times he typically requests a recurring report or assignment, and even his general "recap" preferences (i.e., when he wants the whole play-by-play versus only the decisions he needs to make). If you spot any clear trends, simply tilt your work to match his leanings—and then stretch out in the warm approval of his good graces. Learning to anticipate questions and issues in this way will ultimately grow your planning skills and begin to teach you the discipline of "managing your manager," which is an exercise you'll be practicing for some time to come.

And never more tactfully than when you find yourself disagreeing with your superior's decision about an issue. Although you probably question his judgments about as often as your own to have ever joined the company, it's critical that you very carefully pick your battles, recalling what happens to squeaky wheels at the entry level. For the select few that you do choose to fight—after taking into full consideration his schedule, mood, and any anticipated concessions you may be in the market for in the near future—respectfully present your case *one time*, and let him take it from there. We'll get into how to best position your arguments in the final SURVIVAL BY SUBJECT section, but understand for now that it absolutely never involves forcing the issue.

This is another one of those only-works-in-college habits: Whereas professors actually invite challenges to their viewpoints (sort of), a protracted argument is the last thing your boss wants. No dispute from a career freshman, no matter how rational or brilliantly constructed, is ever going to be received well by an in-charge who's already declined once before (holding true to the parental dynamic). It's important to recognize that a manager's accountability usually extends pretty far upward, requiring him to consider the stances of highly illogical people who have the ability to fire him. And maybe it's even more important to recognize that your manager is also one of those people to you.

we never talk anymore

It sounds curious, but you can't assume that your boss actually knows what you do with most of your days. (Without consulting his Palm Pilot, odds are he can't remember the bulk of his). A midlevel manager's schedule is often stretched to the point of silliness, and you're probably only one of a dozen employees who he has the time and energy to forget about. This, naturally, can cause self-focused career freshmen to feel shortchanged and neglected, preoccupied that their supervisors don't like them or are unhappy with their work. And while that may be the case, chances are much better that he just hasn't found the opportunity to say anything yet; there's usually more talking than you'd prefer when things aren't going well. Alongside, too, an escalation in the level of oversight: from negligent to neck-warming.

So make it a point to periodically circle back with your commander, even if you have your arms comfortably around your assignments and feel good about the progress you're making. It's not a manager's responsibility, understand, to ask you what you're doing and how you're doing it—even though that, of course, is his job. Rather, it's up to you to track him down, tell him, and then use his detachment to your advantage: Since he's not around to know exactly what's going on, you've got plenty of wiggle room to reasonably massage the particulars. Provide, then, not only detailed status updates about clients, deadlines, and next steps with your work, but also humbly—yet confidently—explain your recent successes and ever-so-slightly overstated accomplishments. No matter what your business card says, you hold the most important sales job in the company: yourself.

If your boss is amenable, you might even consider formalizing the process with a meeting schedule, whereby you can chat for 15 or 20 minutes once a week. In addition to providing a forum for consistent feedback (and the first word about upcoming engagements), these quick sit-downs will give you some solid face-time and demonstrate your commitment to open communication and a top quality product— the signature of any good sales call. Plus it'll afford your manager the time to organize his thoughts about your work, or force him to actually have some if he's not there yet.

Some career freshmen go overboard here, however, and constantly update their supervisors not so much to get their input or share pertinent information, but to slyly highlight what mission-statement-altering ideas they've come up with, or intimate how the company would fall into financial disrepair without them. Not only a flagrant abandonment of all humility and reason, even the most benighted boss can usually see right through such thinly veiled attempts at self-promotion, quickly developing a blind eye to the offender. Remember, you only undercut your efforts by perpetually tugging on your superior's shirtsleeve; plus that savior image is reserved for your manager to unpersuasively convey to his own bosses.

shh, here he comes...

There are countless ways to rattle a manager's cage, and it's often difficult to predict what exactly is going to shake him up. Since you're bound to have your hands on the bars any number of times in any number of positions, it's much more efficient just to concern yourself with avoiding those practices certain to cause a quake (relishing the process of discovery for everything else). We'll get to all of the major tremors over the course of this section of the book, but I'd like to touch on the biggest one here... Surprises!

Bosses absolutely hate bombshells, and this is for two primary reasons. First, it undermines their credibility: if they're not properly apprised of what's going on in their department or with a certain project, the appearance is that they haven't got it together. Which, of course, they probably don't. Notwithstanding, springing something on your superior during an important meeting or right before a deadline—heaven help you in front of *his* directors—puts him on the spot, and forces him to dance around whatever traps you've unwittingly left scattered about. (Which, if the holiday parties are any indication, is an awkward, pained bebop that nobody really wants to see).

The second cause of supervisory distaste for revelations is probably best captured by legendary British author H.G. Wells, who reflects, "No passion in the world is equal to the passion to alter someone else's draft." Indeed, there are few things more gutturally satisfying to a boss than making changes to an assignment—whether it means substituting words, changing graphs, restructuring pages, or throwing the thing out altogether. Just so long as you have to stay up well into the morning to do it.

The rush comes from the company-sanctioned—and usually quite arbitrary—exercising of their will, which is probably the only area of their life where people actually listen to them. Still, there are several reported instances of good cause on file, where a manager has needed to re-bake a report to prepare it for public consumption, or to throw a dash of this or a hint of that into a presentation to get it just right for an executive powwow. Without his time in the kitchen, no upward-looking midlevel leader can ever prepare the dishes of an Iron Chef; nor you dodge the edge of the knife.

So whenever you're the keeper of a matter that requires the contribution or approval of your manager, tell him as early as you have to, as many times as you have to, in as many ways as you have to. "It's virtually impossible to communicate too much," explains Jim Broadhead, chairman and chief executive of FPL Group, one of the United States' largest public-owned electric utilities. "I've never heard a single [boss] anywhere complain that he or she is being kept too informed." Nor an employee complain about having to do so after a good managerial haranguing.

Because of the multitude of your superior's other eccentricities and idiosyncrasies (which are now yours for all intents and purposes), the few tactics mentioned in this discussion will only get you so far. The best strategy for everything else is simply to apply the keen and continuous observation you employ in gauging his preferences—grasping at his motivations and rationales, his likes and dislikes, his strengths and weaknesses. When you work to understand *who*, exactly, this person is that you spend most of your waking hours striving to please, it not only adds a layer of purpose and personal interest to the chore, but even positions you to spin his attributes to your advantage when the situation permits.

And even after you make it that far, you're still likely to notice sometimes-dramatic shifts in typical personality traits, depending on his stress level, workload, personal issues, the business cycle, and other such factors. So keep an ongoing mental portrait of your boss, and take a brushstroke to it every time you spot something new. Eventually you'll be able to step back and see the whole picture, but for now just take it color-by-color.

coworkers

now play nicely, kids

Companies responding to a recent survey by the National Association of Colleges and Employers indicated that the ideal entry level job candidate, first and foremost, "knows how to communicate, interact, and work with others effectively." University grades, creativity, entrepreneurial skills: all sit behind the tall, obstructive head of people-savvy as far as firms are concerned. It may surprise you, but your first few money-givers are much more concerned about how well you're going to function with your fellow associates than how well you'll, in fact, perform your job. It's not unlike the parent who tolerates a messy room if it keeps the kids from fighting.

At the entry level, corporations hire based on raw, unfinished potential and then coach for skill, with no real expectations of you deeply understanding their business or your role within it. (That much is evident by how much of its droopy underside you're initially charged with holding up). Rather, they gauge your aptitude to do so based on your college and internship successes, and whatever post-grad working experience you may have; basically, if you're trainable then you're desirable. Where they're rolling the dice, instead, is with your ability to integrate into the collective working unit, for which there's no reliable pre-employment indicator.

And they never stop scrutinizing once you arrive. Humble Honeywell ex-chief Larry Bossidy, in fact, had it at the top of his shopping list when searching for fellow execs: "Do I see a person who can work well with others? Do I see a person who's shown some interest in others? Are these the people who can share their knowledge with other people and do it gracefully and willingly?" he asks. True from the top all the way down, one of your primary goals as a career freshman is to accept and be accepted by your officemates—especially considering that coworker relations is the first (and last) place your boss eyeballs in evaluating what kinds of projects to put you on. The thinking goes that if you're broken here, nothing is going to work right anywhere else. Which, in fact, is usually the case.

Thankfully, it's practically never too late to repair even a seriously damaged dynamic, and doing so assuages the biggest apprehension—or frustration—of everyone responsible for you being there. In addition, approaching your fixit efforts with that patented positive attitude is a lustrous way to show you can put the needs of the team first. Not to imply that you go disguise your individuality or affect a style that doesn't feel right, but that you pull out of your repertoire of identities whichever one says the loudest that you enrich the culture of the workgroup. (The one that says it with a straight face).

Similar to an influential legislator—or loudmouth brother or sister—all it takes is one well-entrenched colleague to gradually shift team sentiment against you, pushing into peril not only your advancement opportunities, but even your job security. I've personally worked with very talented, MBA-level people who were let go principally because their styles didn't mesh well with those of their associates and superiors. With your own political maneuvering, then, it's your job to shake all the hands and kiss all the babies you need to in order to maintain your position as a vital party member. Oh, and always remember to wash with soap and hot water.

but there's no "I" in a lot of words

"Teamwork is a bunch of people doing what I say," I once heard a ranking manager jokingly (but not) comment. What makes it funny, of course, is that he's right. As you well know, the unit of business work is the *team,* and you've got no choice but to band together with your group around whatever assignment tumbles down the pike—regardless of how impractical, insipid, or inane it (or they) may be.

The setup is obviously very different from college, where you can typically choose whom to talk to, if anyone at all, and where the quality of your work almost always begins and ends at your desk. Moreover, in school you only have to deal with assigned group members for so many weeks before you all move on. In the project-based working world, by sharp contrast, you rely heavily on others to complete their work (accurately), to inform your tasks, to field your questions, to abide by group operating decisions, to maintain their focus, and to adhere to the timelines and guidance of team managers—for as long as you all shall work there, until layoffs do you part.

The winning strategy in this hand-in-hand kind of environment is to accept your subsumed role, striving not necessarily to shine but rather to *support,* which will ultimately earn you the recognition you deserve. And you do that by positioning yourself where you can add the most value to both the group and the firm: in the gaps created by your team's interlocking attributes. Just as companies do in the marketplace (and as you'll do again when building your brand), you have to assess your strengths vis-à-vis the unfilled niches in the squad, identifying those potential matches that will delineate your place going forward.

Assigned work is obviously just that; this agenda informs how you can organically grow your role through the types of assistance you offer, the personal initiatives you undertake, and where you stand with respect to certain issues. In filtering your individual objectives through those of the team, you also help ensure that the two are in synch and, ideally, offer the potential to synergize into larger group-wide programs. It even aligns your interests directly with your boss' (i.e., perfectly), which helps when he catches you walking in late. Again.

Begin by carefully reanalyzing the nature of your group: What specifically does it exist to do, and how do the people within it traditionally go about their work? What is the team's operating discretion (e.g., does your manager say, "This is what has to get done and you need to find the best way to do it," or, "This is what has to get done and *here's how* you're going to do it..."), and how have the formal and informal processes taken shape around that? Who are the key opinion-molders, where are the pockets of power, and which cliques most impact the crew's dynamic? Knowing all this, how can you most effectively situate yourself; where does it look like you can post the strongest backing? How can your unique assets be channeled to help to make the tribe stronger and more productive?

Your group, of course, will progress and transform with the personal growth of its members, the arrival and departure of core teammates, and the type of work that flows through the pipeline—meaning that your role is never static and that no leadership position is ever protected. You can establish your candidacy for advancement, then, by consistently monitoring how the gaps move over time as a result of these shifts, noting where your own evolving strengths can best plug the prevailing holes and stabilize the troop. Equally true in most areas of life, figuring things out at the workplace isn't an event, but rather a difficult ongoing process. Like apologizing to girlfriends.

my, what green eyes you have

Being a top performer and team harmonizer isn't without its repercussions, however, and you will inevitably face jealous—even scheming—coworkers as a result of your enviable triumphs and goodwill. And while it is your professional (and, assuredly, personal) goal to be liked by your equals, it's frankly preferable to be liked by your betters should you be forced to pick. Plus even then the choice will never be absolute.

You're naturally going to alienate—and maybe already have—a certain cadre of cutthroat career freshmen and sub-par seniors simply by being your ambitious self, yet you misspend your hours and hopes trying to curry back their favor. That esteem isn't worthwhile and will never be properly recouped, and this is just one of an uncontrollable many issues that people will continue to have with you—usually for reasons only they know. (And even they're not always sure themselves).

Your duty, instead, is to maintain your equanimity and professionalism until things shake loose, not allowing yourself to be dragged to their level; I mean, think of all the experience they have on you down there.

Still, while you shouldn't apologize for your success, you shouldn't put it up on the marquee either. Force the subject out of conversations with colleagues when it arises, and certainly never boast around the office about any special perks or entitlements you may be enjoying. Not only is humbleness important for management to see, it's almost more important for your peers to see: give them no reason not to like you other than modestly accepting the rewards they're not offered. Everybody knows the playing field isn't level, of course, but if you can maintain the comfortable illusion that it is via your unassuming demeanor, you'll tilt the turf even further in your favor.

Which you can gain full traction on by generously syndicating credit for the group's winning work. Even for those projects that you primarily shouldered, if you unrestrainedly recognize the team for their part—which is just the kind of selfless and cost-free act emblematic of an all-star career freshman—you'll line them up behind you one-by-one in solidarity (plus set yourself up nicely to have the favor returned in spades). What's more, smart managers know the score no matter how you try to spin it, meaning that your efforts to deflect the limelight will actually only intensify the glowing sheen it casts on you. Provided, of course, you can get the "smart manager" part taken care of.

mentors

you can't pick your family...

If bosses are like a parent and coworkers like young siblings, then mentors are like that revered older brother or sister—but who never minds you tagging along and that you actually get to choose. They've been-there-done-that galore, screwed-up aplenty, and cajoled "dad" in bulk shipments, which means they can forestall the litany of mistakes that litter most young professionals' rap sheets. Plus you never have to worry about them taking the car out when you need it.

Smaller organizations frequently don't have formal mentorship programs, but the big boys all do—to provide you the best chance of supplying them with a good return on their investment. No matter where you've alighted, though, chances are you'll have to search out an advisor on your own, as firm-assigned mentors are a mixed bag at best. Some dutifully (though not always vigorously) defend your cause and show you the ropes, and others are mentors only in name, which you may have unfortunately already found out. Since most Fortune 500 managers don't have a choice about shepherding career freshmen through the Entry Level Rite of Passage, grunts often don't figure into their schedules outside of airport downtime or drinking binges at the local tavern.

So to begin with, it's essential that you recruit a mentor in whom you feel entirely comfortable confiding. The issues plaguing young professionals are foreign, complicated, intense, exasperating—and absolutely irresolvable when mincing words or doing a political dance to save face. On the contrary, your adviser is out to save face *for* you, and one of their major functions is to make you feel safe telling or asking them whatever you've got on your mind. Odds are they had a very similar question or concern when they were in your position, and one of the principal reasons most mentors want the job is their earnest desire to support early-goers where they, themselves, had to go it alone. Your successes should be vicarious vindication for your counselor's entry level errors, so don't pick someone with whom you'll be preoccupied trying not to come off as green. Full value requires full disclosure.

Keep in mind, however, that a mentoring relationship is transactional, meaning it's equally important to buy into someone with the depth of experience that's going to significantly inform yours. There's certainly no drought of advice out there; just good advice, and candidates available to send you astray with the best of intentions abound. So make sure yours boast some solid years behind them, and have demonstrated their understanding of your firm's workings and the business world in which it works (as graduate degrees can hint at). Their own bosses, however, are typically interested in them for the same reasons—and usually for problems of greater financial concern and broader time commitment than yours—so it's also not uncommon to scratch out your top picks during your search.

Not to worry, as you'll meet at least several qualified contenders while building your network of associates, and it works in your benefit to retain each of them in some capacity. As a career freshman, you require an insistent amount of time and energy to be benevolently volunteered, a disproportionate number of strings to be charitably pulled, and an unprecedented rate of elbows to be impatiently thrown; finding all of these wonderful attributes singly personified is a rarity—and just when you need them even more exceptional—so this is where your "advisory team" comes into play.

Regardless of whom you designate as your primary mentor (which is really a de facto, non-binding choice), you need a relatively deep pool of perspectives to draw from concerning important decisions you're confronted with, as well as to spread out your questions and requests such that you're not an undue burden. And while this team can and should include individuals at outside companies, it's crucial that you have at least one vocal, influential advocate in your firm. Come promotion time, the only way senior decision-makers can usually differentiate between you and the rest of the office furniture is if they have trusted people singing your entry level praises.

One, obviously, should be your manager, another should be a mentor, and preferably there ought to be two or three others from different functional areas who you've gotten to know and impress. Some will avail you as a result of working together on certain projects, and others you'll have to independently watch and woo on your own. We'll talk about that courtship process next chapter. Which, yes, sometimes does involve dinner and a movie.

operating instructions

Mentors, first, are an invaluable resource for leading you to the right people to talk to in pursuing your interests, as well as helping you secure the assignments that will highlight your skills and keep you challenged. (They also work pretty well, by the way, when it comes to some of that ranting and screaming you should be practicing).

Functioning as both a conduit and a champion, an adviser should leverage their relationships for introductions to the gatekeepers of the great engagements, as well as campaign on your behalf for the duties that will stretch you and stagger others. Clearly any (positive) dealings they've had with the people to whom you directly or indirectly report will help the process along, so look to those mentors first when you're in the market for this type of aid. (Or to those people first when you're in the market for this type of mentor).

Notably, however, it is not an advisor's role to secure any particular assignment or project placement, but instead to provide the entryway, offer their counsel for traversing it, and leave you to your own two feet from there. "I tend to think mentors are more adjusters. They help calibrate and adjust the direction you're going in…," explains Harvard Business School professor Allen Grossman in *How They Achieved*. "That's often very important, because if you're a sailor and you're off course by five degrees, 1,000 miles later you're in deep trouble." (And kicking yourself for giving the Exxon Valdez navigator a second chance).

In addition to making the handshakes happen, a mentor should also tip you off as to what kind of grip is best. Or if you should even extend your arm at all. Their history with the company has likely offered them at least a broad sense of what the powers that be are all about, including their differing professional objectives, working styles, personality types, and so forth. Hitting an advisor up for the proper approach before a first meeting will allow you to hit the right individual right in their sweet spot—and then inform the weeks and months of service in front of you once your uncanny kinship prompts a hasty request to fill one of their project's vacancies.

Yet while it's your task to adapt yourself to the methods of whoever's at the helm, it may be in your best interest not to join the crew to begin with. As a result of obdurately ignoring my manager's spot-on advice about Bill, for instance, I discovered that even the highest profile, most coveted projects can rapidly deteriorate into a torturous and belittling entry level existence. Although I suppose that's true any time you have a team headed by a would-be psychiatric patient.

In that vein, it's also an adviser's place to endow you with insider advice about the biggest trials and traps you face as you continue forward as a grunt. They know the loose floorboards paneling most new assignments, so if they're not quick in pointing them out then you need to be quicker in asking; even a nonspecific, "What do I need to watch out for when dealing with...?" will usually get things going. And very often the best information in this category of counsel isn't necessarily technical in nature, but rather procedural and political, whereby you gain the advantage through better understanding how the organization functions around the area in question.

Then your mentors will help you bend to fit. It's a guarded, self-protective position against criticism that unnecessarily holds so many career freshmen rigidly in place, and that any good counselor will begin to limber up through their difficult, yet tactful development of your operating proficiency. Unabridged honesty is the signature of any true mentorship, and it usually calls for experienced and discerning eyes to see what you don't know to look for—or what you've conditioned yourself not to. Plus there needs to be a genuine interest in your betterment to take the time to slap you around. Everything's done in the name of your future, of course, and there'll be enough high-fives to cushion the blows.

Finally, this candor ought to extend to discussions concerning your future career directions (i.e., not with the company). Seasoned mentors know that entry level shelf-lives are brief, and will be more concerned about your success and development as a professional more than your role in the organization, per se. As such, they should gladly and freely offer up their experience and network of contacts when you're ready to move on—and you should greedily and unapologetically tap into those resources. Plus maybe send a card.

Your passions may lead you to realms unknown to your advisors, of course, and in that case they ought to be there with pom-poms and their contact information, cheering you on and encouraging you to call them with any questions you might have in the future. Good business colleagues work like that. Plus they never know if they might need *you* someday.

only what you learn

drift of discovery

American folklorist and Harlem Renaissance inspirer Zora Neale Hurston writes, "There are years that ask questions, and years that answer." That thought was my rock when I was first beset by the entry level. It offered not only a reassuring stability, but an even greater sense of what it meant to be human: Amidst my angst and doubt, I understood that I was simply adrift with everyone else in the natural ebb and flow of life. Disobedient and feral as the cycle was, I recognized the period of questioning I had sloshed into, and was strengthened by knowing that the shore couldn't be far off. In fact, it was probably the only thing I didn't have a doubt about.

For long. Initially certain I would earn my wave to life's enlightening reply just by virtue of living through the storm, I started to see that I might not be able to passively wait to wash aground. I had already moved to a new city, new company, and new line of work, yet was still splashing aimlessly about my assignments, coughing up my pride, and floundering with my outlook on the future. Every stroke I took seemed to lead to another uncertainty, and it occurred to me that perhaps it was because I didn't have a set direction in mind (what with my course being principally left up to the wind and gravity and Internet résumé postings). The years of question, I began to suspect, may very well dump me off on some rocky beach of unacceptable explanations if I didn't figure out for myself where I was really going. Besides under.

Still, after a difficult stretch of some long-overdue deliberation, I was only left shaken in realizing that my exodus to the Silicon Valley was little more than a directionless escape from a bad situation. Absent the sizeable payday and braggability of being a geographically-certified dot-comer, there was no more compelling a reason to jump there than to most any other firm or locale; my motivations were entirely superficial and my dreams entirely unconsidered. Not that I knew what those dreams were, mind you, but just that I wasn't properly looking for them. Profoundly disappointed in myself (and the weather), I pledged that whatever I did going forward it wasn't going to be arbitrary. Although I *was* ready to tell the company where to put its fiber optics, and go make my way through the fogginess back in sunny Southern California.

Recognizing that this next step required more front-end contemplation than I was planning to afford it, however, the labor market graciously plopped itself on top of my company's cellar, sprinkling a fresh layer of dirt on my head. My landlord also couldn't help but join the cause, and bolted the doors with his obscenely large lease termination penalty. You know, there's nothing like an unexpected economic downturn and some unread fine print to give pause for deep reflection. And to put the kibosh on yet another big, random move you may be tempted to make.

Imprisoned, I resolutely set out to find some type of guiding objective, convinced that this was the world's way of telling me it was local. Ignorant, I was also wholly unprepared for the months of agony that persisted, convinced that this was the world's way of telling me it saw me cheat those couple of times in college. Near my breaking point, the vision at last came to me in a rush, of all places during a particularly unpleasant late-August meeting with my manager. Which he decided to call, understandably, following a several-thousand-dollar booboo I had recently made. With the summer sun piercing through his untinted office window directly onto the back of my collar—exaggerating the atmosphere and prompting an accusatory squint in what were already smoldering eyes—the goal felt almost like a portent: I'd better learn everything I can about this business.

My aim was sure to pass muster with the company. Neither grand nor sweeping as I had anticipated, the direction turned out to be exceedingly practical—even simplistic—but did promise to transform my daily circumstances into something that didn't hurt so badly. Finally, I had discovered the chance to at least tread the waters of fate, and maybe even begin to make my way out to some resolution. Plus to stop butchering my silly job.

I started with the obvious, looking through books, magazines, newspapers, and Web printouts about the field I had chosen to commit this early portion of my post-graduate life to. Coming home to a stack of material each night, it felt almost as if I were back in school studying again—and no more than when I found myself fighting heavier eyelids and further wandering thoughts with each turn of the page. Too often waking up at 1 a.m. with my cheek stuck to some chalk-dry scribbling about "e-security" and such, the exercise only more completely confirmed the fact that I selected this profession about as haphazardly as I did my one college biology course, and that the reading was going to have the same effect.

Still fully committed to my cause nonetheless, I began to engage the people I met around the workplace in conversation, safe in the knowledge that I'd never before fallen asleep standing up. I figured that I had a much better chance of absorbing words that I could hear and put a face to, and might actually grow some good relationships in the process. Plus I was hanging on to the lingering hope that buried somewhere in their otherwise dispassionate take on things, my colleagues might offer me a true spark of enthusiasm about the high-tech business and a compelling reason as to why I should stay there.

Turns out they were looking too. Yet they were still able to pony up some indispensable advice about success on the job, with the firm in general, and in the business realm at large. Not to mention pull free that last thread of doubt about me hanging around a day longer than I had to.

Sensing I had really hit on something here, I decided to try the same technique with the people I met in my outside life (if you want to call it that), hoping for more frank and nonpartisan input from folks who weren't getting paid to deal with me. I was also eager to glimpse beyond the narrow confines of my profession, desperate to find that the energy and excitement about this thing we call work hadn't escaped everyone. So whomever's ear was amenable to the tug, I asked about what they did for a living, how they found their way there, what they enjoyed (and didn't) about their work, where they were going with their careers, and, of course, if there were any openings at their companies.

Some of the discussions never found their way out of the specifics of my position; some turned into anxiously-told autobiographies; some revealed conception-changing truths about survival as a young professional; some led me to new places, new people, and new books; and some were just two individuals sharing their thoughts about life. I was also relieved and joyed to find that the passion for work was plenty alive; it was just quiet about it, inconspicuously residing along the fault lines of gruffness, cynicism, and don't-you-hate-your-job-too sentiment shared by Americans and celebrated by *Office Space*.

My eyes began to open. I grew to see the size, complexity, and unimaginable depth of this world—so many lives, so many perspectives, so many types of work, and so many unique interests and goals. There was so much to discover and understand, I had found, that what started off as a straightforward approach to a backward situation blossomed into an overpowering realization:

The years will answer only what you learn from them.

As a career freshman, you navigate the ocean of confusion and struggle in which you're sinking through an unyielding commitment to continuous learning. This transition period is traversed only through new understandings, but which will remain hidden in the people and papers floating about your life until you actively go out and grab them.

It's here that your years of answers—of freedom and happiness—are tied up, belonging to those whose experience is available for no cost other than a few minutes or a few dollars. And it's ultimately in striving to clutch the corporate realm as tightly as possible that you not only secure a definition for your daily trials, but also a direction for your greater aspirations. Plus you get to keep your stapler.

The philosophy builds on top of itself and starts at your cube, where the more you understand about your position, firm, and industry, the better equipped you'll be to perform your assignments, negotiate workplace politics, undertake good initiatives—see how to structure your efforts to your advantage (and avoid a charred neckline). In this sense, toiling at the entry level is really no different than studying in college, and your lot is more quickly advanced by viewing each day in the office as a day in class. Um, wait. An elective. Well... Just work with the analogy, okay?

Moreover, the better you grasp the economics and operating procedures of the working arena, the better positioned you'll be to find your long-term success within it. No matter what your trade, it's *all* business (including education, nonprofit, and sometimes government work), and your career advancement is inherently wedded to knowing the proper ins and outs. So not only will seeing your job outside of its vacuum help you excel within an organization, but it'll also assist you in identifying potential opportunities for your own ventures—to say nothing of running them more effectively once you do break away.

But that's not enough, of course. The purpose of an occupation isn't simply to make a living—no matter how good—but to make a living by doing something you **love**. And before you can find that livelihood you're passionate about building, you first need an in-depth understanding about who you are as a person, what you value in your work, what you hope to accomplish over the span of your career, and what the marketplace even has to offer you. By not exposing yourself to the myriad environments, teachings, and people that abound, you deny yourself the opportunity to uncover fields, philosophies, and mentors that stand to shape and possibly even transform your ideals and vocational goals. Remember, only when you stand open to life does it really start talking back. Plus it gives you something to do on Saturday nights when you don't have a date.

Finally, it seems that learning is one of the things we were put here to do. As humans, we're not only hardwired to understand our existences on a conscious and spiritual level, but those who see and know more about the world tend to lead fuller, richer, more enjoyable lives. I obviously don't have the answers to the mysteries of our incarnation, but I do think that one of the simple ways to try to make sense of everything is to experience as much as we possibly can during our lifetimes. Even if we never realize the meaning of it all, we can at least go down swinging, right?

But I digress. While there's undeniably a certain gestalt to this whole matter of learning and life and work, our immediate needs are decidedly more focused. The business at hand is to outswim the entry level by "outlearning" it, and the balance of this chapter is accordingly devoted to the strategies and tactics for doing so. Which were all inspired, improbably, by the amazing Ms. Hurston—who I'm guessing never envisioned her words supporting a careworn young professional through his corporate ordeals. Much less yours.

the student of old

If you ever watch a budding pupil, like a first-grader, do their homework, you can almost see the wheels forcedly creaking round and round right behind their eyes. Whether it's the rush of new synapses forming in their brains or just the simple obstinacy of youth, these prepubescent academicians are doggedly intent on doing things by themselves. And if it means they have to tear right through that doublewide lined paper with those extra-thick pencil erasers, so be it; the point is that they figure the stuff out on their own.

Now, if you ever watch a university student struggling to complete an assignment...you probably want to do it from a safe distance. Between the incessant (yet admirably creative) cursing, frantic phone calls to fellow students, gallons of caffeine, and repeated flipping to the back of the book for the—c'mon, be there—completely inscrutable answers, they just want to be done with it in the quickest, dirtiest way possible. And if it means liberating some information from an "undocumented source" here and there, so be it; the point is that the grade looks good.

What happens to that childlike steadfastness—to that giddy satisfaction in the simple discovery? Maybe the bloody competition nurtured by our system of higher education slowly erodes the unblemished goal of learning into the unbending demand for performance, ill begotten or otherwise. That's certainly the paradigm Big Business operates under, so maybe there's even a favorable argument to be made here in the name of good preparation. Regardless of why or where everyone crooks, however, two facts are abundantly evident for all career freshmen: You will remain a student for the rest of your years, and you have to rediscover that student of years ago.

While you may graduate from school, you absolutely never graduate from learning, and the model for your continued scholarship is best informed by those too innocent to shortcut across the field. As all of the guided processes and informal arrangements in college—the lifelines, the loopholes, the links—abruptly give way at the entry level to the lonely, singular onus on you to obtain knowledge, your success rests squarely on your determination, rigor, and zeal. Also a touch of that shrewdness and ingenuity you picked up on campus.

In short, it means tirelessly scavenging for information wherever you see it to be gleaned, whenever it makes itself available, however you can get it. Which also, notably, imposes no limit on the count or kind of subjects to study, prescribes no fixed amount of information to memorize, obliges you to take no exams (not directly, at least), and designates no pre-selected people to guide you. It's the kind of educational freedom that makes for not getting one.

So know what it takes. For beginners, the patchwork collection of data, leads, and ideas you gather will be disjointed and fractional at best, requiring on your part a clever and calculated sewing together. The DNA of the process, also, leads to certain efforts being invested frustratingly far ahead of the curve, as you build knowledge in areas and ways that won't be relevant to your daily life for some time to come. Moreover, the program demands considerable personal commitments of time and energy, usually at the expense of certain other leisures and luxuries. Hmm, maybe it is kind of like college.

But you enroll with the affirming understanding that it isn't for a grade, to impress a recruiter, or to keep the folks quiet, but rather to enrich your career and appreciation of life. You learn as a young professional in order to bolster your position, broaden your vision, benchmark your decisions—to begin to build the life that you want to live. And to do even more wonderful things that rhyme.

Plus by searching out your new knowledge ravenously and endlessly—seeking always to differentiate yourself by what you understand—you also get there more quickly, fighting through the ambiguity and hardships with unlikely aptitude and efficiency. Whereas you can only build experience one day at a time, information assembles just as fast as you can find it, meaning that you beat them sooner by knowing more. Which also, in turn, makes you more interesting at parties.

Above all, it requires a self-promise to value your lasting intellectual and professional development ahead of all other entry level objectives (save, perhaps, for not doing bodily harm to your boss). Paul O'Neill, former chairman of aluminum giant Alcoa and short-lived iconoclast Treasury Secretary for the Bush administration, confirms it: "In the best people I see a commitment to continual learning," he says. "I don't mean education, necessarily, in a formal way, but they are people who are constantly in search of new information and new ways they can integrate it into a framework that they carry around in their head." (Where, for a loose cannon like Paul, portability is a must).

The devoted building of that framework ideally prepares you not only to meet the requirements of your current job, but also your promoted job, your job with a new company, your job in a new industry, and ultimately your job doing the work that you were made to do. That's an attractive proposition in a place where the curriculum is no longer printed and bound.

changing majors

So you're a student again, and a freshman at that. While highly meaningful to your overall character, your bachelor-sized knowledge of whatever academic subject you landed on (for many at the behest of parents, the suggestion of friends, or because your beer spilled on that section of the catalogue) will probably be of most use to you now in your back pocket. Even if you're among the few who've actually entered the industry college ostensibly prepared you to join—a logical aspiration, but frequently as sensible as the choice that started everything—classes have begun all over again for your new major: The corporate world.

It's a punishing, hands-on field of study, with nobody to buy last year's test off of or to write your papers for you. (At least not with what you're getting paid). But that's not the route to go this time anyway, where the call to study couldn't be more pronounced: As a young professional, your learning curve is never steeper, your flexibility to assess a company without involvement never greater, and your need to build everyday knowledge never stronger. Really, if there's ever a demand for understanding and the freedom with which to supply it, the entry level is the place.

Which requires looking all the way around. You fail if you scale the boundaries of your lowly position only to perch yourself complacently atop them; mastery means up-and-over, looking also to hurdle the margins of your firm and the industry in which it plays. Your ability to successfully negotiate a trail through the working underground, remember, lies in your appreciation of where to blaze it—an unlikely task if you don't first see where your organization is trying to set fire itself. Besides to the list of promises the recruiters made you.

You need the context of the issues that management is concentrating on to completely inform where and how you fit into the business equation (which also helps, incidentally, with elevator small-talk). And with that solid clench on what keeps your boss and his brethren awake at night, you not only distill those initiatives and areas of research that will generate the most value for the company, but also develop another avenue to predict the kind of help your manager needs before he tells you he needs it.

Throughout the learning process, however, don't forget that the company's not in the business of teaching you their business; that was the job your school already botched. Any knowledge you accrue in the course of doing your work is considered gravy, an indirect benefit of employment. In truth, your firm cares about your education only insofar as it'll help you make them more money. So if it's too distanced from the dollars, even the most radiant line of personal coursework will be only dimly received. (Blackly, should it inhibit your practice at the numbing tasks they actually pay you for).

You have to be clever with your intake of information, then, seeking it out in unorthodox places and at inconspicuous times. There's not a report you photocopy, for example, that you can't learn something from; there's not a hushed conversation in the hallway from which a little strategic eavesdropping won't yield new insights; there's no (public) file cabinet you can rifle through without finding some important tidbit about the company; there's no evening business class at your local university from which you can't gain immense value—and maybe that Saturday-night date—by sitting discreetly in the back.

Don't break any ethical ground, certainly, but know that there's nothing wrong with employing your college-honed cunning when it comes to bettering your position. By building your knowledge in this catch-as-catch-can fashion, in fact, you most effectively construct that bridge for perspective, adding layers of depth to your work through understanding it in a more sophisticated way. Which, of course, provides for more confidence in performing your assignments, giving presentations, speaking with superiors, and asking unsuspecting business students out to coffee. So not only will your hungered learning about your surroundings feed your professional endeavors, it'll even fortify your self-esteem, which is probably trending to the anemic side at this point.

In an effort to get yourself completely healthy and up to speed, the following three nutrients will be the most important components in your diet of information, offering a triple-burst of energy, strength, and stamina as you paddle your way through the entry level:

- People
- Reading
- Training

the company you keep

they won't bite (hard)

A professor's job to her well-paying students is principally just to convey knowledge. Or at least to show up and talk for an hour. Yet for the size of the price tag, one-on-one interaction is much less frequent than might be expected (and it's not like the podium is so teeming with life after class as to preclude a quick scholarly exchange). Attendance, too, at welcoming, bite-sized discussion sections—complete with their own single-serving teaching assistants—is often optional, which somehow gets lost in translation as "opt out." Even raised hands during lectures are about as common as coherent explanations for midterm material.

Rather, most collegians favor the passive standby of "listen now, read later"—or, more appropriately, "listen when awake, read before exam"—and prefer to lay their confusion bare to equally uninformed course enrollees. As opposed, naturally, to the folks who actually write the tests. In fact, it generally takes near hysteria (or an unexpected C) before students will break the "In Case of Emergency Only" glass maintaining the divide and voluntarily go visit their educators.

Which usually isn't all too effective a strategy at the entry level, where the fire alarm gets flipped on along with the lights every morning. In scrambling to the nearest exit, the people in your environment will, instead, be the absolute most useful and important guides. By carefully watching what they do, casually drawing them into discussion, and critically considering their advice, living, breathing humans will consistently deliver the best return for your learning efforts. (Although, unlike school, there's no scheduled time for them to shut up and let you leave).

Older professionals, as I discovered, tend to imbue an elsewhere-unfound sense of history and wide-angle perspective into their career advice; younger managers can offer a strategic, midrange sense of how businesses really tick, often with direct application to your position; seniors usually have a tactical, politically sensitive take on how to realistically step up to the next level; even peers bring to bear more relevant advice than in school, where everyone's been screened with the filter of adding value to the company—as opposed to whatever formula that let in some of the intellectual smurfs you shared classes with. Which, yes, in some cases included the professors.

But I'm obviously not the first to pioneer this technique, and certainly nowhere near the best. My dialogues were a mere pittance compared to the work of former PepsiCo CEO Donald Kendall, for example, who spoke to just about everyone who was willing to talk back when he was first starting out. And often at great personal cost: He tells a story of his early days laboring at a factory in Pittsburgh, staying up until all hours to yank free the insights of the lead supervisor: "He trained more people who received promotions than any other plant operator," Kendall explains. "He used to talk with me until one in the morning. I'd work all day and, at night, sit down with him." Donald, later on, had similarly gabby relationships with head personnel in just about every other part of the country he landed in—and it ultimately landed him at the top.

Still, while businesspeople can provide a depth of insight, direction, and feeling unavailable through any other medium, they don't make it easy. Very often their input is unstructured, incomplete, biased, misleading, and sometimes just plain old wrong—even maliciously so. And while you shouldn't ascribe to spite what can perfectly well be explained by stupidity, it nonetheless takes talking to enough folks to find the gaps, fill them in, and toss out the excess. Which would've been nice to do in college when professors tried to pass their mushy opinions off as hard truths.

grow by example

Among the best information you can tease out of pe[ople,] what really doesn't take much coaxing at all to get t[o,] their histories. Everybody's favorite subject to talk ab[out is] them-selves (especially authors), which turns out to be an increaibly useful phenomenon when they have something to say that actually applies to your own life.

And that's easy to come by as a young professional. The ropes you have to climb at the entry level are tall, rough, and most signifi-cantly, well traveled; they've been ascended, pull after agonizing pull, by all those who've come before you. No matter what their professional rank today, those scars are assuredly still highly visible and freely available for story time. People just love to proudly reminisce about how they've overcome hardships—and few other times of life offer such rich fodder as the first years in the corporate arena—so use their rope-burn to prevent yours. A mistake learned is a mistake avoided, remember, and about as cheap and easy a way as there is to outstrip day-by-day experience. Not to mention the safest.

So in canvassing your network of associates (which we'll discuss building next), figure out who's been where you are and done what you're doing, and then tap their experience and knowledge for all it's worth. Learn about what and whom they competed against, where they stumbled and where they strode, how they approached their challenges strategically and psychologically, successfully and unsuc-cessfully, and how they've ultimately ended up where they are now. Then invest the time and energy into mapping their memoirs onto your miseries, supplanting your worries with some of that hard-won wisdom. Seldom will it be a perfect fit, but you don't need one of those—just enough raw material to sift through and adapt from. Hey, whatever saves on the calamine lotion, right?

your network sponsors

Whoever first uttered the phrase, "It's all about who you know," (in addition to enjoying some disgustingly fluky back-scratching arrangements, surely) is responsible for articulating one of business' most fundamental tenets. Building effective, productive relationships is how you open up professional channels and position yourself to garner the feedback, opportunities, and contacts you need to be successful. As well as invitations to go play golf. So stringing together a network of talented, influential people—out of whose trust and respect will all that naturally flow—is an absolute entry level imperative.

But it'll probably only start off as a trickle (and especially if you're late for tee times). The effort to grow your acquaintanceships must be concerted and directed, slowly building on top of every interaction. Some, of course, are going to be casual encounters around the office, at conferences, or in local hangouts—which you can coolly leverage to find out what they're up to—and others will require some orchestration on your part, perhaps in the form of an invitation to lunch or drinks. However the combination should play out, though, the goal is to move each conversation (gradually and genuinely) that much deeper into the areas in which you need to make the most headway.

Which frequently runs you into another contact. Which is also just what you want: A business network, by definition, is a system of interconnected people, meaning that the broader yours reaches and the more diverse its makeup, the more valuable it becomes (hence the appeal of trade groups). So when it comes to veteran players, a colleague's sphere of influence usually picks up where theirs ends—and meetings are only too happily arranged for gung-ho career freshmen. To maximize your access to the essential information, leads, and future opportunities, then, use each associate as a springboard to the next. Like you did with classmates who had hot friends.

Sound a bit crass and mercenary? Of course it does. It's also standard industry practice. Professional relationships are utilitarian first, and anything else second. There are times, to be sure, when a genuine camaraderie or mentorship will develop out of your efforts; but most often your contacts are just people in your corner, which is right where you need them to be. We'll get further into it in Chapter

Seven, but in general friends are friends, and business is business.

Then what can you offer in return? That is, if all of these success-ful businesspeople are doing *quid pro quo*-style favors for you, what's in it for them? Nothing; not right away, at least. While networking is a barter system, the entry level is a place where large trade deficits are tolerated and debts readily forgiven. Like mentors, people are going to work with you at this stage because they were once there: they remember who opened doors for them when they were first starting out, and want to pay it forward, as it were. Your hearty gratitude and admiration is all they really expect, and, once again, they never know exactly whom *you* might know.

That said, always bear in mind where you sit on these individu-als' totem poles. If you think they're important then they probably are, which means that your top concerns are clinging to life at the bottom of their to-do lists. Yet, at the same time, favors requested out of the blue tend to stay out there, so the line of contact also has to remain relatively unbroken. (People, in spite of everything, still want to be valued for who they are and not necessarily what they can do for you). So be patiently persistent, respect their space, and generally just sort of linger in the background. Happily, there'll always be something to listen in on.

at least they're not $100 anymore

The top people in any company seem to always be in the know, as if hooked up intravenously to a newswire and the *New York Times* bestseller list. Not only do they understand their own business inside and out, but can also usually tell you what's going on (or not) with their competitors, suppliers, and clients, in the industry as a whole, in related fields, in popular culture, and probably in your cubicle.

But there's no science (or intricate medical procedure) to it; in-stead, it's typically the straightforward result of them scouring some combination of books, newspapers, magazines, trade publications, industry newsletters, and a handful of Web sites. Chosen based on what they see management reading, what comes recommended by the critics, what's going to be of value to their position and firm, and just what interests them, these titles and periodicals can frequently put them at a level on par with the technical (though not experiential) knowledge of their superiors.

That's a good place to be, and this is a great way to get there. But it takes considerable dedication to stay current—especially during the days when the minutes actually feel like minutes. For starters, you're faced with the initial burden of figuring out the right things to be poring over, which usually means some careful snooping and interrogation. Then comes the time and out-of-pocket expense of actually going out and making your purchases. And it really hurts when you, gulp, have to figure out which shows you're going to shut the TV off for to actually stay literate. The payoff more than justifies the ardor, though, and it can even be, dare I say, a tax write-off. No, sorry, I meant to say fun. Plus there are usually a few books that can function as a low-cost alternative to prescription sleep aids.

Rest assured it's not always that big a challenge, and particularly when you can put some creativity to use. Thumbing through your industry's trade rag, for instance, or the *Wall Street Journal*—the mainstay of business information—is a great way to invest your downtime at the office. Corporate libraries, also, are usually stocked full with vintage and semi-recently released titles available for free checkout, saving you $20 here and there. What's more, building just an hour of reading into your nightly routine (or your this-assignment-can-wait-until-later routine) can get you through a couple-hundred-page book in a week, and even more quickly if you only scan for the gist.

The point is to keep pace with your industry, keep up with your coworkers, and keep looking smart and well-informed in front of your higher-ups—which a little intelligently placed effort here will do. And more: In addition to helping you stay on top of all the hot buzzwords, phraseology, and industry lingo, your exposure to the works of good authors and journalists will even improve your own communications and writing style.

As well as your assignments. The startup I slogged away with, for example, entered into a channel alliance with a giant consultancy—before anybody knew what they were doing with the Web—and, to my astonishment, I was given part of the account. Not knowing how these types of structures really worked beyond what the press releases told me (i.e., nothing), I went out and bought a great book on the subject. It was a quick and comprehensive way to learn about the different arrangements, interests, and strategies surrounding the practice, and an equally good way to show my initiative to my manager. So when the first roundtable took place, not only did I understand what they were talking about, I even had some good nuts-and-bolts ideas to contribute. (That's what *I* called them, anyway).

As the case had it, I never attended another meeting and my role in the deal turned out to be little more than glorified administration. But that's beside the point. (And not necessarily unreasonable for a non-MBA trying to break into the wheeling-and-dealing world of business development). The take-home idea, rather, is that because of my reading, I walked away with knowledge of a vital business practice that I'm now equipped to put to work for myself.

Again, a lot of entry level investing won't generate current returns, but rather pay out down the line. That means it's important not to allow your early shunts to discourage you from buying into the right habits—and definitely not from buying up the right reading material. After all, that consulting channel has now collapsed, and I can't seem to build my own fast enough.

now that you offered...

As a whole, career freshmen fail to fully apprehend the fact that they're just as much a product or service as any their company designs and sells. They're competing for premium buyers—intracompany and intercompany alike—in a highly selective labor market, and are only as attractive as the relative skill sets and background they bring to the table. Since we already know that the place setting for experience is by nature barebones, the centerpiece of the offering must be knowledge

(Or, as Bill suggested, nepotism).

And one of the most effective ways to broaden, deepen, strengthen, and in general accentuate this core dish is through *training*: any kind you can get your hands on and head around. Whether it's obtained formally or informally, by hook or by crook, your deepened understanding about the techniques and tools in your field not only makes you more valuable in your current position, but also increases your marketability for any job you're interested in going forward. Plus you get the immediate perks of a happy boss, better projects, and—hold your breath—even greater job satisfaction. (All the way from 0 to 1 in some cases).

Furthermore, milking the company in this department is one of the most dollar-sensitive investments you can make. Professional training classes and seminars, as you may know, can be prohibitively expensive (as in the thousands of dollars), meaning that plunking yourself down at two or three of these colloquiums can add an effective $10,000-plus to your annual compensation. So recognize firm-sponsored education as the tremendous benefit it is, and pursue yours hungrily and relentlessly—even if it means lassoing certain people and technologies into helping you get it.

Persuade your manager or mentor, for example, to sweet-talk their superiors into covering a course you found listed in the trades; harass a trusted senior until she shows you how to properly use the new software; approach the authors of a freshly released white-paper with comments and questions that you can potentially parlay into future research opportunities; gush over the quality of another trench-dweller's work to loosen them up for their secrets; take an online tutorial series and use it as a platform to secure new work; provide secondary training to your team to showcase your presentation skills. Bottom line, do whatever's necessary to get the information and skills you need to be successful—and then to make sure the people who need to know about it, in fact, do.

Importantly, whenever you're overdrawing your training budget (i.e., taking non-prepurchased, non-preallocated classes), there's almost certainly going to be some finagling involved. In your pitch, then, you have to confidently explain how the education represents a worthwhile investment of the company's funds, focusing strongly on the new skill sets you'll take away providing for a better, more cost-effective work product. There's a very specific way of going about this (which we'll explore in SURVIVAL BY SUBJECT III), but the point here is that there's no room for timidity when it comes to getting the instruction you need from your firm. Think about it: Do they have any qualms about asking of you what they want? Repeatedly?

Make your all-out swim to learn everything there is to know at the entry level equally as shameless, and the undertow of fate won't have any pull to drag you around with. Although your boss still will. In any event, don't forget to breathe.

survival by subject @ II

the daily grunt

not again...

Y ou're tired. It's raining outside. The coffee is from yesterday. Your company's network can't decide if it wants to be torturously slow or just call in sick altogether. The cubemate on your left is already nerd-wrestling your ears with his recycled commentary about the stock market; on your right, she's engrossed in yet another little-too-loud personal phone conversation—attaché still unopened, computer resting comfortably. Better still, the client has left you a voicemail in a declamatory, almost-religious froth over something they'd doubtlessly figure out themselves if the phone weren't working. And the boss doesn't look much happier himself about the assignment you rushed through yesterday to make it on time for your after-work plans. Which were, naturally, cancelled. Well, it'll all have to wait until you can deal with those 14 emergency-red-text e-mails, which really should've been answered at 2 a.m. when they were sent. You mean you were *sleeping*?

Uh huh, it's the daily grind. Or for career freshmen, "The Daily Grunt"—that game of brinkmanship played each time the access card issues its approving little beep, and swings the doors open to the squeeze of another day. Arms outstretched, it's usually all you can do to hold back your circumstances from situation to situation, person to person. But such is the unremitting life of a young professional, it seems—one of courage, resilience, endurance, and just a bit of luck. Maybe a pocketful of luck. Okay, fine, mostly luck. Still, while it's better to be lucky than good, providence isn't very predictable, and you wield a lot more influence over the matter than it appears. Success at the entry level, rather, is much more fastidiousness than it is fortune: a solid cache of habits, standards, practices, and routines is generally all you need to keep your state of affairs in good working order, and any encroaching conditions well at bay.

So this SURVIVAL BY SUBJECT installment is written to call out some effective ways and means to carry out your day-to-day drudgery, fostering a greater sense of personal control, a healthy reduction in errors, and an overall calming of the nerves. Until, of course, the client slips into another tirade. In that case, you might consider passing her off to one of your local colleagues who can outtalk her.

quality

welcome to the firm

My first consulting assignment out of college was to format a document. No, not write it—*format* it. Suspecting that UCLA might take their degree back if they caught me doing this, I meticulously lined up each paragraph and bullet point, sized the font just right, and ran the spellchecker about four times. It was perfect. When I was about to send it off, however, I was informed that the client had a lower version of the software, and that the report would have to be resaved downward so she could read it.

I quickly did so—anxious to get it out before the close of business on the East Coast—and reattached the document to the prefab e-mail verbiage I was provided with. After giving the message a final once-over (hoping to heroically uncover an error in the ready-to-serve composition, of which there were none), I pulled the trigger and escaped for some badly needed coffee. Driving home that night, I surprised myself in actually feeling a little proud of how I knocked my first project out of the park, trifling as it was.

When I walked in the next morning, I was greeted by the flashing red light of my very first voicemail. Excitedly I entered my security code, eager to hear what was sure to be my manager's praise about the stellar job I'd done. Instead it was the *partner*. With an *urgent message*:

> Hi Michael, this is Richard.
>
> Um, the client wasn't very pleased with the document you sent over yesterday. She tells me that it was a mess, and that she could hardly make heads or tails of it. So I had Julie [the senior consultant on the job] stay late last night to fix it up and resend it.
>
> Next time try to pay a little better attention to the details, huh. All right, have a good day.

I almost lost my breakfast. Sheet white and sweating visibly now, I frantically checked the "Sent Items" folder in my e-mail system; the problem had to have been on her side. But alas, I was horrified to discover that when I saved the document to the lower version, all of the formatting I had done was, of course, lost. In my unthinking hurry to get it out the door (and arrogant wish to poke a hole in my superiors' writing), I ended up dumping a company-logoed piece of garbage on top of a key strategic customer. Who just so happened to have my reporting partner's home number.

So within 24 hours of beginning my career, I had managed to upset a client, alienate a coworker, and cause a top member of the company to have egg on his face—over an assignment I originally scoffed at. Needless to say, I developed some serious OCD with regard to proofing after that.

Yet during my first performance review, well over a year later, the "attention to detail" specter came out to haunt me. When I defensively asked for some clarification, though, guess what they pointed to; I hadn't been able to come up with a good excuse for that yet. Still haven't. It was a hard lesson about the stickiness of screw-ups—particularly the little ones that are so avoidable, but that leave such a bad taste in everyone's mouth. And that also make your boss' telephone ring during dinner.

to the nth degree

There's an oft-told story about Bill Marriott, chairman of lodging giant Marriott International, getting a call from his father while trying to build the firm's flagship hotel in New York City. His dad, with seeming impropriety, informed him that the carpeting by the pool in one of the Virginia hotels needed replacing right away. In the middle of negotiating the biggest deal in the company's history, Bill promised his pop that he would take care of it later, having observably more important matters to tend to. "Son," his father replied, "if you don't take care of the little things, you won't have a company." The carpeting was fixed immediately.

The point of both these stories is to highlight the importance of doing the small stuff well. Regrettably, it usually doesn't get noticed when you do, but it most certainly gets seen when you don't. Typos, grammar errors, inconsistencies, general sloppiness—these are the tiny, completely preventable things that get attached to you far more quickly than any success (they're trying to knock you down, remember), and that in the end can seriously impact your boss' willingness to give you the kind of work you want to do. Well, at least the kind that doesn't cause cranial atrophy. Well, at least right away.

It's completely unlike college, where you can turn in what you already know is a "B paper" intending to make up for it on the final; everything you do at the entry level is, for all intents and purposes, a final. If you're supposed to photocopy a set of presentations and staple them a certain way, for example, then the staple absolutely has to be put in just so. Because if you can't even do *that* properly, then how are you going to fare with the more complicated projects—like those that involve, say, three-ring binders or catering orders. Forget about words and numbers.

Let the excellence of your work be your defining characteristic at the office, just as it calls out the best companies and goods in the marketplace: "So, the number-one thing, maybe the only thing, we judge day-in and day-out, is the quality of our product," confirms Walt Disney head chief Michael Eisner, who leads of one of the strongest, most recognizable brands in the world. Just like Mike, then, make it a given that whenever you lay a hand on anything, it's going to come out in its highest form: not only vetted for mistakes, but reflective of the concern, thought, and extra touches that are the signature of a great trustmark. (Leave your cutting to the lines in Eisner's theme parks).

And don't be fearful that if you specialize in simplicity so well that's all you'll be given. (Finally, someone who can alphabetize)! To the contrary, by doing the ridiculous little assignments well, you'll find that before too long your assignments start not to look quite as silly. Although your colleagues still will.

again, easier said

When you're not excited and engaged by your work, however, doing it well becomes a new kind of challenge. It's not that you can't make it perfect; Koko the sign-language gorilla probably could. It's just so undeserving of your consideration that you have a hard time forcing yourself to put much of it there.

Instead it's simply a chore. And the definition of a chore, as we all know, is a menial duty you're forced to carry out for a paltry sum of money—if any—and that you generally complete only well enough to shut the taskmaster up (which barely works well enough at home, let alone the corporate entry level). The situation, more seriously, can be quite unnerving for career freshmen, who are accustomed to turning in a competitively viable product in the cover-your-answers university environment. When the new output never seems to meet their old standards (e.g., catchable mistakes gliding by, only researching things halfway out of sheer indifference, big slumps in productivity owing to advanced stages of monotony), they begin to question their abilities and grapple with the attendant frustration, confusion, and dissatisfaction that follow. With the boss not far behind.

It's a slippery slope that can send your work ethic skidding and advancement potential right off the cliff. Since it's so easy to careen out of control, the effort to keep steady and on-course must be one of desperate devotion, employing any and all means available. If it helps, for example, try to view the work from the organization's perspective: Perhaps the proposal they have you cleaning up is for a huge piece of business they're trying to win, in which case you're the frontline for ensuring that the firm puts its best face forward to an important potential client. Such as with learning, seeing your position in the full context of the company's operations can add a new urgency and flavor to your duties. Wherever you find your traction, though, keep in mind that your personal sense of worth, integrity, and accomplishment are on the line here, and that it's your job to protect those assets. Even if it means using them.

Although don't expect any real credit for doing so. As difficult as it is, you further have to accept that this isn't the venue to defend your intellectual property rights—even if you're the only reason your manager keeps his job. Everything you do as a career freshman either directly or indirectly has his name on it, particularly when it shines or twinkles. As discussed, that means you're the man's de facto publicist: patching up all of his unsightly mistakes instead of wringing your hands in anticipation of the fallout, however much fun it might otherwise be. Remember, any ship with enough holes sinks eventually, and it's your place as an entry leveler to keep dutifully bailing out your foundering boss until that time comes, should you be on board with one of those types. When it does, the dinghy will come looking for you.

errors

bombs away

But nothing's ever that clean. Perforce, errors go uncaught. Discrepancies escape unnoticed. Faults lurk unrecognized. (Your boss got hired, didn't he)? Such is the stuff of humans, and of the corporate ones in particular. Yet while you're fated to send your fair share of luckless t's off into the world uncrossed, and to leave certain i's languishing sans dots, they don't suffer in vain when you aim to understand why, where, and how they came into being.

You unlock the value of your gaffes by exploiting what they have to reveal—using their teachings to pinpoint those areas where you need to install better controls or put forth more attention and concern. Though it never seems true until well afterwards, there's nothing intrinsically wrong or bad about mistakes; no more than there is anything inherently good about accidentally getting something right (except, maybe, on exams). The only true fault is in falling again because you didn't take the time or have the courage to figure out where the problem was. Paying dues intelligently, understand, means hanging on to what you buy. Including, for a while, your absurd job.

And one of the most basic elements in doing so is keeping things in the proper, yes, perspective. The broader part of it is easy enough to understand (and usually of little consolation), but maybe I'll strike a chord this time: The sun rises in the morning and sets in the evening, never forget, in just the same, trusty way on the days where you couldn't have possibly mucked things up any worse as it does on those that you couldn't have imaginably done any better. And every other day besides. The more times the globe takes another whirl, in fact, the hazier the memory of your faux pas becomes—conveniently, in the minds of those whom you're concerned about much faster than in your own.

In the business world, long-term memories aren't very, and even the unbelievably disastrous debacles eventually work like SAT scores: They may be kept on file somewhere, but not because anyone would think—or want—to look at them. As far as most people are concerned, you're only as good or bad as your most recent triumph or tragedy, and anything can turn around on any given day. (And, sometimes, back around once more). While a dent to my immediate credibility and fun little memory to rehash at an earliest performance review, for example, don't think that my first-day formatting fiasco had any true bearing on my long-run success with the company; that took me at least another couple years to ruin, I assure you. Just as former Apple Computer CEO

John Sculley comforts, "The consequences of mistakes are nowhere near as bad as you fear they are. Even in the toughest situations, the downside turns out to be more manageable than a lot of young people expect." (With the exception, for him, of Microsoft).

Also unanticipated is the second layer of perspective, which is once again wrapped-up in your position as a career freshman: If there's ever a time to lurch, bungle, goof, and in general run afoul, it's at the entry level. Certainly you would prefer to make your gross miscalculations now, as opposed to waiting until you were, say, a manager? Or, better yet, holding off until you were playing with your own money trying to run a business?

Your organization has stretched out a safety net generously lined by its coffers, so this is the time to practice the extra hard stunts. Jumping out well past your reach, of course, isn't going to be instructive for you or appreciated by the firm, but keeping to the easy moves also won't nudge that spacious informal training budget under your feet. Plus it's not like you'll even be a whisper of a memory to the place once you depart, so you get to pack up all of your embarrassments with you anyway. (Right next to those pilfered company office supplies).

In fact, some have even been able to get their break by virtue of their past disappointments. John Peterman, founder of the celebrated J. Peterman Catalog and inspiration for a character on *Seinfeld*, for example, was able to secure funding for his company by way of admitting his previous failures to prospective investors. Venture capitalists know that someone who's never had to recover from a serious setback probably doesn't have what it takes to build a long-term business, which tends to have plenty of those on hand. "If what you're doing is worth anything," Peterman believes, "then failing now and again is inevitable...Failure has been my best teacher." (His next lesson actually came in January 1999 after the company filed for bankruptcy protection; but it's still around today to tell the story).

Michael Dell, CEO of Dell Computer Corporation, would doubtlessly agree with John's sentiments: "One of the first things I learned," he says about creating and growing a company, "is that there was a relationship between screwing up and learning. The more mistakes I made, the faster I learned." And, as evidenced by that "Dude, you're getting a Dell" commercial spokes-dork, he's still learning.

It even helped to humble Handspring CEO Donna Dubinsky, who botched her company's first few months of PDA shipments because she felt a little too invincible coming off of her success at Palm. "Perhaps the only way to inoculate a company against arrogance," she ventures, "is experiencing a setback that sticks in the collective memory." (That, or some really ugly layoffs).

The message is that even the best, most talented professionals commit errors, and that they continue to achieve because they learn and grow from them. Plus theirs are often of the big, hairy, public variety that can end up in newspapers—a consequence you're pleasantly immune to at the who-are-you entry level.

damage control

So what to do about your inescapable, yet entirely acceptable lapses? Beginning at the beginning, which itself seems a peril-free place to do so, the knee-jerk reaction to most entry level howlers is to scrub them up on the quick—and quiet. While obviously preferable to outside involvement, collegial exclusion here is usually bad business and poor politics. And still worse ethics.

Particularly when the mistake affects the product or service the client receives, your cover-up can get you fired even quicker than it takes you to devise the plot—human resources paperwork, dirty looks, and all. Calculated silences have to be just that, and the math usually works out to everyone's benefit when you come clean. As Mark Twain quipped, "When in doubt, tell the truth. You will gratify some of the people and astound the rest."

Don't come across as inordinately guilty, of course, but explain the circumstances matter-of-factly and then *be accountable* for your mistake. You'll earn an enduring measure of respect for doing so, and further strengthen your credibility in turn (which isn't just made of sugar and spice and things you did right). Blaming extenuating circumstances, other coworkers, the computer, unfavorable trade relations with the EU, or just dumbly pleading ignorance wastes time that nobody has—now even less of—and your verbal two-step only draws more attention to the problem you want to make go away as quickly and unnoticeably as possible. Your calm, reasoned expressions of acknowledgement, instead, demonstrate good ownership of the wrongdoing, and help everyone to maintain their composure. Including your boss. And especially you.

Unless the problem is getting worse, delay informing the other players in the matter, however, until you've done your part to understand what exactly went wrong; the more informedly and intelligently you can speak, the more contention you'll curb in the impending dialogue. Although you're obviously not going to have that prep time when the error is brought to light for you—the only reliable procedure in which case is to stand up militarily straight, make eye contact with unwavering sangfroid, and try your best to *look* like you're not the sort of professional who could've done such a thing. Even though there you are.

Best case scenario, you can turn the situation on its ear with a big mop and a forward-looking stance: Using your effective cleanup as an upside-down opportunity to impress your manager, you'll close the lid on the issue if you can also come back to him with some solid recommendations as to how to prevent future foul-ups in this department. Because if an individual of your caliber has managed to gaffe, then just think what all of the other mental giants you share office space with are bound to do.

And when they indeed follow through in their own right—sooner or later, and sometimes on a level that makes your catastrophes seem Romper Room-esque by comparison—unaccusingly work to help them save face, which will yield endless gratitude and Rockefeller-sized deposits in the favor bank. Yet while you should never shoulder their blame or allow yourself to be craftily implicated in anyone's offenses but your own (you can fill the quota just fine, I trust, so be watchful here), you may however need to tumble at times for your supervisor, for which Culture Club has the right approach.

You're locked at the hip with this guy (your manager, thankfully, not Boy George), and the preservation of his reputation is tantamount to the preservation of your own. So in those instances where you're left holding the bag from one of your boss' blunders, absolutely never point your petulant finger at him in front of others—a veritable Milk Bone for gossip hounds—and make every effort to skirt the issue of fault altogether. In fact, there are few better ways to secure your captain's love and respect than by graciously swabbing the decks of his ineptitude. Certainly you don't want to fall into a pattern here, but even if you do it's already clear the respective directions both of you are headed. Toot, toot.

accountability

new title, same money

Being "accountable" means a lot of things to a lot of people, but to your boss it means only one: You own it. Whatever you've been charged with carrying out—large or small, day or night, will you – nill you—you've accepted full and complete responsibility for its proper and timely execution. From soup to nuts. Come hell, high water, or hot date. Period, full stop.

Fashioned from a collection of managerial observances and conversations, as well as a mix of your performances and interactions with teammates and superiors, your perceived level of responsibility prompts in-charges to make all sorts of unregulated extrapolations and conjectures. Especially about how you'll do with things like certain assignments and clients, at various levels of pressure and responsibility, and with complex equipment and tools like fax machines and file folders.

Accountability, then, is your foundation, the underpinning for all of your efforts. It's only on top of this base that you can build credibility and trust, and only on top of those merits that you begin to realize your goals in the company. Persuading your firm, however, that they've invested in a dependable and upright career freshman is probably the biggest immediate professional barrier you face at the entry level. And, like so many other developmental pursuits at this stage, is an endeavor subject to remorseless scrutiny and swift collapse upon faltering: Again, you've got no history to buttress your falls, no buffer of glories past to cushion failures present. Not the mistakes that are genuine and expected, of course, but those that rear for reasons of negligence, slacking, disregard, and the like. In other words, the kind that your love of the work predisposes you to make.

So this is where you become a manager. Taking whatever lessons you can from your own commander, you have to view the *impressions* and *expectations* of others as your direct reports: a rowdy, madcap bunch that you're now charged with keeping in line, in check, and in front of you. Any action you take (or inaction, as it may be) has to be filtered through the eyes of your staff, instilling the confidence that you can be depended upon to successfully meet the business needs you're liable for. Whether or not you really can yet.

As long as you're striving to get there—which includes shoring up your unproductive habits and bulwarking your commitment to quality—you can cobble things together until you arrive. (Every good actor, after all, does their heavy share of behind-the-scenes work). Your top priority in the interim, however, is to cultivate the widespread belief that you've got it all handled, like most young bosses try to do. And, for that matter, parents.

follow up or fall down

Actually, it's not enough to be a manager; you need to be a *micromanager* when it comes to looking after your impressions. Only an insufferable taskmaster can guarantee that nothing slips under radar here—which is where supervisors, of course, like to hang out. When they're not right behind your desk silently watching you not work.

People always forget what they mentioned, scheduled, and requested, and nobody is better at this than corporate managers. (In fact, I'm convinced my former superiors were in charge of training). To their credit, frontline overseers usually have enough knocking around in their melons to justify their astonishingly limited capacity for recollection; but that doesn't excuse you from following through on what they may or may not have said. Or thought they said. Last week, I think it was. Maybe.

So it's your duty to get your chief to clearly and in no uncertain terms articulate exactly what it is that he wants from you with any given project, preferably in writing. (In duplicate and legally notarized, wherever possible). Remember, your assignments at the entry level are second-hand; your manager's the one ultimately on the hook for getting them done. You were only hired to help him get there. And exactly there—not someplace your unique rendering of whatever he asked you to do takes him. His bosses have already pretty well made up his mind, meaning that your value will come through best in the quality with which you deliver on those orders.

And should your by-the-numbers assignment be sizeable enough, you're further responsible for going back to him to verify that you're moving forward correctly, and with the proper priority given your outstanding workload. By consistently reminding your boss in this way of the directions he's provided before you follow them too far down the road, you help to preempt all of that expensive and time-consuming backtracking young professionals are so vilified for. Plus it'll help illustrate your ever-tightening clutch on the firm's operations. Oh, and you might have actually misunderstood him, if you can picture that.

Although a manager's memory seems to kick in implausibly well when yours doesn't. And, through some dark and unexplainable force, bosses almost never fail to check in when you haven't had the patience to. Another one of the entry level's spiteful gags, I suppose, because few things goad an in-charge more than a career freshman who begins an answer to his question with, "Um, I handed it off, but I don't know…" or "I'm not quite sure what happened with…" Okay, why not? Didn't you follow up and check? You mean you didn't think the 30 seconds it takes to pick up the telephone was worth being absolutely certain that this issue was settled?

Not until now. Obviously too late, so you have to make getting confirmations about meetings, timelines, project specifications, and every other crumb of daily minutia a regular habit. While immersing yourself in the "adminisphere" often feels wasteful and unimportant, the cost of a fuming manager, bungled assignment, or missed deadline is incalculably greater than one or two annoying, but ultimately painless e-mails, calls, or trips to a coworker's desk. And especially so because those irksome little tasks will help to maintain your boss' directorial distance and faltering remembrances.

But even they're not a full warranty against an unexpected explosion or meltdown. Lamentably, it's your added responsibility to maintain a comprehensive "CYA" file, standing (coarsely but suitably enough) for "Cover Your Ass." This device is used to guard against a colleague's or client's false understandings, whereby a folder is kept of dated, documented evidence regarding certain conversations, scheduled delivery dates, outstanding obligations, required approvals, out-of-scope requests, and items of that ilk. You put it into motion, importantly, only when you're absolutely forced to; it's much more of an insurance policy than a policing technique. But it can be that strategic bucket of cold water to toss on an overheated associate's head about an error or oversight they, themselves, made. (Although if your manager is vehemently insistent—in the face of all evidence to the contrary—that you're wrong, then you're, of course, wrong. And you really should've known better).

Capping off your secretarial tyranny should be the assumption of responsibility for those things that haven't even happened yet, which is the mark of all great impression managers. These individuals elevate accountability to its highest level, anticipating those duties likely to fall under their jurisdiction based on how they see things playing out—and then taking the steps well in advance to be in place. So to follow through in your own right, you have to be equally sharp-eyed, keeping focused on the pipeline and what it might spit out at you.

Do you have an upcoming off-site conference, for example, or feel a brief sickness coming on (cough, cough) for which you'll need to line up resources to cover you? What troubled engagement might you be suddenly pulled into, and how would that conflict with your current calendar? Can you feel a crunch or see a seasonal rush coming up for which you should be prepared to bury yourself in hurried assignments and late nights? Your staying on top of these things is also something that managers manage to remember, but this time for all the right reasons. Right up until they forget again.

how "zz" got on top

Psychologist Alfred Adler, best known for identifying the "inferiority complex" (from which so many of our business leaders suffer), was one of the first pupils of Sigmund Freud to break with his mentor in the area of predicting people's actions. Rejecting his sexually frustrated teacher's idea that we behave based solely on past experiences and development, Adler instead held that people act based on their expectations for the future—what they subjectively believe to be true, regardless of its factual basis. Sure to have badly hurt Freud's super-ego, Adler's beliefs were broadly upheld, probably sending his id on a triumphant tear through the local bar scene.

Trading on the finer points of the human condition, as the best always seem to do, sales guru Zig Ziglar (real name, no beard) some years later infused this flavor of mind juice into Corporate America, popularizing the classic "under-promise – over-deliver" strategy. It's a basic accountability technique, whereby the salesperson simply keeps the client's expectations ever so below the level they know they can deliver on. (Which also works, incidentally, with significant others). For Ziglar, that meant consistently coming back to his buyers ahead of schedule and with more than anticipated—which, in turn, meant happy faces and hands on wallets. Pretty brilliant and unexpected for a guy with parents as cruel as his.

By continuation, you have to be exceedingly judicious here with your entry level projects, taking into account all possible delays and hang-ups, and considering the time required for whatever above-and-beyond touches you might want to include. So insofar as you have some flexibility with the deadline, tacking on, say, an extra day to even your most conservative estimates will budget for ample breathing room and unexpected setbacks. Plus it'll also afford for additional proofreading, revision, and add-on time—and still position you to get everything handed in early. Trust, goodwill, and sanity are sure to flourish.

Yet your under-promise may not be quite as far under as you think. Things almost unfailingly take longer than estimated, and for their part career freshmen are notoriously optimistic about turn-around schedules. Really, it's almost habitual that young professionals mis-scope their projects and fail to figure in common everyday time-sinks, including meetings running long, people dropping by their desk, odds and ends eating up the hours, and quick client calls turning into a protracted series of explanations, reiterations, and say-ings-again. So if you sense that you're going to be delayed with an assignment, your accountability depends on letting the right people know as soon as you realize it. Remember, you're probably only the first or second step in the process, with plenty still to be done on the top end once you submit your piece. That snag amounts to a bottle-neck for the entire project, and the owners need to be apprised of the holdup so they can adjust the schedule or assign additional resources accordingly. (Lest they have to stay late at the office and actually work on it themselves).

What's more, the over-deliver part may not be so high up there either. Entry levelers are also reviled for being big talkers, oversell-ing their skills and no-probleming their way into assignments they need a secret decoder ring and psychic advice from Miss Cleo to figure out. While it's important to confidently market what you can do, of course, and not to appear stubborn or indifferent to seniors in need of a rescue, taking on more than what you know to be feasible is bottom-line bad salesmanship, and Zig would've fired you on the spot for doing so. (Although Adler might've bought you a beer afterward to cheer you up).

The product in this case has absolutely no chance of measuring up to the artificially high expectations that have been set for it, and your accountability has equally dim prospects for recovering from the overstep. I can remember at the end of a summer internship I did for a big compensation consulting company, for instance, my manager telling me how he was generally pleased with my performance over the past months, but unimpressed with my Microsoft Excel abilities. Never having keyed a single formula to that point, but barefacedly telling him during the interview that my skills were "progressing" (and I'm sure I would have gone so far as explaining how I wrote the source code in order to get the job), I never had a prayer of living up to the standards that I, myself, had established. Nor was I offered the chance to try again.

Worse still, the difficulties commonly don't stop here, with impression-minded career freshmen carelessly tossing out slippery information so as not to look unaware—and completely wreaking havoc on expectations in the process. When the issue's internal, granted, the mistruth is usually of less import, often resulting in just a spate of under-the-breath namecalling. When the bosh is peddled off to a client, however, the situation is entirely more consequential, where money may even be lost should the firm be held responsible for meeting whatever obligations were inadvertently agreed to.

Several times I managed to violate this protocol, too (let it never be said I did things halfway), most memorably right after joining the ill-famed Silicon Valley startup. Feigning to know what I was talking about in the least, I let it slip out during a meeting with a top client that our software could do something it still wasn't very comfortable with. Just having heard about the feature an hour prior, what better a time to open my mouth than in a room full of executives, not the least of whom being my boss' boss.

The customer's attention now piqued, I had the inexpressible displeasure of then watching each and every company member in attendance sequentially take their turn backpedaling from my wayward remark, periodically puncturing me with a venomous stare in between sentences. Which, of course, were gentle love gazes compared to the tongue-lashing I brooked after a slightly disenchanted client got on the elevator to go home, looking as a gentleman caller might who didn't get the goodnight kiss he was hoping for.

So for the sake of everyone's accountability, it's probably best that you don't volunteer the information you don't have (or aren't authorized to talk about), and opt to deflect any contentious questions with a pat response like, "Let me find out, and I'll get right back to you." To my knowledge, there's not one client or manager in modern business history who's ever been dissatisfied with that answer. But who knows, you could get lucky.

ethics

a tale of two companies

Modern business ethics first came into vogue during the 1980s, when corporations began to seriously concern themselves with avoiding SEC entanglements, legal potholes, sticky press fiascos, and the like. Some even worried for reasons that had nothing to do with public relations or money. But not too many. So seminars were held, articles written, studies conducted, and classes even incorporated into b-school curriculums; it was almost faddish. Having principles became posh—kind of like fidelity being the "in" thing to do with marriages. (Or is that out now, I can't remember).

Over 20 years later, we're worse off than before we started trying to play it straight—what with the financial sleights of hand, increased offshore (i.e., tax-evasion) dealings, insider trading run-ups, and under-the-table stock allocations. The terms "accounting scandal" and "corporate governance" actually *mean* something to the everyman these days. Before you know it, kids will be asking why the 25 shares of General Electric they got for Christmas aren't trading at a higher multiple.

Yet while business ethics is a whole other book altogether (some shorter than this one, most in narrower circulation, and all less believable), I think the stories brought to us by two organizations that faced a kind of moment of truth in recent times frame our pending discussion quite nicely. I'll begin with the two-to-a-block Starbucks Coffee Company, who ran into a major ethical crossroads back in 1994 after a massive frost in Brazil ruined most of the green coffee bean crop they live on. Starbucks, like most java retailers, buys their beans wholesale in the form of "futures contracts," or commitments to buy scads of the stuff over time at a fixed and discounted price. The too-chilly kernels, of course, sent the cost of futures soaring, but at a time when—if you can believe—the foam-and-jazz dealer was having difficulty meeting their numbers to make investors happy.

So here's the dilemma: Does the firm buy up a stash of cheaper, lower-quality beans (a difference in taste the average coffee drinker would never detect) and protect their earnings, or do they lock into sky-high contracts that'll hurt their income statement over the next several quarters and potentially scare off critical future capital? As chairman Howard Schultz puts it in his autobiography, *Pour Your Heart Into It*, "We would have saved a ton of money, but we would have had a different kind of crisis on our hands."

Now contrast this decision-making with that of ex-energy hulk Enron Corp., who stepped up from staid power generator to free-wheeling trading giant in the 1990s, hawking everything from electricity to unused bandwidth to "weather derivatives" (which I don't fully understand, but more or less amount to betting if God feels like rain or not). The new Enron marketplace was a revolution, and the company went hard to work creating things that took even more paper and lawyers to swap.

But making markets is a big, expensive business. For most companies, sizeable growth means borrowing some amount of cash; for Enron, then, it meant borrowing stacks. So much, in fact, that they began to think their copious shareholders, bondholders, and creditors might start to get a little squeamish about all of that debt—nearly $40 billion worth by late 2001. (I can hardly type the number myself). So here's this firm's pinch: Do they temper their growth to keep the finances in hand, or do they go further into arrears and risk upsetting their stakeholders?

"Just don't tell mom and dad," went the chorus at their Houston headquarters. Using some creative accounting (an oxymoron if ever there was), Enron set up dozens of dubious partnerships—with fun names like "Chewco Investments," after their favorite furry *Star Wars* character—in which to shelter the liabilities and do a nifty sidestep of the balance sheet. It was even more fun for certain top executives, who netted tens of millions in additional personal income from cooking the books.

The thing about public companies, though, is that they're accountable to the *public*, who's generally pretty fussy when it comes to other people spending their money. Catching on in October 2001—after the firm lopped a nominal $586,000,000 off of previous years' earnings—it took an aghast populous less than two breathtaking months to yank down this Texan power cowboy, angrily kicking it under the shelter of Chapter 11 (the third-largest such case in history, behind WorldCom and Conseco). The debacle even knocked the Big Five down to Two Pair, as Arthur Andersen LLP's hand-over-the-heart denial of any wrongdoing was undermined by their, oops, methodical shredding and deleting of thousands of Enron-related audit documents, digital files, and e-mails. Regardless, now there are only four giant accountancies pestering graduating seniors on campus, proving there's an upside to everything.

Two different approaches, two different outcomes. One required sacrificing an extra quarter for your morning grande drip, and the other forced you to watch your share price plunge from $90 to a couple dozen pennies. Had then-Enron leader Kenneth Lay been able to admit his borrowing problem in time (surely there was some sort of executive 12-step program he could've signed up for), perhaps his company's stock would have ended up being able to cover more than the price increase for a cup of Mr. Schultz's brew. Which he now sells more than $3 billion worth of per year. Some even to me.

bigger than expected

Ethics aren't convenient. And that's the whole point. They're there to make things hard when the easy way also happens to be the wrong one. To keep on the straight and narrow with your exchanges, then, yours have to be consistent, encompassing, inflexible, and based upon a bothersome acceptance of decent Western values. But being that upstanding individual when you'd much rather have a seat isn't a matter of looking good or not wanting to get caught;

it's instead a question of your own respectability, virtue, and sense of value as a person.

And, just as importantly, as an employee. But if there's a place that can shiver your principles down to room temperature, it's Corporate America: a grasping, clutching institution where work is done without meaning, where advancement comes at all costs, and where moral compasses point toward the bank. As a career freshman in particular, where the sense of betrayal and frustration is so pronounced, the urge to make your own rules where you can feels almost justified—like a vigilante capitalist in a way, just taking what's due.

But what, exactly, might that be? Your very capitalistic agreement of employment is at-will, and in force under your acceptance of the standards of conduct the company expects you to adhere to, counting those pertaining to fraud, theft, plagiarism, and delinquency. Compensation and non-discrimination aside, no stipulations are ever made as to what the firm is obligated to provide you in return for your services, including type of work, advancement opportunities, training, or even general regard for your presence. And while they may be representatives of the organization, the people who make and break the promises have absolutely no bearing, legal or otherwise, on the covenant. If that were the case, headhunters, managers, and executives would all have to be honest, and I wouldn't have enough to write about.

Your ethical post, rather, is to staunchly uphold the faith of that commitment, under even the slickest of circumstances—which the top people all find a way to do. For instance Mike Volkema, CEO of blue-chip office furniture-maker Herman Miller, who explains, "Good leaders are required to have a nonnegotiable set of core values that allow them to do the right thing, and make the right decisions, in those moments when it's most difficult to do so."

And that can be just about anytime. Padded expense accounts, inflated timesheets, misappropriated work, false representations to clients (company management exempted from none) all mingle freely about workplace, cultivating an atmosphere where duplicity is not only tolerated, but often steered through the crowd with a cradled arm. Indeed, in getting away with it, sometimes it's not even clear whom you're getting away from.

But it's much bigger than that. It doesn't matter how much they have, how little they'll miss it, or how unfairly they've treated you. It makes no difference the amount, the type, or the nature of the transgression—especially when you're standing in an unemployment line or, better yet, a courthouse. This is about your integrity, what you stand for as a dignified and learnèd human being. From that conviction comes your moral strength, which is something that's felt and respected each time you're unwilling to take the shortcut, that easy way out, those few extra dollars. Plus it's pretty hard to keep focused on what's in front of you when you're always looking over your shoulder.

Honesty is the overarching principle under which the best businesses and people in the world conduct their affairs, and most of them have more than enough to show for it. Mr. Schultz of Starbucks can certainly vouch for that. Actually so can Enron's ex, Mr. Lay, who might be willing to testify that honesty is necessary to continue conducting any affairs at all. If he doesn't go and plead the Fifth again.

branding the bottom

metals, livestock, and you

Companies sure do their damnedest to make you feel like you're their top recruit. Steeping in an artificiality that Corporate America has cooked to perfection, a firm will lavish you with smiles, attention, and prime rib until you can't help but believe this place wants you as badly as you now think you want them. The small army they send of well-spoken, well-dressed, well-oiled professionals gunning to get you onto the team assures it: Never mind the 28 other candidates; those interviews are just to create the appearance of fairness. No, it's *you* they all want to share in their successes, their wealth, and their liquor.

Hit with that compelling story of challenge and excitement—struck by the idea of a place where the people are close and genuine and care deeply about your future (if not your arteries or liver)—you can't help but fall right into it. And before your signature dries on the offer letter, you're hurriedly presented with a cheap token gift, a prewritten welcome note, a delayed start date, a raft of policies and regulations, and a six-digit employee number. Welcome to the firm. Back of the line, please.

One of a kind? Only to your parents. To the company you're one of many, not especially unlike any of the other unsuspecting career freshmen they inveigled into signing. Just another warm body, really, in their undifferentiated collection of young flesh, all doing the exact same gruntwork (each in their own unique and vastly important way, of course), and any of whom is easily substitutable when the numbers work out. In fact, if you were being traded on a formal exchange—which isn't necessarily to say you're not—you would be considered a *commodity*: a bulk product that's low-priced, indistinguishable from its counterparts, and not highly valued except in large volume. Coffee, pork bellies, sugar, and highly intelligent college graduates... Sounds like a nicely stocked apartment to me.

But this isn't right. You're individually talented, independently motivated, and indisputably distinct from the masses; while the firm may have sold you a bill of goods, you're certainly not one of them. So how do you move yourself out of the perfunctory commodities market, demonstrating the significant and tangible value deliverable only by you? What do you have to do to break free from the noise and clutter—to capture the attention of the managers empowered to move you forward? What's the path to making the company actually believe its own knotted story?

black sheep get bought

We all know what brands are, at least from a consumer perspective. The best ones are easily recognizable, stand for a certain quality and style, and say a lot about what we're willing to spend to impress people we don't know.

More technically, however, a brand represents a clear set of promises and associations that have been built up in the hearts and minds of customers for years. We've come to know and trust these companies because they have consistently offered us the products and services that deliver the experience, benefits, and identity that we recognize and aspire to have. Speaking to us in a way that's personal and memory-driven, often to the point of precluding any other choice, a strong brand offers a mental shortcut to the right answer, to the leader of the category, to the place where we want to go.

How do they get there, though? There are plenty of great products out on the market—as there are plenty of great people at the entry level—so what props one brand atop another? Young & Rubicam, a leading global advertising agency, wondered the same thing, and decided to develop a database of more than 13,000 brands in 33 countries to figure out what's what. Called the Brand Asset Valuator, they picked the 35 most important dimensions of a brand to look at (we take their word there are that many), and have run all sorts of complicated and impressive mathematical formulas and statistical equations yielding large insights and larger billings. But down of that mountain of data rolled one predominant and critical theme: Strong brands are strongly differentiated.

Which is exactly what needs to happen at the office. You have to position yourself as a decisively unique member of your class, manifestly apart and above the under-esteemed cluster you share a job title with. Your name must be the top-of-mind choice for quality and delivery when your manager is looking to staff his most pressing and sensitive projects. Carrying an ultra-premium value to your cost, the aim is to be considered the prized member of your executives' career freshman collection, kept on the mantle instead of the shoebox. In short, you need to become a strong brand of your own.

The stronger, in fact, the more successful. Dr. David Aaker, our country's foremost authority on brands, ranks certain companies' brand values in his latest book *Brand Leadership*, pointing out that nine of the top 60 firms in the world have brand values exceeding 50 percent of their entire market value. Roughly translated, that means more than half of each of these organizations' worth is in goodwill—in the name alone. Premium players like BMW, Nike, and Apple have brand values that surpass even 75 percent.

That level of recognition is built over time and out of superior products, of course, but the incredible performance of these companies demonstrates the power that a solid, well-differentiated brand confers. Especially among an entry level set of competitors who have no idea what they're doing yet. And particularly for a manager who's as frustrated as they are.

on building a brand

why are you even here?

To transform yourself into a matchless brand begins with understanding what, in fact, makes you so matchless. The entry level is overstocked with heaps and piles of career freshmen—overrun with a nameless, faceless mass of young professional humanity. So your brand has to break through in a compelling, vibrant, and exclusive way, offering the kind of value that will have a cumulative effect over your tenure. As Aaker explains, "The difference between good and brilliant cannot be overstated. The challenge is to be noticed, to be remembered, to change perceptions, to reinforce attitudes, and to create deep customer relationships."

And you meet this challenge first by clearly articulating your *value proposition* in everything you do, or your unique and important reason for being. This is your statement of purpose: what you have to offer the company, the highly individual ways in which you offer it, and how it's meaningful and rewarding to your manager and seniors (i.e., your customers). The key is to understand their mindsets, motivations, preferences, and tastes, and then work to convey your value proposition—the essence of your brand—in a way that's more clear and forceful than your competitors'.

In developing this deep knowledge of your market, you also earn the feedback that's going to help you prioritize and adjust your positioning, bringing your brand in the closest possible alignment with your vision of yourself and the core strengths that your customers are most interested in. Such assets might include:

- *Results-Oriented*: Resourceful, quick and effective, mindful of the end purpose.
- *Smart*: Mentally active, applies knowledge efficiently, consistently learning.
- *Approachable*: Cheerful, warm, easy to meet and deal with, relationship-focused.

- *Dependable*:   Reliable, willing to do what it takes, comes through when needed most.
- *Sincere*:   Earnest, genuine, gratifying to work with at all touch-points.
- *Accomplished*:   Meets established goals, sets the standard, gets things done.
- *Influential*:   Knows how to approach issues, has sway among peers, a spokesperson.
- *Credible*:   Honest, worthy of confidence, extends boundaries by way of trust.

It's through a defined set of filters like the above that you distill your core message, so invest the time into studying the business environment and your place within it, evaluating how and where your brand position will have the greatest impact. What unique group of attributes and characteristics, you should ask yourself, can you reliably own and grow over time? Who's your closest competition, and how can you best wield your strengths to distinguish yourself? Where are your weaknesses, and what steps can you take to complement and toughen them? When *is* the right time to add more toner to the printer?

Empowered with this information, develop your value proposition critically and tightly, scrutinizing your brand for gaps, soft spots, and places where you're stretching a little too far. The final product should be a thorough, succinct, and easily understood statement about what makes you individually valuable, how you get there, and why everyone should believe you're so important. Especially you.

Keep in mind, however, that a brand trickles down from the most critical, make-or-break assignments all the way to how you handle phone conversations, write e-mails, and carry yourself in meetings. It's all well and good to have a high level vision for your persona; but some of the most essential execution is in the mundane, recognizing the impact that each of your actions and comments stand to make vis-à-vis the value proposition you're promoting. So I guess that means, technically speaking, finally listening to all the stuff your mom told you to do growing up.

but you promised!

Once you know what you're basically selling, your mission is to flesh it out with something that your customers can hang on to—and that they can measure you by. This is your *brand promise*, or how you pledge to deliver on your value proposition. The place where the abstract meets the actual, there's little you can do here by way of explanation or rhetoric to influence how your assurance is communicated; it, instead, takes shape as does your performance, unmistakably conveying the functional and emotional benefits (or detriments) that your customers can anticipate when selecting you as a contributor to their work.

A functional benefit, to explain further, deals with the tangible, deliverable-driven value you offer: top quality assignments, consistent on-time delivery, good follow-through and sense of accountability, and so forth. Emotional benefits, by contrast, create the human connection that transcends the black and white of the actual work, bridging person and product: Will your manager and seniors feel wise and validated for trusting you? Does being associated with your work confer status, respect, and reassurance? Do you offer a personally satisfying and rewarding interaction? It's not enough, then, just to offer a job well done, but rather a job well received—an integrated package of nitty-gritty and touchy-feely.

Do it right and out falls *brand loyalty*, which is the ultimate goal and at the heart of any brand's value. Since roughly 80 percent of your work will come from about 20 percent of your customers (or so says the ever-present "80 / 20 rule"), and since there are only so many hours a day that you ought to be doing this stuff, just a handful of satisfied seniors and managers will ensure that you reliably get the kind of work that you want. Probably more than.

Indeed, while you always want to bring the top people into your fold (or be brought into theirs, as it were), stretching your brand promise too thin weakens the pledge immediately. It takes knowing your boundaries and limitations, pushing back on those assignments that threaten your ability to deliver up to—and beyond—expected standards. Because trying to recover a brand is a lot like trying to resuscitate... Well, just ask Enron and Andersen how hard they were huffing and puffing.

don't I know you?

People love familiar things, which accounts for most prolonged sufferers of bad jobs, dysfunctional relationships, and Tom Green movies. When it comes to brand building, however, the recognizable is richly rewarded, where people will ascribe all manner of positive, frequently unfounded attributes to things they think they might know from somewhere. Even if they haven't had any direct interaction with the brand whatsoever, should the logo, tagline, colors, or whatever set off some sort of flickering light bulb in a dark room, most individuals are prepared to say it's better than the rest. And many times prove it with money.

That's the power of *brand awareness*, and the case for you growing your presence at the office. As some brand managers say, it's how big the billboard is in your customers' heads; so for a career freshman on a swarming strip of street, that means you need something, say, building-sized, preferably with malnourished models posing in lingerie. Absent that, you'll have to settle for ensuring that every office-goer whom you're capable of having a pleasant interaction with, you, in fact, do.

Even if only in passing. All it takes is enough smiles and quick hellos in the hallway (resisting the overpowering impulse to look at your watch or the picture on the wall you've never taken the time to appreciate) to make sure you're not only vaguely familiar, but also have quite a lot to show for those humiliating years of wearing a retainer and headgear. At heart, loyalty stems from creating positive experiences, and any off-putting encounter—regardless of environment or circumstances—is going to send your efforts into fibrillation.

Also keep in mind that workplaces today are a tangle of associations, acquaintanceships, and links, and you never know exactly whom you might be impatiently tapping your foot at while waiting for the copier. Just as you're hard at work building relationships with those individuals sure to get you somewhere, you should be equally diligent about exchanging even the briefest of pleasantries with the strangers who may be able to get you even further—once you realize how they're attached to the friends you already have.

Moreover, you're feverishly trying to build your credibility at the entry level, for which a burly brand awareness is like a long-needled shot in the arm. Getting yourself known (for the right reasons, obviously) is a marker for the value that you're capable of delivering, and a loud statement about your ability to draw a crowd around you. The goal is to get people buzzing, discussing your work, inquiring about your availability because they heard about you from one of their trusted colleagues.

This interplay naturally leads to better, more enjoyable work, and sets you up nicely for inclusion in higher profile opportunities—which, in turn, will get your name out there even more prominently. Spiraling rapidly upward, each subsequent project you obliterate and make feel stupid for bothering you can then be touted for increased publicity, building your reputational power and causing you to grow in height by a good foot and a half, easy. And all this because you rattled some rusty bell in a drafty and long-abandoned head.

a niche business

Over time, even well-known, well-respected companies lose favor when their individuality fades—the so-called stale or stagnant brands. This means you need to ask of yourself the same question that corporate brand managers ask each new publicity cycle: What is it that makes this product distinctive, exciting, and relevant? (Which, for them, is generally followed by, "Still nothing, huh? Okay, how much do we have to pay someone famous to say they like it?").

As a career freshman without the money to blow on full-page spreads and 30-second TV spots—and whose customers work right down the hall—it means, instead, constantly defining and redefining your *niche.* This is the compelling little corner of the universe you own that's both attractive to your buyers, as well as reasonably defensible against would-be gatecrashers. And one of the most effective strategies in carving out your unique place at the entry level is developing a weighty expertise—linking your brand to a strong functional benefit.

Holding a superior position on a key attribute is an extremely powerful asset—being the top researcher among your peers, say—as it generates heavy interaction with all the right people, as well as adds value to the company in a way that only you can take credit for (in the most humble way). The function should be something you're genuinely interested in, to be sure, but positioning yourself as the go-to guy or girl for an important kind of assistance not only elevates your current role, but also yields solid entry points into other departments for a potential future move.

As with groupwork, survey the market carefully to uncover the openings left by competitors, and see where your best skills can contribute the most value. But don't only target their weaknesses: recognizing how others keep hold of their chunk of managerial mindshare offers a standard against which to gauge your own approach and progress, and highlights best practices toward developing a better alternative, a refined set of tools, or a new kind of application. In most cases, keep in mind, the wheel has already been invented; you can propel yourself forward quite handily just by putting your inimitable spin on it.

But make sure your turns are balanced and in alignment with your workload, and that your efforts are prioritized according to what your customers most prefer. As a rule, it's smartest to situate yourself as the top-of-mind career freshman for just one essential function at first, guaranteeing that the big names dependably turn to you for a product you can deliver on in a memorable way. As says Robert Kagle, founding partner of Benchmark Capital (the Silicon Valley VC responsible for funding companies like eBay and E-LOAN), "I've seen a lot of companies fail for lack of focus. I've rarely seen a company fail for being too focused."

Once you've very purposely fashioned that initial place for yourself, procuring the right kind of future work tends to be much more of a hands-off endeavor. Again, the mastery of your specialty is seen by your superiors as an index for your capacity to master many other, often-times unrelated tasks. Some that even require use of the frontal lobes. However, as we'll talk about when discussing personal initiatives, your above-and-beyond work only counts when you're going above and beyond someplace your company actually cares to.

the company that keeps *you*

At the center of the best brand strategies, also, are calculated associations with other strong brands. Called the "halo effect," one brand will link itself to another and piggyback on the goodwill, hoping the angelic image of the supporter rubs off on the supportee. That's why you see so many sponsors of the Olympics, for instance, as companies want to be seen next to athletes with physical supremacy, ironclad courage, and superiority at a sport that people are willing to watch only once every four years.

There are those individuals in your office that management pays even closer attention to, and not with any less reverence. These are the superstars, the standard-setters, the designated repairmen for things that someone else broke. I like to call them "Midases," because if they touch you you're golden. Indeed, a connection with one of these precious-metalers leads to an instant solidification of your credibility, the casting of a radiant hue on your brand awareness, and a royal passageway to the top assignments. Because "in modern times, it is only by the power of association that men of any calling exercise their due influence in the community." Or so believed American statesman and Nobel Peace Prize recipient Elihu Root, whose modern times were the early 1900s.

There's assuredly at least one Midas within your reach—or, rather, the other way around—identifiable, in part, by the glittery showers of praise, the reliance of the team on their work, and the degree to which people shut up and listen when they're talking. More often than not, Midases also tend to be welcoming people and make a habit of ensuring that those around them are successful, meaning that an honest, unassuming approach will generally be well-received and well-rewarded. In fact, by shadowing those who lead and teach naturally, you'll further learn the behaviors that will win the respect and trust of your colleagues—both of which are necessary for any leadership position of your own.

The goal is to get your Midases "referenceable," or in a position where they'll actually evangelize your worth, vouching for your abilities when management asks them to opine on certain assignments and staffing decisions. At this point, you've advanced beyond passive association to the level of *endorsement*, which is one of the fastest and most effective ways to build your brand at the office. (And with friends they want to set you up with). But at the same time, you have to keep a careful watch on your linkages, making sure they're doing their job and not dragging you down: Can this relationship provide a point of differentiation? Can this connection be owned by my brand over time? Does this association resonate with my manager and his peers? These are all questions you should be asking yourself from day to day, quieting those once kings and queens who may have fallen from grace.

Remember, career freshmen have the stigma they do because too many of them have duly earned it—playing, slacking, and generally behaving in the amateurish, slapdash way one might expect of recent college graduates. There's undoubtedly the mandated portion of these children in your department, so it's critical that you keep your dissociated distance, lest their bad equities leach on to you. They may be fun, but sometimes the people who you'd most like to have around, unfortunately, are the ones you can least afford to. Kind of like ex-lovers.

fresh face to the world

If you build it, it's true they'll come; but that doesn't mean they're going to hang around. Your brand has to evolve as you do, and as your company shifts in response to the ever-renovating marketplace. Indeed, smart organizations are always reinventing themselves to stay current, fresh, and significant—yet while maintaining their core values and integrity. Well...they're keeping up, at any rate.

When the bottom fell out of the consulting industry during the late 1990s, for instance, its top players were forced to seriously rethink how they were going to market. With their bread-and-butter enterprise software implementation businesses sputtering, many looked toward alliances, venture capital, back-office outsourcing, and other confusing things they now claim to be "leaders in." Same for the big computer-makers, like IBM and Hewlett-Packard, who grew their professional services divisions hard to make up for slumping hardware sales.

Your own approach should fall along those very lines, as you adjust your focus to meet the changing business needs, and as you prove to excel at more sophisticated tasks. Repositioning yourself around that new kind of work, moreover, not only increases your value to the firm and staves off rivals, but also allows you to shine the brightest at the assignments you do best. Some entry levelers, I hear, have even talked about "enjoying it"—but I can't confirm those kinds of rumors.

And while on the topic, it's important to note that colorful and exciting brands, like Virgin, aren't exempt from reassessment either. In fact, irreverent founder and chief executive Richard Branson shed his venerable music label in 1993—which housed cash-cow acts like Janet Jackson and the Rolling Stones—to expand into air travel, railways, clothing, telecom, and even cola. Although I don't think any other CEOs besides Branson have dressed up in costumes or posed with nude models for press. (At least that's what he told his wife it was for).

The point is that the best companies are constantly building, trans-forming, reshaping, and doing whatever else they have to do to stay alive and competitive. When you treat your personal brand with the same urgency and flexibility—when you're always standing at the in-tersection of what you're good at and what the market wants you to be good at—you ensure yours is a value that's enduring and significant. And even more practically, you also help ensure that you don't get too bored and listless, which of course is the bigger problem at the entry level. Come to think of it, maybe you can ask your company how 40 percent career freshman turnover at around $20,000 a head fits in with their global brand strategy. But not too loudly.

survival by subject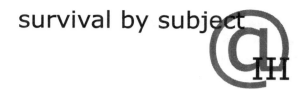III

dancing the dance

jigging for dollars

Politics is about money. Anyone who tells you differently doesn't know what they're talking about or has something to gain. Oftentimes both. Just look at the workplace, which fatuously mixes together people and paychecks, courting the elaborate and addled dance that ensues: handshaking, hedging, backslapping, backstabbing, brownnosing, jockeying, pushing, shoving, death threats. And those are just the basic steps for the extra buck—which, never mind, is worth closer to 70 cents after taxes.

Speaking of theft, you can pay a visit to this nation's capital for as good of proof of the cash connection as there is. Our political machinery is oiled, smeared, and dripping wet with the greasy funds of special interests, foreign concerns, independent lobbyists, pork barrelers, and the slipperiest palm moisturizer of them all, Big Business: Jiffy Lube for the United States government. (Enron, in point of fact, was the biggest underwriter of Texas political campaigns).

Now, if federal legislation were tied more tightly to its merits, moneyed petitioners would have a hard time figuring out whom to bribe, venal lawmakers would lose their will to obfuscate, truth and reason would prevail, and a wide stripe of our bitingly clever political pundits—the happiest byproduct of Washingtonian corruption— would be out of a job. So this we don't want.

If rewards at entry level, on the other hand, were nudged even fractionally closer to the fundamentals of perseverance, talent, and creativity, early-stagers would find a real motivation in their labor—a purer sense of enjoyment and fulfillment and a drive to succeed not fueled by fear or money. But that's the only kind of control Corporate America has over their youngsters. So this they don't want.

They'd rather have you dance—just like every other W2-waving worker jigging for dollars in their own right. But by learning the moves to this complicated, aggravating, frequently distasteful, and absolutely necessary shake-about as a career freshman, you'll be able to slide, shimmy, and shuffle with improbable grace and ease when the company expects you to only flop clumsily around. And even if you're not overbothered with the extra change jingling in your pocket (and have no penchant for senseless bureaucracy or moral elasticity), most of your colleagues and superiors are (and do), meaning it's their disco.

Your goal at the entry level is simply to make it from one end of the floor to the other without landing on anyone's feet or spinning in their way, and it's the goal of this final SURVIVAL BY SUBJECT edition to teach you the choreography. Granted, the music's going to be a little different anywhere you go; but with a little improvisation and practice, these basic steps always impress. Besides, it'll give you the jump on your fellow demagogues should you ever go into public (dis)service.

office politics

goliath in slacks

You can think of your company as a person: a big, lumbering, eccentric individual with a very peculiar, but reasonably predictable way of conducting itself and dealing with certain situations and issues. It's got a unique personality, specific likes and dislikes, particularized tastes and preferences—just about everything but an astrological sign.

(Though "Cancer" quickly comes to mind for some reason). As with anyone else, getting along with this giant means figuring out where and where not to go, when and when not to go there, and how to properly make nice when you've caused it to scowl, shout, stomp, spit downwind, or wake up grumpy and try to sit on you.

Management's nervous that you won't. Just as they're twitchy about you being able to play well with your coworkers, they're equally restive about your savoir-faire in picking up on the uncountable organizational foibles and oddities they don't have committed to a thick regulatory binder. Sure, they'd love to tell you all about them, but it's not that easy to say in plain English that "right" very often doesn't mean "correct."

How, after all, are they supposed to phrase the idea that most of the stuff going on in the office is the sinewy consequence of informal arrangements between people and departments, wound together in a snarl of unspoken rules and norms? I've done corporate communications for a while, and I don't have the slightest idea how to make that sound like what it doesn't mean. Which is the whole point of corporate communications.

So, once again, you have to read where everything is actually written: in between the lines, of course. These are the spaces wedged in the gaps of the formally mapped food chain, hovering on the outskirts of the process flowcharts, and loitering about the power plays, personal alliances, and political bents of your firm's personnel. Who, for instance, is doing impression management for whom? How do things *really* get moved through the system? Which executives and managers are deciding who works on what projects *in practice*? Where are the areas with the negative political capital, and who's responsible for the misadministration? Where does your department sit in the company pecking order? Did your boss get dressed in the dark this morning?

"It means understanding the lay of the land in an organization," explains our favorite Carnegie Mellon professor, Robert Kelley. "Part of it is knowing whom to trust and whom to avoid. Part of it is knowing how to navigate all of the competing interests within the organization—recognizing which ones will come into play and which ones you can safely ignore."

But it's not advisable to overlook much about giants. Even their small appendages are plenty big, and hurt just fine when they land on top of you—which they have a way of unexpectedly doing. Too many times do we see a career freshman thrown blindly into a highly politicized engagement, skewering the powers that be with their incautious slips of the tongue and uncalculated dealings with the enemy: "I was just trained on this last month, so I don't really know what I'm doing yet. This is our boss' first big project, too," I once heard a tenderfoot plainly remark to a top client executive, assumingly trying to build rapport or commit arson.

Especially given that certain layoff and promotion decisions are based squarely—almost entirely—on how judiciously an entry leveler interacts with important customers and company heads, you always need to be in the know on what's at stake, who's on the hook, who's watching, and how things ought to be done according to whom. Easily enough, the best move is to walk right up to the right people and ask point blank: your supervisor, your seniors, your peers, Midases, extra-departmental staff, everyone.

You'll probably get just as many takes as people you question, but that's to be expected; the trick is to categorize the varying perspectives, piece together your political map, and then properly account for the topography as you do your work. Keep in mind, the issue isn't which spin is right (although your manager's certainly has pole position); the idea is to recognize that the viewpoints *exist*, and that you do your best to individually accommodate each of them. Plus then remember what you said to whom.

write it, say it, regret it

Not long after I started with the Silicon Valley startup, management decided to restructure payroll and shift my job function to hourly pay from a salaried model. It was, in effect, a demotion for the group, and the company air was thick with gossip, controversy, and my holy indignation. Taking the move as a deep personal affront, I stayed up until 2 a.m. that morning carefully composing a pointed letter to the vice president of the department: explaining how the company wasn't valuing me properly, detailing what needed to happen by way of a resolution, and more or less flexing a political muscle with the strength of an underfed eight-year-old boy.

Receiving it as might—well, as a top Internet firm with an uppity twentysomething twit might be expected to, I was subsequently told that if it weren't for my VP's 25 years of experience in dealing with up-and-comers like me, I would have gotten my comeuppance right on the spot and been forced to clean out my desk before day's end. I did so by year's end anyway, but at least that was of my own volition. Mostly.

I still can't explain how those *Jerry Maguire*-type memos seem so brilliant in the sleepless haze of late-night self-importance, but I am quite versed in the consequences. Indeed, mine is an exaggerated example (to which I seem to be repeatedly held hostage) in the importance of exercising the furthermost level of caution when committing your thoughts to writing. Remember, your opinions can be misconstrued under the best of circumstances, so giving them tangible, re-readable, reproducible, distributable constitution when you're all foamed-up probably isn't the best way to soothe the umbrage. Unless you want some federally subsidized time off, that is; then only a high-ranking veteran's kindheartedness can stop you.

The upside of the written word, however, is that it provides for reflection and reconsideration if you give it the chance. The self-destruct button is just a mouseclick away nowadays (surreptitiously calling itself "Send"), so employing your uncommon restraint here and giving it the hour, the day, the week—however long it takes you to consult your advisors and put your best faculties to work—will ensure that you maintain proper corporate communications protocol and never say what you really think.

A whole other challenge altogether when it comes to dodging vocal misdemeanors, which enjoy only the spongiest, most cooperative of filters before speedily fleeing from your brain into the world at large. And at the entry level, just about everything passing through your lips is a strike either for or against your professional judgment, confirmation or disproof of the decision to bring you aboard, one inch closer to up or out. So, to quote publisher Malcolm Forbes, "Knowing when to keep your mouth shut is invariably more important than opening it at the right time." Particularly during formal meetings, important discussions, and those toxic gossip rings. (Which, not inconsequentially, throw into jeopardy your reputation, your future, your moral fabric, and hence your chances of ducking a call from Jerry Springer).

Seniors' credibility and position in the company provide them with some verbal wiggle room, and managers' still more. But as a career freshman in provisional standing, you'll live (or not) to rue any wayward remark about your company, its quirks and blemishes, your colleagues, their quirks and blemishes, and of course your commander, who oversees all that mess in his own idiosyncratic, blotchy way. The faux pas will unfailingly be recalled and dredged up at the most untoward times, like conversations about project placements, big assignments, and to be sure, performance reviews.

Regrettably, your understanding about the company and the people it houses is still substantially tapered and from a bottom-up vantage point, and what you may consider to be an acceptable protest or deserved criticism, the firm may view as unchecked ego or outright insubordination. It's not until after many months of watching organizational discord that you'll have a fair assessment of what kind of disagreements—from which kinds of employees—are agreeable to your employer. Who you're unlikely to keep hold of long enough to seriously figure it out.

like playing on the freeway

Still, for what political understanding you do amass, it's essential that you restrain yourself from playing with it, and this is for reason threefold. First, people in general tend to like nonpartisan, easygoing colleagues. It's always good to be liked, and it's especially good to be liked at the entry level—at least until you've got the clout, history, and a sizable coalition of people to back you. Up to that point, you have to pick your issues with ardent self-possession and foresight, avoiding unpopular positions or commingling too closely with individuals who take them (as in bad brand associations).

Second, managers have an undying respect for employees who simply put in a solid day's work without making any unnecessary waves. It's always good to be respected, and it's especially good to be respected by your first couple of bosses. Knowing that they can count on you not to become entwined in the dangerous plots of your cohorts—and have presence of mind enough not to let the client in on exactly how little you or your company know what you're doing—inspires miles of confidence and brawny recommendations for the most sensitive engagements. Plus your boss is the ultimate reason you will or won't get promoted.

Third, because you're probably not going to fully understand the political machinations of your office until after it's too late, you can get into a host of trouble long before you realize what you've actually done. It's always bad to get into political trouble, and it's especially bad to get into political trouble at a company where you don't have the pull yet to get yourself out of it—or a sense of where to even start tugging. Still, career freshmen can't seem to stop here, embroiling themselves primarily by way of going over heads and stepping on toes.

Unsatisfied with the time, consideration, resolution, or whatever other measures their taskmaster has (or hasn't) employed in response to a particular concern, young professionals are notorious for approaching his superior in hopes of a better fix, sending a contemptuous breeze through the boss' hair. Or, in a fit of overzealous self-determination, they've also been known to prioritize themselves all the way into the deputation of another manager—usually lured by some of that coveted manna of the entry level, challenge.

Obviously both are exceedingly tempting, but neither is at all acceptable. The word from your chief is, for your purposes, the word on high, and only the most unlivable of circumstances he mulishly keeps unsettled should prompt a consultation with his higher-ups. Really, should it even get to that point, the relationship is by all guesses irreparably damaged anyway, probably pointing to a transfer to ensure that your best interests continue to be met by the company.

And for those instances where an interdepartmental principal tosses an enticing morsel of work over the fence, not only are you are absolutely beholden to your boss and require his full approval, but you even have to do it according to his timetable. The receipt for your labor is sitting in his desk drawer, remember, meaning that it's completely his prerogative how he puts you to work. Or doesn't. (You may be in storage for an upcoming project). Regardless, your overseer has his own interests in keeping other managers happy, so many times an arrangement can be built; but he always has full architectural discretion.

Still further, you also have to be ever-conscious of who owns what, or whose toes are exposed. There are myriad functions in a company, all of which have somebody who's tasked with getting them done—not necessarily an evident fact judging by the results. So, being an ambitious newcomer in search of an attractive, defensible niche, this looks to present a robust market opportunity; which it does and it doesn't: While the openings may fall right in your wheelhouse, the political curves can send them right out of the strike zone. A function, after all, is only as functional as your ability to make it accomplish just what it's supposed to, and that never includes the ire and retaliation of the dozing outfielder who dropped the ball. So it's critical that you use the proper channels and get the go-ahead from the rightful, if lackadaisical owner. Give them the chance to save face and spin it as "assistance" or "a great learning opportunity," and everyone wins. Not the least of whom, interestingly, being the firm.

Above all, though, keep in mind that every asinine policy and idiot employee was the troubled decision of someone else, that you really won't be at the company for very long, and that no matter how poorly the place is run, it's *not* yours to fix. Besides, even if you did, it would just end up confusing management.

initiatives

how busy do *I* look!

The people who advance, according to Walter Shipley, former chairman of Chase Manhattan Corporation (now J.P. Morgan Chase & Co.), "are those who take the initiative and are self-motivated to anticipate what the next need is, or anticipate how they can be supportive." Most career freshmen, instead, only anticipate their manager handing them something that they'll end up measurably stupider for doing, and usually aren't too far off the mark. As a result, many will look to delicately milk their assignments for an extra day or two, or attempt to escape detection by busily occupying their desks: shifting, shuffling, and analyzing reams of vacant paper, perhaps with a spreadsheet or word processing program unaccountably open.

Not only delaying the inevitable, this tax-returnish practice of deferral serves to stifle your boss' confidence that you can handle anything much beyond sluggish gruntwork, or unconvincingly pretending not to be sitting idly all afternoon. And even if you're a star in the ambitious constellation of entry levelers who promptly approach their manager for more orders once they've run out of them, it still says nothing of your ability to read into your department, your company, the market, or in between those carefully-ruled lines. Certainly you don't have carte blanche to take on whatever task you see fit; but you do have license to help stutter the cycle by asking your manager to sanction a dynamic independent activity.

"Wouldn't it be great if..." "What we really need is..." "I wish we could..." These are the mating calls for entry level initiative, however overused and whiny they may be. Perhaps an adjunct to your niche—or even a signpost toward a branded specialty—when you ask to commit yourself to an extra undertaking that's effectively already been asked for, guesswork about the idea's value is all but removed. It's sometimes called "working in the white space," where a job is initially unforeseen by management, but then increasingly defined through the fractious griping of their laborers. Yet it nonetheless continues to stand unclaimed, primarily on account of everyone playing dead when it comes to actually doing something.

As a young professional with the narrowest latitude for grievances—and with not much wider a selection of engaging pursuits to choose from—this is one of your most eye-catching chances to make a real impression with your manager, and possibly a real difference in the department. Even if you have to do it (and you will) on your own time. Particularly if business is slow and you've captured upon the opportunity in a compelling way, you can sometimes plant a towering flag into uncharted ground while your peers are planting their wallets into towering happy hour bar tabs.

But you need to ensure that the home front is properly secured first. The importance of making your assigned work the top priority can't be overstated, as the sexy stuff only looks that way when your boss is whistling along with you. No matter how much the initiative may enliven you, demonstrate your intelligence, rub your elbows with management, or curb overpopulation and famine, it still has to come after you've finished typing and distributing those meeting minutes you took down. Contrary to your intentions, you'll be handily punished for giving short shrift to the duties that allow the company to actually issue invoices and pay your salary twice a month.

Nobody (important) is going to be impressed either if your ideas aren't tied to a significant part of the business. To quote management guru Peter Drucker, "What gets measured gets managed," meaning, in this context, that you need to make sure the company is going to take a hard look at your self-guided work before you devote too much time and energy to it. Social and community activities, like food drives and team-building retreats, while warm and fuzzy on a nippy winter's day are just as soon left out in the cold by firm execs. (Besides, it's HR's job to organize those things, come up short, and then sport the corporate bull's-eye around the office). Rather, you should be focused on your department's performance-based goals, determining how and where your projects can promote those ends effectively, practically, and cost-efficiently.

But, at the same time, you also can't get carried away and dilute your efforts. In addition to keeping them in line with the needs of the organization, it's equally important that you keep your ventures limited, directed, and closely cropped. "If you spread yourself across too many initiatives," explains Elizabeth Dole, former American Red Cross CEO—and wife of the Viagra-popping, Pepsi-swigging, Britney Spears-ogling former senator and presidential candidate, Bob—"you will have been working night and day and you'll wonder what you have accomplished." (You'll probably wonder, too, what your significant other is doing while you're away).

It's not unusual to hear about overeager entry levelers bargaining their way into an overwhelming squall of work—even with just one banner-waving, two-drink-minimum-evading scheme—so make sure you've carefully scoped your projects before approaching anyone about them. A poorly executed initiative often looks worse than no initiative at all; then, at least, the doubt remains.

the only case is the business case

Your ability to get most anything of personal interest done as a career freshman rests on how well you can prove the business reasoning behind it—a practice your employer assumes you to be grossly incapable of. Understanding the firm's financial workings at all, for that matter, challenges the customary perception of you needing a wet nurse and after-lunch nap (which you may already take just the same, eyes closed or not). So by positioning your overtures in line with the company's revenue stream, not only do you speak a language that people are actually going to listen to, but you also stand to bowl over your onlookers. It's sort of like a toddler skipping past googoo-gaga right into discounted cash flows.

Enter, then, the *business case*, which sets an initiative up to address at least one of the two most fundamental issues to any organization: how it will save them money or help them make more of it. Your individual benefit is relevant only insofar as it expedites either of those, including instances of personal conflict; even here the company is only worried about morale, productivity, quality, and customer satisfaction, all of which translate into dollars. So no matter what it is that you want to accomplish, it has to demonstrably grow the business to get the green light. And you've got to prove it with numbers.

That means carefully straining your interests through the firm's when defining your issues, and constructing your arguments around the improvement of key business metrics: faster turnaround times, more streamlined operations, lower incidence of errors, improved communication, wider margins, additional client billable hours, and the like. Good business cases also call out the opportunity costs of not moving forward with the recommendations, as well as account for any potential downside where applicable, persuasively explaining why the risks are warranted. Bottom line, whatever revealing underthings it might be hiding, a proper rationale is always suited in black tie only—preferably ornamented with your manager's preferred presentational flower in the lapel.

The technique is equally effective for those things you want to drop as those you want to grab. After redeeming some measure of my credibility at the startup, for instance, I was asked to take over a chore that several lobotomy patients had already balked at in a tentative outsourcing agreement. Beginning to babble and drool uncontrollably on my desk, I realized I had to promptly wrest myself from its kung fu grip in order to keep my own name off the waiting list for the procedure.

So I put together a business case, appealing to the company's softer, gentler sensibilities; you know, the dirty, crumpled, overadorned kind that cause people to lunge and bite each other when you drop them. My brief memo to the VP went something like this:

Susan:

After reviewing my log sheet, I've found that this new task consumes somewhere between seven and nine non-chargeable hours per engagement. At my billing rate of $200 an hour, this is upwards of $1,800 of work that we're absorbing without recompense.

Given our average package price of $35,000, my

commitment to this activity represents more than a 5 percent discount to the client, as well as a margin erosion of over 2 percent to the company. Further, the duty leverages effectively none of my core skill sets, and inhibits my ability to ramp up in areas where I can add more value to the organization, including analytics and modeling.

As such, I recommend exploring alternatives; perhaps we might transfer this responsibility over to the Business Operations group, whose operating cost and expertise better meet the demands of the role.

Thanks for taking the time to think this over.

Michael

Several weeks thereafter, I couldn't help but avoiding eye contact with the hapless ops folks, who were unexpectedly hit with this desensitizing drivel as I was rehabbing. Fortunately, they, themselves, were eventually able to shake loose, freeing my conscience and reminding the firm that its employees aren't going to tolerate just anything that's put in front of them. As you know, even the entry level has its limits— an instinctive, visceral, you-can't-be-serious set of them—and in those cases the victims are the only willing. Or the lobotomized.

ideas in the mist

After looking around your company since arriving, you've probably identified two and a half dozen ways it can operate more effectively. Doubtlessly so. Pick out the other hundred dozen you've missed, figure out how to fix things, convince the right people to change, and you'll be ready to run the place yourself.

A hallmark of corporate politics, it usually doesn't matter so much how well something's going as it does whom it's keeping happy: If the top brass like it, then it works. Whether or not it really does. At all. That's why it's essential you understand who's partial to what before speaking up with your ideas. Even compelling business cases still regularly lose out to tradition, stubbornness, and ego, and there's a whole lot of that guaranteed to be promenading around the office. Keep in mind, if you think you know what you're doing, management's got that many more years on you of thinking the very same thing. And probably being right more often.

"Before you start yelling about how things need to be changed, you have to understand the culture," warns Don Fisher, founder of hip clothier and carefree commercial-maker, Gap Inc. "Don't arrive and think you know everything." (Recurring theme, huh). You may have a dazzling initiative that's already been tried and failed miserably—even if it's worked everywhere else you've seen it implemented—so you have to give the place the benefit of the doubt and honor its ungainly, backward way of running. Experience, like that of the cautionary Mr. Fisher, dictates not fighting the system, but rather learning to work nimbly within its constraints to make happen the things you want. Including change.

No matter how agilely you move in and around the field, however, as an entry leveler even your most brilliant brainchildren stand to be met with annoyance and apathy by those whom they were birthed to please—whereas even the dullest, most fabulously stupid suggestions by seniors will generally be given all due consideration. And far too often are you bound to find your idea discounted while a similar, or even identical, concept will be lauded when offered by a veteran. Credibility can sometimes take an unreasonable amount of time to root, and thoughts, regrettably, are often only as great as the mouth they're spoken from.

Consider the story told to us by Peter Gruber, chairman of Mandalay Entertainment. Their 1988 film *Gorillas in the Mist* quickly became a logistical forest when they realized that the screenplay required the primates to do what was written—to actually "act." (While that obstacle hasn't stopped other Silver Screen performers of comparable talent, the folks at Mandalay were nonetheless concerned). So during an emergency meeting—and, forgive me, it boggles the mind how the concept eluded inquiry to this point—a young intern meekly asked, "What if you let the gorillas write the story?"

The idea, basically, was to send a cinematographer into the jungle with a truckful of film, and wrap the movie around whatever you get. After telling her—with titters more than words—that she was there in spite of her ability to talk, they hours later considered the idea (which was in competition with sticking little actors in ape suits), and ultimately opted to go with the girl's proposal. The result: phenomenal footage that practically scripted the thing for them, a film shot for half the original $40 million budget, and, oh yeah, a Golden Globe for Sigourney Weaver.

Had Mr. Gruber offered the suggestion, on the other hand, the more likely initial response would have been audible gasps of wonder at his flummoxing and uncommonly lustrous insight. Remember this when you're considering revealing a concept you've developed to a higher-up; even beware of fellow entry levelers poised to snatch your purse. People are generally too self-involved to pay attention to the things you don't hit them over the head with, so simply staying quiet is usually insurance enough against misattribution. Of course your own manager may very well end up shoplifting the submission, but he's much less likely to forget who supplied it to him—and much more likely to reward you down the line.

But even then it won't happen very often. Corporate receptiveness is a function of the right idea, presented in the right way (i.e., business case format), being tossed out at just the right time—not unlike a three-window slot machine. In the exceptional instances when you do manage to hit the triple and catch your boss' attention, his interest will probably be lukewarm at best, and heavily influenced by the depth of your analysis, the quality of the presentation, his personal slant on the matter, the time he has to devote to it, the importance of the issue to the group, and the staunchness of the individuals he'll have to persuade. It's obviously a losing proposition most times, so it becomes a game of persistence and patience, much like everything else as a career freshman.

Still, you should keep handing those ideas over, and that's for a couple of reasons. First, your primary goal when presenting an initiative isn't necessarily to get it put into action, but rather to continually demonstrate that you're thinking critically about your firm's business. The real objective here is impression management, and many times a well-fought loss is just as good as a victory.

Second, since it's a numbers game, you constantly have to be putting your visions out there to ever have a chance of landing on something that works—which, from time to time, really does happen. "Merrill would never be where we are today without taking the concepts that the younger people brought to us," confirms the Bull Lynch's chairman emeritus, Dan Tully, evidencing that even the biggest, most successful companies still have plenty of legroom for fresh thought.

And while your best ganders still have to be blessed by the boys with the mahogany-appointed offices—where by blessed I mean credited to—it helps to consider that you, too, might one day be the lucky recipient of some career freshman's stolen insight. Not that Corporate America condones this sort of practice; but they do always seem to be looking the other way, don't they?

promotions & transfers

forget me not

While their corporate medicine cabinet is probably overcrowded with memory-juiced bottles of ginkgo biloba and unpronounceable phosphatidylserine "smart pills," chances are your firm still can't immediately recall the last project you were staffed on. Much less what you did right with it. And while a general day-to-day satisfaction is pretty much all you need from your company at any given time, the cumulative effect of their forgetfulness will often leave you only with that bland, unaffected approval come promotion season. Which, in turn, will usually leave you right where you are, or not too far away from it. Getting all herbally hopped-up, it turns out, really just helps them forget in a more healthy way.

Indeed, the typical organization decides how to move you based primarily on a blurry overall feel, dotted with a smattering of managers' and seniors' recommendations (for or against), and edged with a threadbare assortment of "representative" anecdotal instances they've seen fit to jot down—or seen fit to have jotted down for them. After a couple foggy "oh yeahs" and "that's rights," you're stamped one way or the other and dispassionately dumped onto the doddering stack of other career freshmen having their futures with the company indifferently determined. "Hey, can you pass the ginseng?"

Once again, the onus is on you to aggressively guide the perceptions of the firm, doing the math and building the defense that they have neither the time nor the inclination to bother with. In the business case of your career, you're called on here to illustrate the unique and material value you've added to both your work unit and the company as a whole over the past year—as you know, quantified with dollars, percentages, hard data, gift certificates to GNC, and any other specific measurements of concern. Breaking the rule, if there's ever a place at the entry level where your well-considered boastfulness always has a seat, it's at the performance review table.

What did you help to speed up, make cheaper, do better, or sell more of? What have you accomplished, specifically and numerically, beyond the prescribed pace and precincts of your position? In what tangible, functional ways have you outstripped, outmatched, and outshined your cohorts? How have your personal initiatives impacted your department operationally, financially, and even culturally?

As any good statistician will tell you, certain figures can be overemphasized, overlooked, rounded up, trimmed down, tweaked, turned, and massaged to frame a beautifully rendered, reasonably embellished, and extremely alluring picture. It's vital, certainly, to stay within the borders of truth and reason; but by all means, selectively employ the facts to tell the most compelling story you can tell.

One of my more worldly former managers (who made it to all seven continents before her 30th birthday) has developed a globally applicable tool to help your cause: the "DIGJAM" file, standing for "Damn I'm Good, Just Ask Me." Blunt and immodest, like pretty much everything else about her, it's a foil to your CYA folder where you keep examples of your best work, as well as proof of your here-today, misremembered-tomorrow praise. The binder is even a reliable catch for those congrats you're bound to forget yourself.

Anytime you get a singing e-mail from above, for instance, print it off and in it goes. Same holds for assignments that were particularly successful or that you're unusually proud of, along with those nettlesome problems you helped to unpick—which you should document and date on your own if there's no written proof. Use these credentials as evidence in support of the claims of greatness you make during your review, ideally matching up specific items with each accomplishment and virtue you extol. Like any exam or presentation, it's all in the prep work; so take the time to scaffold your numbers and assiduously plan out what you want to say, including retorts, explanations, and defenses for likely objections and counters.

Especially those levied by way of collegial input. Many managers, in today's always-pressed environment, have taken to farming out much of the responsibility of assessing your performance to a crowd of trusted senior underlings. Not an unreasonable practice—these wingmen *are* typically closest to you and your work—it does, however, present a unique conflict of interest: They may have it in for you. Justified or not, this group can have a profoundly injurious effect on your advancement prospects, and usually don't have the professional propriety to keep themselves from doing so. If they don't like you as a subordinate, after all, they're surely not tickled by the idea of you becoming a peer on equal footing.

All of the marks on one of my old colleague's performance reviews, I can recall, were completely skewed because he could never seem to do right by one particular senior consultant. Despite his work being considered outstanding by most all other counts (including my own, and I was in a position to say after all the help he'd given me), in the end the veteran was just too tight with the evaluating director; she heard exactly what this dodgy saboteur wanted her to hear.

So in your own dealings, it's critical that you either patch up those acrimonious relationships with influential officemates—and it's your job to know exactly who has management's ear—or, if things are completely irreconcilable, that you talk louder than they do to your manager. Besides, you shouldn't be so distanced from your boss such that any outsider might have an undue bearing on his take. As you know, this is your keystone business relationship, and it's your unmitigated liability to ensure that you're consistently on the same page. Which shouldn't be an issue, provided you keep a solid line of communication open with your weekly meetings, informal feedback chats, and passing conversations in the hall. Remember, almost never will a manager ambush you with a review you didn't see coming...if you were looking.

regular or organic?

The idea dragged around by most young professionals is that they have to do just what they're told for two or three years as a grunt, so that they can have the distinct privilege of being told just what to do for the next two or three as a senior. It's the "track" big companies usually espouse, and indeed a crowded and colorless place to go for a jog: What career freshmen generally don't realize here is that even if they beat the pack by six months or a year at the first turn, they're still on a course that empties out into the stultified ranks of middle administration. And eventually the moribund chambers of sub-executiveship, should that be the way they'd like the next 20-plus years to shape up.

The upcoming final section of the book, gladly, is devoted to averting that path and setting you on the one to your passion, the walk of your dreams. But it fits to introduce this part of the discussion, I think, by talking about a kind of promotion standing askew to the thickly foot-trodden route: "organic growth." Completely unrelated to the pricey vitamins and supplements your firm's directors are gulping down with their $6-a-bottle S.Pellegrino mineral water, this kind of intracompany movement deals with formalizing the work you're already doing.

Perhaps a result of the white space getting murkier or your niche splitting its britches, when you're already positioned for and meeting increasingly important organizational needs, a legitimate, business-card-earning role can sometimes crop out of it. You'll usually have to write up a comprehensive business case and job description, bear in mind, and then keep tugging on the one-armed bandit until your boss pays out; but if you enjoy the position and the product adds real value to the firm, then it's an ideal direction to push in. And if you win, you can extend your life at the company in a significant and personally meaningful way, as well as grow your knowledgebase and skill sets in marketable, well-differentiated areas.

Even if you're currently holding fast to the traditional trail, however, you still have to be doing the job above you before you're eligible to get it. Most corporations have tightly defined milestones, metrics, and behaviors that call out a senior from an entry leveler, and the firm's expectation is that the formal induction will follow the existing field-work. It's rare that someone will get bumped up to the next notch based only on time served, or in hopes that they'll now be incented to execute at the level they're capable of. Rather, if a career freshman isn't doing backflips over the unstylishly phrased rubric in the organization's documentation, the better incentive for them, typically, is to land a headhunter who will help them underperform somewhere else for better money. As any good, unscrupulous headhunter has been trained to do.

And whom you may need anyway if the politics don't line up. It's even rarer that a multiplayer promotion is a real contest between candidates, where the nominee with the strongest relationships generally gets the nod—even though their assignments may not be a shake comparatively. If the executives and managers making the decision, however, have worked closely with certain individuals (or have had their seniors do so for them), and only have one or two slots to fill— which is becoming more and more common in these belt-tightening times—it doesn't make sense for them to shop around for a lesser-known competitor who may or may not be a worse fit.

They'd prefer to like the employee first, and then spend whatever time and money they have to getting them up to speed. That's why it's so important to grow your brand awareness, and to keep strong ties with the people who get listened to. Research cited by next-generation magazine *Fast Company*, in fact, shows that in over 80 percent of promotions, candidates have a mentoring relationship with someone higher up the food chain who speaks favorably on their behalf. (The other 20 percent just look better than the outside résumés. Cheaper, anyway).

But you, yourself, shouldn't do any speaking outside of your own merits. Remember, everybody's trying to get promoted, and there are almost always several of you vying for the same manager's love and adoration. It's never going to be handed out equally, to be sure; yet you'll also never capture more than your share—and, it's easily reasoned, far less—by setting out to undermine or discredit a fellow contender. I've never seen that tactic work well at doing anything but dirtying the individual's reputation, and seriously agitating the beehive of people who subsequently (and, for them, highly unfortunately) became their superiors. Instead, by selflessly offering your assistance to teammates and generously supplying your group with extra time and energy, as does every foreseeing Midas, you'll naturally distinguish yourself as a leader near the top of a very short list.

Plus doing so will help ensure that you're "covered in glory" come evaluation time, or that you have a string of recent successes, coups, and positive interactions fresh in people's minds. (Sort of a modern-day Era of Good Feelings, but without having to tour New England or bemoan the Federalist Party). As with pretty much everything else, timing can be the make-or-break factor with promotions, so it's important that you do whatever you can to build up some good momentum going into performance review season. True, you may not be able to control certain projects or tasks, but you can always look for strategic volunteering opportunities, niche extensions, and similar hey-look-at-me activities to give you that extra push.

But before you do anything, make sure you actually want the job—plain, organic, with cheese, or otherwise. Many career freshmen get so caught up in the glamour of getting advanced that they realize only after it's too late that they don't like this new position any better than their old one; oftentimes much less, what with the extra hours, higher expectations, and only marginally bigger paycheck (especially after governmental siphoning).

While it's always important to be stretched and challenged, it has to be in the right directions, for the right reasons, and at the right intervals. It doesn't serve you, for example, when the demands of your role don't provide adequate breathing room for interdepartmental learning, brand building, and networking—to say nothing of maintaining your mental health, physical well-being, or any semblance of an outside life. As later discussed, career paths, while ultimately negotiable and unbinding, should always be the result of careful consideration and planning, and never unmarked ambition or desperate escape. That route is for relationships.

do you guys need another player?

Sometimes an excellent alternative to moving up is moving over—which itself can elevate you even quicker than tripping your way through the congested, narrow-laned track. Also a resort from organizational flight when you're struggling in your home department, a transfer offers tremendous exposure to a part of your company's business that you may have never seriously considered, and that may fit your strengths and goals far better than what the firm initially sold you. (And, really, what wouldn't)?

As you insistently continue your post-college education and chat up the various personnel you run across, bump into, and stalk down, don't be shy when it comes to nudging key managers about potential opportunities for collaboration. Not necessarily in terms of a full-blown position straight away, but just a chance or two to play in their sandbox to see if you like the kids and toys. And not necessarily during your first conversation, either: It usually takes a couple of hey-how-you-doings before it's kosher to give them a better feel for your interests and strengths, and you glimpse theirs.

You'll come away with some good input regardless of whether or not they're on board with the idea of you bothering them day-in and day-out, and through that you can better pattern your next moves. Understand, though, that even if they're not entirely horror-struck at the thought of you calling them boss, it's still not to say a change of venue is imminent. Far from, in fact, after figuring in the department's budget, workload, staff position, political standing, the overall economic climate, and any other candidates ahead of you—if there's even a job to be had. While being on the inside does confer one of the better advantages available, it's hard to secure a good post no matter when, where, or how you go about it.

So you have little recourse here but to hope that the manager is upfront with you and appropriately tempers your expectations. I, personally, was left hanging by one very sly (or deluded, I'm not sure) brand manager who mercilessly strung me along month after month with warm, resounding assurances of her interest; it wasn't until after she got canned two quarters later that I began to suspect she was trying to feed everyone that same soup. It speaks to the need for keeping things on the hush when sniffing around for a relocation—no matter how promising things look. I know it goes without saying, but should you even have an errant, restless night's dream about telling your co-workers, you need to punch yourself very hard in the face after waking up. Twice.

What you obviously want to avoid is word prematurely getting back to your captain, which may not only scuttle a potential trade, but make the remainder of your term under his dominion an exceptionally hellish proposition. Plus don't forget, even if you do get your transfer, you'll still probably touch his department in some way, meaning that the swap should be politically clean and free from bruised feelings. More experienced managers generally won't penalize you for quietly and respectfully shopping, having seen their familiar share of cross-departmental moves, and benefiting from a broader view of the overall gain for the organization and even the transferee. The standing bet, however, is that your manager isn't one of those.

So when the deal is all but done and it's time to break the news, be sure to express your undiminished, 'till-the-bitter-end commitment to your department and teammates, sounding the note that this is strictly a professional transaction. Make your boss recognize that you're at the very beginning of your career, and that you owe it to yourself to gather all the knowledge you can about the business world—diversifying your portfolio of experiences, information, skills, and colleagues. If this objective is better met elsewhere in the company at this point, then you're duty-bound to explore that opportunity. And should it not work out, then you're thrilled to continue learning with and adding value to his group.

For believability sake, by the way, I'd recommend practicing that last line a lot.

all the spinning plates

balancing acts

I t takes a special kind of facial muscle control, I'm convinced, to talk out of both sides of your mouth as well as Corporate America does with work – life balance. Really, I've spent hours at the mirror in practice to no avail. Which is just as well, I suppose, because I wouldn't know what to say anyway; that's for overpriced PR execs to concoct and contort.

My favorite catchphrase of theirs, to date at least, is "work hard – play hard," which accents the façade of a recruiting event almost as well as a slurred rendition of "Auld Lang Syne" spices up a draggy new year's eve shindig. Now, I'm perfectly in tune with the working hard part—as each of my entry level managers saw to—yet I'm still to encounter a group of swashbuckling young professionals engaged in that so-called hard play. "Work hard – drink hard," maybe, but that's as close as it generally comes. Although after a solid string of 70-, 80-, even 90-hour workweeks, the prospect of anything hard outside of a decent liquor does, admittedly, tend to lose its charm.

But firms can't be straight about things and still secure a spot on *Fortune* magazine's "100 Best Companies to Work For" list. No, they even one-up the lip service, running splashy media blitzes about their freshly revamped flextime programs, telecommuting options, mandated vacations, and any other jazzy alternatives they've devised to engender "healthy personal lives" for their valued and respected "corporate family members."

Who, naturally, are punished when they actually use them. No matter what's told to the guests, after the goodnights are said and the front door shut, the dysfunctional culture imposes its unarticulated—yet absolutely unmuffled—dictum about how much time on the job constitutes a proper commitment to the firm. At most of the big meat-grinders, as you know, 12- and 14-hour days are worn proudly around the office as badges of courage, with bloodshot and baggy eyes bespeaking a brave and true team player.

A decent and upstanding devotee, to be sure, who looks upon reasonably scheduled, nonalcoholic after-work activities with a crinkled brow and low grumbles—resulting, as one might guess, from their jealous longing and disempowered frustration. It's a tenet of the new "corporate martyrdom," where overengaged employees try to convince themselves that they don't want liberating outside identities by punishing those who sanely do. "No, I'll slavishly toil here until all hours so I can do the same thing again tomorrow. You go have fun."

You can see the conflict best, perhaps, in the bustling black market for leisure. It generally starts to manifest around 7 p.m., when people begin to drape a spare jacket or sweater over their ergonomically-correct chair, adjust their still-burning desk lamp, deactivate their screen saver, and lay a set of glasses down on some very important-looking papers. At which point they, stealthily, leave. So to best satisfy the obsessive demands for output and loyalty (and to fallaciously dazzle *Fortune*), Corporate America's lifeblood is watching primetime television with digging pangs of guilt. While their bright, active cubicles, on the other hand, are all busy being terribly impressed with one another's dedication.

Career freshmen, in particular, are easily manipulated targets in the arena of overwork. Big Business all too readily plays on that time-honored college lifestyle of complete immersion, where studies, activities, and friends are enmeshed in multicolored, 18-hour days of industry and amusement. Except firms do it in black-and-white, and without all that revenue-threatening glee.

New economy "corporate campuses," for instance, are purposely fashioned to encourage extended stays by the younger troupe without families or good judgment—a throwback to the go-go university environment of gyms, clubs, stores, eateries, and other things to do instead of class. Colleagues, too, are quietly spun by organizations as sort of friends-designate, what with the upbeat sloganeering, outside gatherings, team building exercises, and annoying office birthday celebrations. Yet they'd unplug the treadmills, send back the foosball table, fire the masseuse, dump out the free sodas, take the pictures off the walls, and give you a folding chair if they thought they could get just as much out of you. To them it's all overhead. And to most young professionals, it's not enough anyway: Even the plushiest digs and most fun-in-the-sun kind of corporate culture still leave a gaping void, formerly occupied by some assortment of school-related entities.

Free from the throes of hated blue book exams and 100-page nights of reading, there's so much that entry levelers ache to do. But without a centralized location or fixed schedule to play in and around, they don't know where, how, and most of all *when* to do it. "Because of their lack of experience," Robbins and Wilner report in *Quarterlife Crisis*, "young graduates say they doubt their abilities to prioritize properly and their self-esteem falters as they wonder if they will ever be able to fit everything they want into their lives."

Worried about establishing their professional presence and earning rewarding assignments, career freshmen frequently overcompensate with exorbitant workloads and excessive hours. And without that easily accessible community of like people and liked events to retreat into, there's little reason to go home anyway. Which is obviously just what the firm wants: Those late-night workmate bonds will do wonders for productivity and morale, and probably even help to staunch turnover; people are much less likely to quit on their friends, you know.

Compounding the damage caused by early-stagers' tendency toward taxation, their negligible free time isn't even usually so free. Bartolomé and Evans, of aforementioned *Harvard Business Review* fame, also found that negative emotional spillover will soak a person's private life when work is overwhelming and unsatisfying (entry and level)—"no matter how little he travels, how much time he spends at home, or how frequently he takes a vacation," they add. When there's challenge and reward at the office, by contrast, the duo likens the job to an invigorating workout, leaving one refreshed and energized for the remains of the day.

Considering how often a career freshman can walk to the company parking lot at 11 p.m. with a crisp handclap and jaunty "whew," it suggests that Tae Bo memberships should continue uncancelled, and that this situation needs to be attacked with Billy Blanks-like vigor and intensity. Indeed, given that the two most common triggers for the unwanted overflow are adjustment to a new job and an improper fit between work and worker—two of the business basement's most prized and distinctive attributes—it's clear that this is a serious fight.

And one that, long-term, desperately has to be won. Ample psychological research shows that the patterns for decision-making shaped during an individual's 20s and 30s tend not to change in later years—meaning that assuming a hyperskewed, work-centric lifestyle at the entry level can actually be the inconspicuous start of a very lengthy and destructive cycle. For proof, just give one of the elder drones a call at their desk right before you go to bed; surely they'll have a great story about the *really* crazy hours they used to put in back in the day. (To avoid an uncomfortable silence, however, I wouldn't probe about their weekend plans, hobbies, or romantic relationships).

As it's only too clear, you're going to have to give the firm some of the ridiculous hours they want. And as you're also painfully familiar, some of your personal interests are going to have to be surrendered to those of the organization. It's a reality of work, and pretty much so at any stage. But what's never justified (or safe) is a devotion to your company at the expense of everything else life has to offer you as a twentysomething. Outside of the dim, bleary-eyed sphere of sleep-deprived corporate delirium, there's a bright, rich, and worthwhile world to be known, drunk in, absorbed through the pores. Look out a window, you'll see it. If you don't consistently get yourself out there in some capacity—if you don't pause to put some space in between the spokes after each turn—absolutely everything suffers, and especially that thing you're most trying to keep healthy. Which, regrettably, isn't usually your health.

wherever, whenever, whatever

After more than a century of research on work incentives and boundaries, scientists still can't say how much a person can produce in a day—particularly when it comes to "mental work," because how do you measure that anyway? (Although I wouldn't put the question to your boss, as I imagine there's stack of mental work on his desk he'd be happy to give you as an experiment). Notwithstanding, Corporate America strives to push its employees ever further with each passing quarter: earnings are never strong enough, sales could always be better, market share is still too narrow. Plus Wall Street makes sure the shoving match continues, bullying CEOs into delivering double-digit growth and ensuring that the rank-and-file always have a higher hill to climb.

I certainly don't take issue with productivity; that's what fuels economic development and makes this country so prosperous. The worry, I feel, is in the means by which we get there (and ultimately our reasons for doing it, which is something we'll address in the next section). That life-or-death extra penny per share, those additional thousand widgets, the client account that has to be squeezed for another million bucks: we satiate the insatiable by putting in the kind of hours that even Japan—formerly the world capital of workaholism—can only respectfully bow to.

And that's if they're awake. A recent survey commissioned by the National Sleep Foundation revealed that one out of every five salaried American workers groggily slaps the alarm at 5 a.m. or earlier, and that this country as a whole has reduced average doze time by 20 percent in the past 25 years. It's to the point where, according to the *New York Times*, the typical U.S. citizen gets 500 fewer hours of sleep per year than they physically need. (In addition to, by Japan's standards, at least 40 hours too little of inebriated karaoke).

@ the entry level

Insufficient siestas, of course, lead to lower overall work quality, higher rates of error and oversight, memory impairment, and, we can't forget, irritability. As a career freshman, you get plenty of that without the help of an always-made bed, as assuredly does your boss; a full night's slumber, instead, is actually one of the cheapest forms of insurance you can hold at the entry level. (Next to a desk on a different floor than your overtired manager). More seriously, however, and more to the point, studies in this department have further shown that rising in the wee hours can be a sign of depression, which isn't an altogether surprising finding for people who feel that they can't cram their lives into normal waking intervals. How to interpret the practice with regard to young professionals—who are prone to hopelessness for reasons greater in number and kind than an overload of assignments—remains uninvestigated and unsettling.

With after-office and weekend hours, too, currently spiraling upward with each passing year, we've arguably leapt past the "Organization Man" archetype of the 1950s right into a pervading and perversely celebrated "Overworked Man." At worst this is an uberfocused, woefully out-of-touch, I-left-reality-in-my-other-pants kind of breed: Consumed with their work, defined by the job, and obsessed to the point where their efforts—like all things obsessive—are self-defeating.

You know, the managers who suffer no misgivings about compelling people to stay late into the night; who harbor entirely irrational expectations for revisions and turnaround times; who blow the banal up into the barmy; and who basically run around in a musty state of unadulterated craziness. As many an executive has attested, these wretched individuals are usually halted somewhere in sub-administration, with senior officials bristling at the thought of having to deal any more closely with them than they already do.

My nemesis, Bill—the paradigm of managerial mania—in fact suffered that very fate himself: A lingering contact informed me that he was removed from his regal project shortly after I removed myself, and told in not so many words that while he wasn't going to be fired, the only place he'd ever become a partner would be in a marriage. And we all know how short-lived that frightening union would be.

176

Especially after running out of sedatives.

Though the middle ground here is certainly far better populated at the entry level, the effects of the midnight oil-burning aren't necessarily any less destructive. As workaholics-in-training, young laborers are forfeiting life's lush third dimension out of the almost unfightable expectation to overcommit. It's as if giving oneself completely over to the company's whimsy—day, night, home, abroad, in a box, with a fox—is the only way to survive, much less succeed. And it's put career freshmen in a sleepless, restless bind: travailed, tired, thwarted, and frankly bummed out about it all.

Then, subtly along the path, bummed out can decay into burned out. Consistently putting in overtime, plugging away during lunch, dragging work home, rushing to meet deadlines, not taking vacations, trudging through sicknesses—essentially the higher points of the everyday corporate routine have all been identified as leading contributors to fizzling. Though none has been found riskier than lacking obligations or interests outside of the office, which as discussed, career freshmen can be disquietingly good at.

When there's nothing to define the boundary between work and everything else (assuming there's anything to even keep apart), the stress and pressures of the day never go away. Building in weight and intensity over time, the eventual result can include chronic fatigue, cynicism, anger, hair-trigger swings of emotion, and even heightened self-criticism—all of which tend to manifest on the job. It's kind of like eighteenth-century English statesman Lord Chesterfield's thought, "Few people do business well who do nothing else." Except that modern-day young professionals usually don't do either.

first things when?

priorities in practice

When this madness is stirred together with the my-job-makes-me-weep negativity already spilling out into your personal time—and soaked by the want for something to fill those brief reprieves—it becomes clear that this is a question of *priorities*. You already know how enduring are the habits you form at this stage, and how quickly things can get away from you. Making a good showing as a young professional, then, doesn't mean making a life out of your job—no matter how fiercely prescriptive the firm is about the "right" number of hours. Or how insistent colleagues may be about the "right" number of times per week to go get sloppy with them at the pub.

Rather, it's about locating a balance between the two conflicting sets of wants, and counterweighing the demands of your position against all of the other stuff you can and should demand from life. Part of it is building in rituals and practices, part of it is working more efficiently, and part of it is just drawing the line. Because if the company is going to promote the guy who put in 80-hour weeks for two years straight, you have to ask yourself if that's a promotion you really want.

College students certainly are. A recent PricewaterhouseCoopers survey of 2,500 university-goers, in fact, had 57 percent name "attaining a balance between personal life and career" as their primary professional goal. Atop the ivory tower, it's pretty easy to see the mêlée down below, and a fair majority of to-be entry levelers predictably prefer to keep lock on their liberation. Even, apparently, if it means lagging behind the sharp-elbowed fast track.

After stepping down into the grimy midst of the unwashed corporate masses, however, that shiny idealism quickly dirties and smudges, rendering their pledges as impractical jabber from a group who didn't know what they were saying. In a dramatic about-face, they now in fact want to be *leading* that treacherous speedway. Even, apparently, if it means chalking up their pointy edges and throwing themselves headlong into the bruising fracas.

Or does it? There's a contradiction at work here between priorities and payroll, and it doesn't appear to go away even after the entry level does. A millennial survey by *Fast Company* perhaps revealed the inconsistency best, asking corporateers to rank certain items as a means to achieve balance in their lives. "Making personal life more of a priority" was selected by 91 percent of the respondents, while, in the same breath, 83 percent said they would take a $10,000 annual raise over more free time. What's more, 63 percent of those surveyed said that "learning to live on less money" was a key step for them, while fully 86 percent indicated that thickening their wallets was of prime importance.

Reading this, one is left to think that America's workforce is clinically schizophrenic, incredibly loopy, or deeply conflicted. The right answer is probably a combination of all those, but the last one comes pretty close on its own: Almost every person surveyed on this topic—by magazines and otherwise—also agrees that achieving balance in their lives is their own responsibility, and many express guilt and regret about the choices they've made. So understanding the lie is instinctive; doing the right things about it isn't.

Finding equilibrium is instead about actual, tangible, calculable things you do in your life (besides confusing pollsters with your incompatible objectives). "Your company measures its priorities. People also need to place metrics around their priorities," believes Vinod Khosla, founding CEO of Sun Microsystems. Now a partner at Kleiner Perkins Caufield & Byers, one of the Silicon Valley's premiere venture capital firms (which, incidentally, funded the startup I was with), Khosla works about 50 hours a week when he could easily put in 100. Family, however, comes first to this well-aligned executive, and he makes sure that he's home for dinner with them at least 25 nights a month. "Having a target number is key," Khosla explains. "I know people in my business who are lucky if they make it home five nights a month. I don't think that I'm any less productive than those people." (He's certainly no less rich, with a net worth around a *billion* dollars).

Research on balanced individuals shows that they have widely built these kinds of practices into their weekly and monthly calendars, and stick to them (almost) no matter what. It's the only way that they find the time to do the things that keep them personally energized, engaged in life, and refreshed for work. Plus the technique offers day-to-day visibility into whether or not they're living according to their priorities, and helps them gain a greater sense of control in their lives—where they can't be prevented from doing those activities that bring them pleasure, fulfillment, and release. When the seesaw is perpetually at ground level, by contrast, depression is far more likely to mount, making it not only heavier to push off, but that much harder to even want to try.

Some people find that having a ritual, such as meditation or some quiet reading time, creates an island of silence that sets a calm, serene tone for the day or evening. Some people that drives nuts. Others prefer vigorous exercise, feeding on the adrenaline and increased blood flow to the brain to help keep them stimulated and motivated, all while staying in shape. Some people that makes heave. Whatever works for you, so long as it offers a brief escape from reality (the importance of which cannot be overstated, and for the depressed in particular) and provides a sense of balance, control, and peace.

The overarching point is that if you don't identify, tenaciously fence-off, and then keep careful watch on those parts of your life reserved only for you, your company will steadily graze their way into them, leaving you hewn, barren, and desolate. Believing that the time for balance comes later is both folly and dangerous; never is it easier to become involved in outside activities than at the entry level, where the pull of the job isn't nearly as intense as at the managerial level. In fact, by getting good at your "me time" as a career freshman, you'll be able to more effectively handle the heavier weights and strains levied by future positions. Plus you're more likely to survive long enough to actually see one of those.

like asking for a date

"Learn to say 'No!' It will be of more use to you than to be able to read Latin," advised the regarded nineteenth-century British preacher Charles Spurgeon. Though that can probably be said of most things, the advice rings just as true today as it did back then. My guess, actually, is that the technique was pioneered by the earliest women unwelcomingly invited out to dinner—judging by the skill of the importuned contemporary lady. Regardless, the tool has also been found to work exceedingly well at the office when used in consistent and strategic ways. Failure to put it to work, in fact, can put *you* to work by hours more per day, and ultimately end up tossing you right out of balance. Not to mention dumping you in a table for one.

Managers and seniors love to dress up nice-to-haves as must-haves, with complete disregard for young professionals' personal time; as you know, on-my-desk-in-the-morning urgency is frequently closer to after-lunch insignificance. That's why it's essential you're always clear about which deadlines are nonnegotiable and for what reasons: information that will help you determine where and how you can firmly, but tactfully ward off unnecessary work.

Remember, it's not shirking; it's simply in line with the practices of all in-demand people. Even ones you wouldn't necessarily think of right away: Take NASCAR champion Jeff Gordon for instance, who explains, "I never want to say no, especially to our sponsors. But if I didn't learn to say no, I wasn't going to be able to do my job. And my job is what got me the sponsors in the first place." (Why they all pay to clutter indistinguishably together on an object taking repeated left turns at a blurring 200 MPH is another question).

It's usually easy enough to tell when your boss is adamant about getting something done right away, and when he'd just like to casually admire it sitting on his desk for a while. Directly asking the right questions (and delicately reminding him of all the other admirable stuff you're occupied with) will typically tease out whatever breathing room there is to be had, freeing you up to go carry out your private agenda. The same obviously also goes for seniors, who as a general rule are more unabashed with their requests—and too often shamelessly drunk with power over greenbeans. Who, as a general rule, could do their job.

And whom many times they ask to. As you also surely know, one-ups are notorious for dropping by entry level cubicles unannounced, tugging on a hunk of work they'd be ever so grateful for a hand with. The favor bank balance is, of course, never high enough, so it's usually difficult to pass up a good deposit; but how often do seniors actually pay back those kinds of credits? This been-around-the-block bunch is reviled, as well, for their managerial-like lapses in memory when it comes to career freshmen cashing in on the stuff they stayed late for so many a night: Rolls around performance review time, and where's that recommendation?

So when a veteran rears with a random, unassigned need, keep in mind that your responsibility to take it on extends only so far as your free time and good humor. Even if your plate is only half-full, you still have to account for your extra-office activities and engagements, which should never be compromised for something that's not even yours to begin with. True, the senior may walk away miffed, but you'll have clearly established your boundaries, which in the end are always respected. Instead of delegating down to you, now perhaps they'll do some pushback of their own, forcing the workflow upward. And when that ingrained guilt inevitably starts to emerge, it always helps to keep one thought in mind: How likely would they be to punch the OT card for something *you* asked them to hang around for?

a healthy distance

In still another not-so-long-ago survey of 1,000 working men and women (this one by the Yale School of Management), nearly one in four said they were chronically angry at the office—most commonly because their employers "violated basic promises," and didn't fulfill "the expected psychological contract with their workers." They must've called some of my old colleagues.

Work is personal, and people as a whole have higher expectations of their companies than ever before. They want to bring all of their skills, interests, and values to the job—to root their whole identities in their position. (Presumably because they're not doing enough of that outside of the office, which Corporate America doesn't want them to anyway). Yet as a result, the hurt and resentment cut deep and hard when employers frostily betray their employed. And at the entry level— where balance is also about understanding what you can and can't expect work to do for you—the effects can be even more emotionally devastating: Raw, inexperienced career freshmen, after all, are just doing what the organization is suggesting they should. Plus it's kind of like their old academic schedule; in a raped-and-pillaged sort of way.

"Of all the institutions in society, why would we let one of the more precarious ones supply our social, spiritual, and psychological needs?" asks Joanne Ciulla in *The Working Life*. Reflecting on the dangers of laborers placing such a large portion of their lives into the unsteady hands of paycheck-givers (a fact that most recognize, but persist in doing regardless), she advocates strong outside ties to mitigate the impact of a shakeup. "It is important for people to be connected to activities and organizations unrelated to work," Ciulla continues. "If they lose or change their jobs, they'll have other friends, communities, and interests to support them."

And by friends, she still doesn't mean extra-chummy associates. To grow too involved with officemates isn't usually practical for your brand positioning, and certainly not advisable for your overall social well-being. These kinds of relationships often center narrowly on re-hashing workplace matters—precisely what you're looking to get away from—and can change dramatically after a promotion, transfer, or role-change. At work, don't forget, you're in a hierarchy where colleagues regularly hit below the belt to move up the ladder; even the tight little whisper-and-giggle relationships come untied when more cash is at stake. Given, also, that companies are forever shifting and people always coming and going, companionship seems to be much better found in environments of a lesser flux. (Plus don't you want to stare into a face you don't already have to look at for 10 or 12 hours a day)?

And by friends, Ms. Ciulla definitely doesn't mean your manager. Bosses' praise can tether entry levelers to their desk sunup to sundown, sweating and swearing until things are just so—until they can bask in the radiance of that dollar-driven acclamation again. Some in-charges, with their winning smiles and winsome characters, even have the chore down to a near-truth. It's pushed the manufactured attachment to the point of Sally Field at times: "Oh, he likes me, he really, really likes me!"

Now, outside of the fact that should your manager quit or get fired tomorrow he would completely disappear from your life, I'd be hard-pressed to bet that he truly values you as the multifaceted individual you are. He likes the gruntwork part, doubtlessly, for which he may occasionally beam at you, offer his miscellaneous thanks, and perhaps even extend the sporadic invite for drinks. But if he didn't think you could help further his business objectives, he'd probably stop talking to you. And who can blame him—if this person weren't your boss, would you really care what he thought either?

Big Business spends a lot of money Frankensteining together their mangled families, scrubbing the brains of the kin into believing they've got a second place to call home. Who often do call it that until one of their relations puts the screws to them. But when they then furiously realize the misshapen experiment they're all twisted up in, many can't seem to find life outside of the organization's human resources strategy. So as a result, most of this country's corporateers are also working very hard to enjoy themselves.

As a skeptical and still-distanced career freshman, recognize the situation for what it is and forbear against your company's duplicitous embrace—out of which such monsters are born. Find your own activities, your own friends. Locate a sense of self in individuals and institutions unaffiliated with your field, finally putting your campus-free autonomy to work. Remember, there's an entire world of people out there who can offer your life newfound perspective, depth, and diversity; just not anyone with a financial stake in your comings and goings.

life, after all, is for living

I asked myself a while back if I wanted that promotion—the one that would cost me two workweeks rolled up into one, month after month, year after year. My own priorities at loggerheads, I was unexpectedly led back to my childhood and the writings of Lewis Carroll. In *Through the Looking Glass and What Alice Found There*, this former

Oxford mathematician draws out both the question and the answer with beautiful simplicity: "The rule is," the Queen said to Alice, "jam tomorrow, and jam yesterday, but never jam today."

A widely interpreted paradox, sure, but to me it's meaning was singular: The sweetness of life is in the *now*, which is exactly where I wasn't looking for it. What's already gone and what's yet to come, I realized, are just that; remembrance and anticipation, while core to the human condition, don't in themselves make for the thrill of living. That stuff, rather, is scattered all around us at this very moment (even, on occasion, in the office). Now there is, of course, a balance to be struck between doing and scheduling, experiencing and recalling, working and living—and not that those should be mutually exclusive endeavors. Or even can be, really, if John Lennon was right about life being what happens while you're busy making other plans. But there's only so much jam to go around, and some of it's got to be spread on right now. Sometimes thick.

To work merely for tomorrow's (potential) sweetness is a joyless and thankless—not to mention precarious—way to live. To hearken back entirely to yesterday's pleasures is a lonely, empty way to meet each new sunrise. And to keep up an all-consuming work routine in hopes of a maybe-promotion, I saw, wasn't going to afford me too many worthwhile "todays." Uncertain, though, about where my professional path was heading—seeing as how I was ducking off the fast track—I was further emboldened by an analogy from Brian Dyson, former CEO of Coca-Cola Enterprises: "Imagine life as a game in which you are juggling five balls," he says, "work, family, health, friends, and spirit. Work is a rubber ball. If you drop it, it will bounce back. But the other four balls are made of glass. If you drop one of these, they will never be the same."

With faith, then, I let the right orb fall to ensure the safety of the rest; and it's now rebounded higher than I ever could've imagined. Yet the fragile spheres are the ones people most regularly let teeter, hang in the air, land where they may. In this needed-it-yesterday new economy, we can't seem to give any substantive thought to our recreation and personal welfare, or at least any priority. It's a trend, in fact, that would've befuddled even Aristotle, who held that people do business *in order* to have leisure—which they probably did back when people actually listened to philosophers. Thinking about it, perhaps it's because of some epochal regression that we now can't see past our cubicles; there aren't too many ancient Greek workaholics on record, after all.

As there weren't in preindustrial times either. The lifestyle of laborers back then was much more like the days you only recently left behind: late-morning wakings, leisurely midday lunches, sleepy-eyed afternoon naps, all-night working sessions, all-night drinking sessions. No, the modern era has definitely taken us backward. We no longer understand how to slow down, to take it easy, to seek out the little delights of our existence. To, what some might call, live.

In its time and place, understand, recreation is as proper as anything else you do (and at the entry level, usually much more so than your job). You need the distance from the pressures of work to reflect, learn, play, and gain a sense of who you are and why you're here. Plus you can't take it all so seriously. You're in pursuit of your passion, and that's definitely an earnest business; but you also have to appreciate the nuances and humor in life—especially now, when there's not always that much to laugh at. So not only is it a balance of time and activities, but also a balance of emotion and attitude.

Or it could just be that Kurt Vonnegut has it right: "I tell you, we are here on Earth to fart around, and don't let anybody tell you any different."

IV

@on to your calling

what gets you up in the morning?

just 10 more minutes

What gets you up in the morning? There it is, the question of all questions. Other than "the alarm," that answer of all answers is for most people as slow in awakening as they are on a gray, cold Monday morning. And the idea, really, is no less abrupt or startling than that red-numbered, red-intentioned device inflicting reality on our workforce each dawn—reminding them of the cheerless, lachrymose duties of their employment. Often to a radio-show host as grating on the nerves as the people they have to share those duties with. It's no wonder they make snooze buttons so big.

Randomly ask a person on the street how they like their work, and the (real) answer is most likely to fall somewhere between "It's a job," "It pays my therapy bills," and "Why, are you recruiting?" Distaste for one's profession—sometimes to the point of physical revulsion—is arguably epidemic in size after this latest turn of the century. Yet we see no crack research teams working on a cure, no slogan-chanting activists protesting in front of downtown highrises, and no politicians faithlessly promising more fulfillment at the office if elected.

Maybe it's because they're all stuck at their desks, too. Every laboring American, in the end, will spend roughly 60 percent of their life rendering unto Caesar: working, getting ready for work, commuting to work, thinking about work, thinking about quitting. Considering that we slumber away another third of our lives (or spend that many more hours sleeplessly toiling), I guess I'd also have second thoughts about spending my weekends waving around a "Honk If You Hate Your Job" picket sign in the street. Plus there would be all that noise.

Ask this same person, also, how they decided on their line of work, and the (real) answer is most likely to fall somewhere between "The money's really good," "My friend got my foot in the door," and "Why, are you recruiting?" Words like "passion," "meaning," and "purpose" are virtually unheard in their explanations, as is absent any sense of energy, excitement, or even life. Eyes don't dance, voices don't pitch, arms hang languidly at the sides. Jobs, instead, are impassively and vacantly described by their income, their pedigree, their market position, their responsibility. The "what" they've got down no problem; it's the *why*. Intimate the notion of reason, and eyes suddenly get shifty, voices tail off, fingers play uncomfortably among one another. A subject-changer for sure.

And, amazingly, corporateers will put off the question for years, and sometimes whole lives. Never do they slow down to ask themselves why it is they actually get up and do what they do everyday—other than to pay rent, eat, and buy trendy European garments at $300 a pop. They even go so far as to blankly return to business school, eager to get degreed and begin vacuous, consumptive careers in investment banking, consulting, technology, or something else they talk about a lot on CNBC. Which is also why they come entirely unraveled when something happens—like a disease or midlife—to make them stop and look around. (When, for males at least, in march the hair plugs and exotic auto retailers, if you'll remember). Tellingly, within several years of getting that MBA, most people surveyed still don't find the jobs they have particularly meaningful or important. And they'd much rather have lunch, when asked, with a social leader or humanitarian than the CEO of their choice.

So if they find causes more important than cash, then why aren't they out doing that kind of work instead? Or, perhaps a better question, are they willing to *admit* to themselves they find it more important? People have a knack for not hearing what they're saying, and especially when they don't want to be listening. Owing to the difficulty and risk of introspection in this case, it's unsurprising that the talking and the doing don't match. What turns up along that journey inward, after all, may be painful not only because it doesn't fit with how individuals want to see themselves, but because it may also not align with most of the decisions they've made in their lives to date.

Then what are they going to do—quit their jobs, leave their cities, turn their lives upside down and shake out all the stability and financial security they've sacrificed psych and soma to establish? No, they'll hang on to their denial of convenience until it's forcibly stripped from their quivering hands, thank you very much. Henry David Thoreau may call it "quiet desperation," but at least it's got indoor plumbing, which is more than can be said for the accommodations at Walden.

People (especially auditors) take inventory of everything but themselves, and I think that's telling also. We recognize the importance of accounting for the stuff we make, but have a nagging blind spot about the stuff we, ourselves, are made of. At heart, we're miserably removed from our **values**, what's stored on our inner-shelves, what makes us who we are. All of the big questions are warehoused here: What are you meant to be doing? Why are you meant to be doing it? What'll be your mark on the world? What do you want your life to have been about when all's said and done? To know what gets you up in the morning—to see how to spend your limited time here on Earth—you've first got to know who you are.

It's a deceptively simple concept, yet inaccessible to so many. And to career freshmen with no excuse: this is the beginning, your opening gambit, a point at which Pandora still has the carpenter's claim check for her box. Now, I devote much of the last chapter to covering all the reasons why the entry level is the time to pursue your passion; what we need to talk about before that is what this passion looks, feels, and tastes like. And while I'll tender my ideas about paths, pitfalls, practices, and processes, I'm obligated to disclose upfront that I don't have a magic, plug-and-go kind of formula to get you there. Nobody does. (Despite what their editors tell them).

191

The value I can offer, instead, is to empower you with the perspective and conviction to uncover your professional purpose, and then to rouse the courage inside of you to make it happen. But it's ultimately your responsibility. Dreams, remember, are only as real as the challenges you're willing to face in realizing them; yet success is only as distant as your heart from your hands. And, oftentimes, your feet from the corporate door.

the value of values

on kids & consultants

Disturbingly, more Americans commit suicide on those gray, cold Monday mornings than on any other day or at any other time; it's also when men suffer 75 percent of all sudden heart attacks. The prospect of another week—whether they tell their bodies or vice-versa—evidently just isn't something these forlorn folk can cope with. And while the pattern is morbid and shaking, it's among the more powerful signs suggesting how dolefully distanced people are from the work that makes life worth living.

Which is also nothing new. In his 1972 classic book *Working* (which I got around to reading long after I was supposed to in college), Studs Terkel interviews a sweeping array of laborers—from piano tuner to press agent to professor—in the sociological pursuit of determining what exactly this thing is we do all day (and night) in order to survive. His findings were dour and hard-faced, at best offering a cynical ambivalence about the "violence" that most jobs inflict on body and spirit.

"It is, above all (or beneath all), about daily humiliations," says Terkel in just the third line of this 762-page manifesto. "To survive the day is triumph enough for the walking wounded among the great many of us." Notably, and consciously or not, a number of his subjects doggedly return to the idea of meaning and memory throughout their dialogues—the hope to have their daily bread buttered with both personal resonance and public remembrance. Something, at minimum, better than that "Monday through Friday sort of dying."

It's been more than 30 years now and, sadly, it's not clear what's changed. Terkel's stories are still relevant, still timely, still speak of an elusive truth—a homeless truth amidst the hours of empty, sudsy bar conversation about corporate strategies, coworker relations, competing sports teams, cashmere sweaters, and C-Class Mercedes'. The idea of meaningful work or professional purpose is almost unmentionable here, where the superficial is on tap and consequential imports taboo. So without a disarming veteran journalist serving up the rounds, it usually stays domestic and cheap.

Although a few drinks can actually help. Inhibition sufficiently dampened, those suppressed, seditious thoughts will sometimes bubble their way up to the surface in a miasma of reflection, frustration, longing, and nausea. It's then that professional convictions will come clean, hidden beliefs about money and happiness find escape, and the disparity between life's actuals and ideals emerge with bleak dejection. Only then might laborers well-up, choke on their words, and take that long, hard look at the contradiction they're breathing in and out each workday. In this freeing moment alone is it that the true, exposed, vulnerable individual may share what most uniquely makes them who they are.

At least until they sober up. But by then the beans are all over the table: their belief system, their value set, their deep-seated yet dormant guiding principles from which it's all they can do to hide and distract themselves. They, of course, could be out setting loose their heart and soul full-time—exploring, growing, learning, ranting to whomever might listen until they collapse breathless, in tears, and utterly satisfied. But instead they're in consulting.

There's a story of an American painter, John Singer Sargent, who brushed a panel of roses to his canvas that won wide approbation from fellow artists and admirers. Eager to have his work adorn their home, suitors offered considerable amounts for the painting, only to meet a steadfast refusal to sell. Nobody understood. What they obviously couldn't have known is that whenever Sargent was feeling discouraged and unconfident about his abilities, he would look at that painting and be reminded that he did something great—something that represented his truest talents. It's not unlike the engineer who's been caught proudly patting the machine she's designed (as a parent might touch the head of their child), or the author who's confessed to rereading his book for the fourth time, just to make sure he actually wrote it.

The expression of these individuals' values in their work is what gives it meaning. That meaning is what gives it purpose. That purpose is what makes them passionate. And that passion is what makes it great, what keeps them fulfilled, what gets them up one morning after the next. Validation by others, while deeply affirming, is still secondary; there's value in what they do because they, themselves, find it there. One of humans' most basic needs, in fact, is self-expression, and we as people tend to be happiest and most satisfied when our work represents who we are and what we believe to be worthwhile.

In its purest form, the evolution and growth of that work mirrors our evolution and growth as individuals (which we see quite publicly, for example, with actors and musicians). When a person's profession misrepresents their values, conversely, it blunts and sears away the talent and energy swirling around the maze of their unique, indelible thumbprint (as we also see, albeit less noticeably, with most business-folk). That, in turn, leaves the soul undistinguished, undignified, unremembered, and altogether hollow. It could be, too, why the Fortune 500 dresses so alike.

Philosophers have speculated that if we lived in a utopia where everything had already been built, invented, and discovered, architects and scientists would nevertheless continue to build, invent, and discover—but as a game. It's a provoking thought, and begs the question of what we would do with ourselves if we didn't have to work; for that matter, it throws into the air the very definition of a job. (Especially one like mine). But more to the point, it draws out the idea that when work embodies the true values of an individual, it becomes more like *play*. Intense, meticulous, regulated play, granted, but play just the same. As with children, it would be done for the intrinsic satisfaction of the act, and not so much the material rewards that result from it. How many intricate, long-labored Lego structures, after all, remain standing when it's dinnertime?

It's not the first time kids have gotten it right when we haven't. They wear their values right on their sleeves: fun, learning, testing the limits, lots of food and sleep. There are definitely worse ways to live. And we as adults are making sure we try all of them, as Terkel has documented with solemnity. Yet while the days of crustless peanut butter and jelly sandwiches, whisper-filled afternoon group naps, and carelessly completed coloring books have obviously run their course, their message never grows up: To be happy means doing what you love.

Especially with the big-boy-sized politics and pressures encumbering the working life (particularly the entry level part of it), you have to introspect that much harder, braver, and deeper to come to terms with your values and priorities. Only when you know what fills you up from the inside—as you instinctively did as a child—can you find your life's work, your passion, that true channel for your energies and gifts. As Leonardo da Vinci said (and as John Sargent would agree), "Where the spirit does not work with the hand, there is no art." Or, perhaps more fittingly for that broken, drunken consultant, there's Oscar Wilde to draw on: "The real fool, such as the gods mock or mar, is he who does not know himself."

now *is* later

Although the gods probably never had to worry about the first of the month; and I'm sure they never had to walk defiantly past a sale at Neiman Marcus. Entry levelers, on the other hand, tend to experience a weighing psychological need for reestablishment and personal grounding after leaving college, looking primarily to their careers to settle them down. And when they, of course, find that they can't even get a toehold on things at the office, lately-capitalized career freshmen instead turn to their cash as an anchor, buying up their stability in bulk: Those tony couture ensembles, a car manufactured this decade, an apartment free from insects (like old university roommates), non-collapsible furniture; their "comfort purchases" all say to the world—and especially themselves—that they can play the part. Or at least look it. Besides, young professionals are just getting a head start on what society says they're supposed to be doing anyway.

And we all know how well society has it together. Regrettably, the more fulfilling professions often travel with an entourage of difficulties, not the least of which being a paltry salary. So in coming to terms with your values, you have to traipse your way through to an understanding of where money fits into your life, both time-wise and in the absolute. The latter, of course, is a much deeper issue, and improperly measured without considering your broader material aspirations and the harrowing tradeoffs that come with getting there. Which we will. At issue first, however, is impatience.

Obviously it feels good to have the toys today; if it didn't, we'd probably all have hung around campus for another year to date sophomores and take the classes we really wanted to. But instead we ended up ASAP at the corporate entry level, preoccupied and glower-mugged over a fellow grunt being worth however many more thousand dollars per year than us. Jumping to a job—whatever passion may be felt toward it—that pays still less (and sometimes dramatically) would only widen the inequity, exacerbating the angst and itchiness felt when colleagues pull up in late model Beemers, or friends extend an invite for a steep-priced night of sushi and socializing. Surely following your values as a young professional has its compensations, but like that of a collection of Louis Vuitton handbags or a new 3-Series coupe?

No. But in other ways, yes (and sometimes dramatically). There are a few that immediately stand out: One you can't spend, one you don't want to, and the other you'll probably have to wait a while for; but all offer a richness that the government doesn't print for heedless entry levelers. The first—and in my mind the biggest—is the dividend you get each morning when the alarm doesn't invoke a wave of, well, alarm. Waking becomes a happy jumble of anticipation and comfort, animation and calm. The mind wanders in the shower not with schemes of avoidance and recitations of anger-management techniques, but rather with spinning ideas about how to do things better, how to reach more people, how to create deeper value. Plus there's not all that cursing. Beginning the day becomes a perceptibly different phenomenon, and in a way that adds a fullness, acceptance, harmony, and sense of purpose to everything that comes after it.

Which is appended by a remarkable see-through with respect to the consumer goods and living arrangements motivating most of Corporate America not to take a heavy object to their company PC, or a sharp one to their coworkers' tires. Through the lens of values-guided work, the big-ticket playthings and upmarket apartments are exposed to reveal a cost base extending well beyond the price tag: living the crippling life that earns the money in the first place.

When stepping back, you can now look at the august executive—draped opulently in Armani, bejeweled handsomely with Rolex—not with a distended yearning to emulate, but rather with a pitying understanding of what they're paying to try to get you to. And that deep feeling of "rightness" you earn from living life on your own terms becomes a kind of currency in itself—wealthier than the assets of any well-heeled corporate administrator. Plus you don't have to pawn your soul off in the process. Bonus.

Besides, when you labor for love, the odds favor you eventually getting all that money you don't want, and probably more of it than you ever expected not wanting. In his stirring book *Making a Life, Making a Living*, as a case in point, Harvard business professor turned "MBA savior" Dr. Mark Albion cites a study of 1,500 b-school graduates whose careers were tracked over a period of 20 years. They were dumped into one of two buckets: Category A—1,245 people—represented the folks who decided to take big-coin jobs after graduation and think about their dreams later; Category B—255 people—marked those who decided to pursue their passions straight away and worry about finances second. And at the end of the evaluation, there were 101 millionaires. Only one of which came from the first group.

Though the numbers seem a little too perfect, they're not made up, and they're certainly not coincidental. The people who do the work they value are also the most successful, and that's because their passion predisposes them to do it better. They live above-and-beyond, executing with an unswerving flare and energy, impassioned to excel, exceed, and excite. When compared with the mechanical, unemotional, reluctant way that detached employees will approach even well-regarded, well-compensated jobs, it's plain who's going where.

As former Outward Bound director Allen Grossman believes, "If you're not passionate, maybe self-discipline or whatever set of emotions you have, including guilt, might help you work hard." But that's not enough according to the nonprofit executive and also-Harvard educator, who views true achievement as inextricable from love for what's achieved: "[Passion] is the wonderful ingredient that brings happiness with success." Because of the two, only happiness works as a stand-alone.

In addition to getting promoted faster, zealous workers also tend to find fresh and creative ways to market what they do, eager to get their message to everyone who's willing to listen. Even to those who aren't. And this usually means even more superfluous cash from things like new business ventures, partnerships and alliances, consulting gigs, speaking engagements, book deals, and so forth. Plus the truth of their work has a way of keeping them on top.

A place where vintage rap forerunner Run-D.M.C. still hangs out, for that matter, getting spins from time to time on local hip-hop stations around the country; you know, the kind that didn't exist when they first started out on the street corners of Queens in the early '80s. "It just shows that if you maintain your honesty and integrity, commercial success and longevity will follow," holds Def Jam cofounder Russell Simmons of his biggest act of all time. (The the two remaining members of which, incidentally, still collect a royalty check each time we pick up an album of them paying homage to their Adidas).

So more fully considering your time horizon can increase your paycheck tolerance: True, you may be taking a short-term dollar hit, but longer-term you'll be building skill sets in an area you love—which stands to have a far stronger financial, emotional, and personal impact. It might even leave behind one of those immeasurable social marks. The money, in the end, is really just a way of everyone saying thanks.

bending and buckling

The most basic premise of ergonomics (which, I glumly found out in college, takes a lot of math and has to do with more than just car interiors and office furniture) is that the machine should be designed to conform to the person. Any contortion or human adjustment required is considered a failure on the part of the contraption, and generally results in improper operation, discomfort, distress, and over time, injury. It's even been the primary cause of sunken ships, melted-down chemical plants, over-irradiated cancer patients, and squished people when gas pedals in cars have been placed too near the brake.

Countless more people, however, have been senselessly smashed by their careers for much the same reason. They've unnaturally manipulated their values and priorities to fit their jobs, and suffered devastating psychological and physical harms as a result of the bad engineering. Data cited in Charles Handy's book *The Hungry Spirit*, in fact, shows that 42 percent of all American laborers feel spent by the time they head home, trapped in the debilitating cycle of working to get exhausted, to go to sleep, to do it again. Swimming in negative emotional spillover and choking on the toxic office environment, engulfed employees (and particularly early-stagers) also report slowly losing the traits that have heretofore defined them, including their laughter, their optimism, and their willingness to get up and get at it everyday. Or to even get up at all.

Those working according to their hearts, by contrast, seldom tell of such symptoms, and usually quite the opposite. They instead tend to describe high levels of excitement, release, and replenishment from the hustle, enduring markedly lower levels of stress and anxiety. That, in turn, results in things like heightened feelings of pleasure and accomplishment, more rewarding interpersonal relationships, improved concentration and learning, healthier sleep and weight patterns, and even fewer sexual problems. Over the long run, passionate craftspeople also seem to do less dying from things like strokes, heart disease, and trauma to the head due to repeated self-flogging. So practicing a labor of love, it turns out, isn't only immediately fulfilling for the soul and one day the pocketbook, but also exceedingly practical for your overall well-being.

It even helps to naturally calibrate that elusive work – life balance. Shelly Lazarus, chairman and chief of marketing giant Ogilvy & Mather Worldwide, discusses in *Lessons From the Top* how the wrong profession stymies employees and cultivates intense resentment, keeping workers from the things they love and find important. When people have a deep appreciation for their trade, on the other hand, it's not to say that the exchanges go away, she continues, but that both sides of the decision take on a brighter complexion.

"Because even when you have those difficult moments and you have to choose between something you want to do in your personal life," Lazarus explains, "at least it's an approach / approach problem, which is much more satisfying and fulfilling than to have an approach / avoidance conflict with the whole thing." Laborers are also more effective at the office, don't forget, when they actually want to be there—which studies have shown to reduce workweeks by 20 or more hours—leading to fewer of these kinds of conflicts anyway.

Not that your passion is necessarily a panacea, however. There's a lot of rubbish that rides shotgun with most ways of earning a living, including, assuredly, your calling; it's the nature of the beast, and life besides is never that neat and tidy and tucked into the pants. And not that it even should be. But when you're doing the work that you were made to do, the aggravations and disappointments don't set you all aflame, but rather light a fire under you to get stuff fixed, to get your affairs in order, to make sure your unique vision stays alive and intact.

You can liken the idea to someone pinching a pressure point: Sure it hurts, but it also makes you jump up and kick whoever's got their hand on you. It's in this way that your true profession strategically squeezes your values, muscling you forward with a devoted ambition, urgency, and insistence. The wrong job, by contrast, just strangles life away, throttling you through the cycle of defeat: antagonism, anger, frustration, desperation, and eventually hopelessness. And nobody's ever changed the world, or even their lives, when they weren't, at a minimum, supremely hungry for something.

# of bone & belief

within and above

So it makes sense, by all measures, to cast aside your betrothed pay-check and begin that run-in-the-park relationship with your values. But with the literature and apparatuses to help you uncover your calling being so abundant and conflicting (and sometimes silly), it's not always clear how to even start dating. You can't stroll down the self-help aisle, for instance, at any self-respecting bookstore and not be euchred by the woozying selection of soi-disant shrinks, all of whom claim to have somehow accomplished what more than 60 years of severe, university-level research hasn't been able to. And not that college investigators are necessarily folks to be venerated in this department: The best they've been able to come up with so far are the acronym-heavy Myers-Briggs Type Indicator, and imposing-sounding Strong Interest Inventory.

Now, while it feels reassuring on some level to think that your calling is an "ENFJ" away or that you can have your passion pre-dicted by some distance-learning Ph.D., a formulaic approach for something as wildly abstract and richly disparate as human beings probably isn't going to account for you and your vicissitudes. It seems to me, instead, that the process needs to be much broader and looser—less dogmatic and prescriptive. And I don't think it has to be that complicated either.

Looking around the right corners and under the right rocks, in my eyes, is rather about understanding a simple partnership of two: the Natural and the Spiritual. One is an everyday satisfaction, redemption, and joy; the other is a deep feeling of truth, greater pur-pose, and fulfillment of a mission. They're both embodied by your values—just on different levels—and both are inextricable from one another, like mind and body, nature and nurture. You can only get at them by turning yourself inside out, but which happily doesn't call for completing nearly as many ink-depleting exercises or two-column tables as others might suggest. Just let your heart and your gut be your notebook, I say, and watch for when they sing and jump as we continue our brief discussion.

the natural

It's there if you want to see it. That pastime, industry, interest, subject, amusement, distraction—whatever—that warms you up from the inside, sometimes makes you lightheaded and butterflied with anticipation and excitement, and can bore people to actual tears as you wax, ramble, digress, and altogether blather on about its particulars, minutiae, and trivia. (Perhaps, like me, you've already lost some friends as a result of your recidivism). An apologist, however, you're not; when the mind is abuzz with everything to be discussed, considered, and picked apart, the outward rush is almost uncontrollable—and just too satisfying besides.

You're certainly no economist, either, when it comes to practice: Oh how often have you turned the clock face to the wall, left the fridge unusually unattended, treated your bedroom mattress as if you were already an overused midlevel manager. The threat of ever becoming which, suddenly, seems flimsy and intangible when you've perceptibly set foot in that out-of-bodyish "zone," surprising even yourself by how naturally everything flows to you. But you've probably staggered most people made privy to your brilliance, who've no doubt pointed out your uncanny instincts and characteristics conducive to the field— that innate sensitivity and connection to its intrigues and finer points. And you can't help but feel in your bones that they're right.

Still, it's not like opinions have any real seat at the table, as the experience leaves you feeling personally complete, energized, and hungry for the sensation again—when you can be that truest version of yourself one more incredible time. In the interim, though, you can train without tiring, attend lectures and watch programs without dozing, study its ins and outs without repeatedly checking to see how many pages are left in the article or chapter. (Adding all the more conversational fodder to your alienating dialogues). And as you take repeated intermissions to fantasize, there's a distinct, touchable sense of one-day reality and attainability—not just romantic visualization or wistful aspiration. No, there's a real feeling that this is your particular and special connection with the world, where you slide right in without force or contravention. This is that love – work cocktail you can drink down with full gulps and get drunk on its authenticity, dizzy and emotional with a physical and psychological harmony and integrity.

At least that's how passionate people describe it. (Plus this is what those questionnaires and tests are getting at anyway). So if it's not directly evident what it is that you feel so intensely and confidently about, you at least now have a broad awareness of what to be looking for. Still, if you really only share a nodding acquaintance with your values, it can take a healthy stretch of time to get here; yet it's essential to honor the duration and discomfort of the process—being honest with yourself and holding firm and true to all the stuff you're made of. That's the only way, after all, it's ever going to be properly put to use.

But there are a couple of important caveats here. First, while it's a beautiful thing when you love the work you also have a natural ability for, you however deaden your calling when you labor away at something for no reason other than you happen to be especially good at it. Look at Academy Award-winning filmmaker Francis Ford Coppola, who reflects on what some see as his greatest accomplishment with regret and despair: "People are shocked to hear that I think of *The Godfather* series with sadness," he confesses. "I see those films almost as a personal failure."

Coppola's heart, it turns out, doesn't beat for jumbo-budget, blockbuster Hollywood movies; yet he nevertheless allowed all of the acclaim that his trademark pictures received to pull him in a personally unsatisfying direction. "Their success led me to make big commercial films—when what I really wanted was to do original films, like those that Woody Allen is able to focus on," he explains. Without a values match, as made blindingly clear, even the best-regarded work will leave the creator passionless and without fulfillment.

Conversely, if you're drawn to something you make mistakes even thinking about, your lifelong happiness yet depends on following your passion into the dark. And maybe even back to school. Yet wherever that fussy route ends up leading, it's a path that has to be walked, and straight to completion. Tempering, of course, against the demoralizing "straw-man" risk of setting yourself up to get knocked down, it promises an existence generous with reward and excitement when you're patient, honest, and fair with your abilities.

Besides, the people who want it more just about always get it—and the best bosses are only too happy to offer it up. One of whom being Ace Greenberg, affable ex-chairman of securities giant Bear Stearns, who explains, "If they don't enjoy going to work, I don't care if their IQ is 30 points higher, the guy with the inferior IQ—who loves what he is doing—will beat them to death." Not that smarts would be what held you back (or that IQ tests are any more valid than "type indicators" or "interest inventories"), but it demonstrates that smart managers will consistently take heart over skill. Probably, in part, because they also know the gap between the two never lasts for long.

the spiritual

The second element of your life's work, in my mind, is wrapped up in the idea of God (or that greater power—by whatever name—connecting all things, giving us our metaphysical sense of existence). Even for an American populous in which agnostics and atheists number fewer than 5 percent, the subject nonetheless remains controversial in the fullest, so please bear with the discussion. As an avid consumer of religious teachings, I see beauty from West to East, and would never presume to advocate any particular faith—and wouldn't know which one to choose even if I were to. But I can't write a secular book because I'm not a secular person.

In fact, the countless volumes of holy scribblings in existence would themselves suggest that we have some sort of distinct purpose here—a mission, a destiny, a *calling*. Now, whether you believe that our souls have multiple incarnations or just one go-around, we are each irrefutably ordained in this lifetime with certain unique aptitudes, ideas, dispositions, and all of the other shared but personal spots of humans. And somehow they, in turn, all convene to create our wishes and dreams and most hopeful visions for how life will turn out.

Neurophysiologists, of course, are all still shrugging their shoulders and leaving early for lunch; but that's not to say the process is random or inadvertent either. Consider our equally brainy evolutionary scientists, who contend that the probability life came into being out of pure luck is roughly zero. Doesn't it stand to reason, then, that the chances we have the values and skills we do out of jolly accident are about the same? (And if not, explain how you eluded genetics and made out so much better than your parents). Indeed, I maintain that our priorities and flairs are of a higher divination, whatever the mustard-splotched research papers (don't) say. And while we've inopportunely missed biblical times by a couple thousand years—when God seemed to be a lot more talkative—I'm content to take the fact that these amazing things exist inside of us as evidence enough that He wants us to put them to work.

As a result of my cancer scare and its attendant epiphanies, personally, I feel that God has shown me my life's calling: helping young professionals find theirs. (An idea to which in college, by the way, I would've politely smiled and discarded the flyer, as I did with most of the fluff I was accosted with on Bruin Walk). But here I am, and here you are reading me—which, admittedly, feels pretty fantastic and significant. Most importantly, though, it feels *right*, and I believe that's because I'm sharing what God most wants me to share.

Which also suggests that our abilities best serve us when they serve others. Your dreams aren't only for you, understand, but for those whom your vision might touch, inspire, and motivate. Being a good steward of your gifts means giving of them freely, visiting your talents upon those who can best benefit, learn, and grow as a result. I'm in no way any kind of theological scholar, but it seems to me that there are few crimes after breaking the Original Ten that might irk the Supreme Being more than being selfish with your endowments.

Certainly, though, you don't have to be a beacon to humanity to lead a meaningful life or to use your inner-stuff in the proper ways (and not that I'm one of those either, by any rowdy stretch of the imagination). While the most rewarding jobs do tend to be those in which people directly help others, values-driven work makes no stipulations about its larger impact—political, social, religious, or otherwise. So long as you're being the person you want to be and doing the work you find important, then you're leading the best life you can be leading. And the one, most probably, that God intends.

Nineteenth-century American writer and physician Oliver Wendell Holmes perhaps captured the issue best when he said, "Most of us go to our graves with our music still inside us." That's one of my favorite quotes, and one of the saddest, too. People have so much beauty and magic within them, and yet so little inclination or nerve to peer in long enough to find it. They disallow their truest talents to ever surface, and in doing so deny themselves their own happiness, fulfillment, and liberation. I mean, if God gave you a melody, don't you think He meant to hear it?

decisions, decisions...

the error of trials

So we want to do right by God, our fellow human beings, and—with apposite self-interest—ourselves in shaking free our values, pouncing on our passion, and living its joys out loud. But, as we also know, life is never that neat and tidy and tucked into the pants; and, one more time, not that it should be. Callings are fickle, and often refuse to come clean until well after we've slogged through the muck and morass and gotten our boots satisfactorily muddy. Yet how else would we earn the perspective to recognize our dreams when we finally set foot on them? Or acquire the background to put that insight to work? Or even understand how to properly honor and revere our visions for the magical stuff that they are?

You bet. Now try telling that to the quagmired young professionals who can't move their legs. Or to those who struggle loose, only to feel like they're crossing the entry level Rubicon with each career decision they make. Or to me, for that matter, when I was drowning in the Big Five. As do the majority, I took the first port I saw during that rocky storm—principles be damned—and, also in line with most, ascribed a paralyzing finality to my choice. But, short of taking a contract out on Bill, it seemed to be the best (i.e., easiest) option in a busy crowd. While I couldn't be sure of the consequences I was anchoring myself with, I at least knew they were worth 40 percent more a year than the ones I was getting away from.

"Twentysomethings often feel that the only means they have for navigating the seemingly endless choices looming ahead of them is trial and error," confirm Robbins and Wilner in *Quarterlife Crisis*, "which is really just a productive-sounding euphemism for guesswork." Had you read me that line at the time, I would've personally put together the support group to commiserate and eat pastries. But today it's plain that there's nothing so sordid or abrasive about guesswork that we need to call it something else (and not that "trial and error," if you ask me, sounds any more fruitful). The process of discovery, rather, is a natural and important one—central to the human condition and the adventure of living, however you want to look at it. No, since the waters can't be tested without getting a little wet, the problem can't be with the prevailing philosophy; yet it most certainly can be with everyone shutting their eyes when they jump.

A surprising number of early-stagers profiled in the ladies' after-college collection are floating haphazardly around, or making floppy, one-off sort of lunges at their dreams—frequently in the name of some gangrene-averting "fluidity." Moreover, the neglectful ex post facto assessments as to how good their decisions turned out to be seldom inform what their next choices should look like. Good thing doctors don't work like that, else we'd probably still be going in for bloodlettings to drain out the little stomach gremlins causing our bad humors.

The surest path to your passion, instead, is by way of a planned and disciplined approach to your experiments and tests. If modern medicine got that way by using its uncountable errors to provide feedback about where to go next, it follows that modern calling-finding should work the same way. Plus it's the approach that just about every passionate worker has directly or indirectly proven to work. Well, at least the ones who don't believe in gremlins.

a matter of course

Speaking of days long ago, there's a story of Socrates visiting the public marketplace in his native Athens, and being asked upon his return what the trip had taught him. "I never knew there were so many things in the world which I don't want," he replied.

Now there was a guy in touch with his values. Of which, noticeably, no serious mention was made with regard to career decision-making in *Quarterlife Crisis*. Yet while your early ambles about the employment store are sure to return results similar to a wunderkind Grecian at a dumpy bazaar, you clarify your scientific-method job hunt when you conduct your search according to your priorities. We'll spend the next chapter discussing the more strategic and tactical issues surrounding your crisscrossed career path, but the foundational rationale is based right here.

To know yourself is to know your steps, and when supported by the confidence of your convictions, any road you take—no matter how it winds up—is walked with tremendous certainty and scarce regret. Otherwise it's only predictable that you might second-guess and backtrack as a young professional, fraught with worry, doubt, and guilt; noodles flop around as a matter of course when happenstance is the vocational counselor of choice. "It's not hard to make decisions," conversely, "when you know what your values are," as Roy Disney blithely puts it. Advice well taken from a man who didn't build the Magic Kingdom with his brother by dithering around in mouse ears.

Coming to terms with your mores, as you know, requires some highly durable patience and continuously straightforward introspection; making decisions in line with those principles, by contrast, calls for rugged discipline and brute strength. Too often the nearsighted professional turns that career freshmen end up taking run head-on with the priority-based choices they simply didn't have the self-control to carry out (like the age-old college conundrum about whether to go out or stay in and study). Quick money, a reputed firm, familial pressure, an emergency exit: all are usual suspects when visions are vitiated.

Even picking the right one out in a mental lineup still doesn't mean that it won't attack again (or that it won't get one of its buddies to do it instead). Prevention, rather, is a process of identifying vulnerabilities and risk factors, and then taking the right steps to defend against intrusion.

We'll also talk about how to do that in following chapters, but it ultimately comes down to filtering your choices through the prism of your values and aspirations. At the end of the day, the overall quality, depth, and enjoyment of your life is at stake, which in itself should be enough to brace your internal fortitude. Plus you can always reflect on how good test day felt in school after a confused night of consumption. (You know, maybe that much *hasn't* changed since graduation).

Still, life is about constant growth, and any one career decision—no matter how momentous or ground-moving it appears at the time—is just another step in your progress. So while honoring its immediate impact, it's essential that you equally moderate the enduring influence you assign to it. Practically every seasoned professional has been there at some point or another, having to reconcile themselves to an unexpected loop: being "reorganized" within the company, getting laid-off, quitting precipitately, accepting the wrong position, finally poking their boss in the eyes, and so on.

Whatever it looked like, the shakeup forced these individuals to reassess what were probably fairly solidified, mentally-invested career plans—often with mortgages, families, and related cash commitments riding on them. Yet not only are they no worse for the whirl today, but are actually better prepared for the next unforeseen upheaval coming at them down the line. When it comes to work, keep in mind that just about everyone lands on their feet sooner or later. With sooner not necessarily being better.

Plus, like everything else, the apprehension subsides with experience. "The kinds of things I would have feared 20 years ago don't really bother me as much today," muses former Apple Computer chief John Sculley, talking about the differences between obsessive entry levelers and laidback long-termers, who tend to take things more in stride because they've been through it so many times before. "You learn to essentially handicap the situation and think, 'Well, if that goes wrong, can I tolerate it?'"

Former Hambrecht and Quist CEO Dan Case (who, in quite a gene pool, split a mom and dad with AOL Time Warner ex-boss, Steve, before his untimely passing in June 2002) always could, sharing a similarly laissez-faire attitude as the Macintosh maverick—and surprisingly so for a securities analyst. "'What was the worst thing that could happen?' I would ask myself. If it didn't work out, I'd start again." (It also helped, I'm sure, that he didn't have to worry about disappointing the folks, what with his brother's job at the pizza joint).

Even the irritating minority who heard their calling while sipping on embryonic fluid has still had to consistently make their decisions by the yardstick of their values. Just because they're more attuned than most people to what those values are doesn't mean that their choices have been any less thorny or testing; it's that they've allowed their hearts to guide and strengthen them during those difficult moments, relying on priority-rooted decisions to shape their worlds. Although I bet they still can't figure out what to wear to work most days.

king kasparov

I was watching VH1 recently and caught an interview with R.E.M. frontman Michael Stipe, who was discussing the filming of the rockers' groundbreaking 1991 video "Losing My Religion." The director, Tarsem Singh, originally had an elaborate, storyboarded plan for how it would all come together; after a day of filming, however, apparently nothing was turning out right and tensions were running high. So what's a shot-caller to do when his arrangement flubs in front of a musical force? As Stipe recalls, "So he went into the bathroom, threw-up a couple of times, and came out and said, 'Okay, we're doing it like this...'"

It's probably one of the best metaphors for careers that I've ever come across: You think you know how it's going to play out, but you never really do until you're right there in the mix—and then you vomit. Even for those projects and jobs that adhere as closely as possible to your tightly-worded internal script, the fidelity is never perfectly true and the outcomes never fully expected. Now, was Tarsem any less a professional for what happened? Perhaps *more so*: he didn't abandon his vision, but instead shifted its execution to fit the actual circumstances that life decided to throw at him. The love of the work wasn't weakened; he simply adapted, grew, and learned. And the best part of it is that he walked away with key professional lessons that he can incorporate the next time around (along with six MTV Video Music Awards and some extra Pepto-Bismol).

That's the nature of plans: they're never static or set, but instead are always reshaping, evolving, and changing—just as you are as a person. And that's the whole point: to keep your goals and priorities straight amid a swirling and ever-metamorphosing world. I liken it to playing chess, where you always have to be thinking three or four moves ahead. Throughout any given match, your strategy changes completely—usually several times over—after your opponent forces you to reevaluate the board. You may have to temporarily shift to a defensive posture, for example, because a weakness in your structure has been exposed; or perhaps the challenger has inadvertently opened himself up to attack, for which you need to subtly realign your men. Then you have your three or four moves planned in a direction entirely *unplanned* just a short time ago.

As you keep going, you're also sure to get checkmated—usually several times over—forcing you to move all of your pieces back to where they started from. Yet over the long run, it doesn't matter. The objective of chasing the king (i.e., pursuing your passion) is the same no matter how many games you have to play to get there (and when you're up against the proper competition, it's not supposed to be a quick trouncing anyway). The idea, understand, isn't necessarily to know the answer, but to know that you've always got a next step in arriving at that answer—no matter how many steps away you may be. So long as you try things out with a values-based sense of direction and let your strategy flow with the natural development of each match, no move you make is a wrong one. I call it "plan-to-change:" a simple and powerful method that doesn't define the path itself, but rather the *process* to the path, which never veers.

As always, the best know the routine. Chuck Knight, celebrated former CEO of Emerson Electric Co., for instance, on more than one occasion put together long-term designs for his organization that he completely revamped after only a short time. "Anybody who takes a five-year plan and puts it in the wastebasket after one year and does it over has to be a little nuts," Knight admits. "And I've never seen a plan that didn't get better in that process."

The begrudging Francis Ford Coppola, once again, is also a reluctant ruler of this domain. While filming *Apocalypse Now*, his currently West-Winged star Martin Sheen suffered a heart attack, threatening the director's vision for the picture and leaving him shaken for the first time during shooting. (It rattled Marty, too, reports have it). Ultimately undaunted, however, Coppola employed the plan-to-change technique expertly: While Sheen was recovering, he pulled in a double and shot most of the material from behind, leaving the audience unaware that they were admiring the fatigues of a spun-around look-alike. "To keep going in a crisis, do a 180-degree turn," Coppola advises—this time literally. "Don't look for the secure solution. Don't pull back from the passion. Turn it on full force."

But that obviously takes some risks. More specifically, it takes some *smart risks*: ones that match your value set, that are ultimately bearable should you fail, and that present a true opportunity to approach your dreams. In chess language, to get the board position you need to execute your strategy, sometimes you've got to expose your queen to capture. Oh, it's definitely going to hurt if you lose her; but you've still got another 15 pieces at your disposal, and this is just one game.

Besides, it's not going to turn out exactly the way you have in mind, and you already know how much you stand to develop and learn—probably in unexpectedly significant ways. So the justification for not sliding yourself out there is usually oversupplied by fear and confusion, and understuffed with logic, flexibility, courage, and all of those other markings of masters. Plus since most of your regrets are about the things you don't do—the moves you don't make—it's always more psychologically satisfying, if nothing else, to know that you took a gamble on your values and lost. (Much more on that later).

But nothing, either, is to say that entrapping your initial passion is going to keep you fulfilled for good. As we keep doing life, it tends to have a remarkable way of showing us things that we never imaginably saw coming, but that fundamentally shape our character and send us back off at an angle to our original intentions. Sometimes in a completely opposite direction. And if not by way of a great change experience, then through the process of aging, which itself often guides us to work with a greater meaning and purpose (as we implicitly recognize that mortality isn't going to break its date and we'd better get on with what's important).

First loves are always special; but at the same time, it's exciting to know that the chess game never ends—that there will always be the search for an ever-deepening calling. It's incredibly comforting, too, to also know that the rules never change, no matter how many matches you end up playing. So long as you always keep those three or four moves in front of you—regardless of what the king is made out of—it's a contest you never have to retire from. Or ever want to.

maps & chats

Yet it takes more to win at chess than just to have a fuzzy, if-he-moves-here-then-I'll-go-there kind of structure to your path—even when it looks those requisite few steps ahead. There's flex *because* there's firmness; shifts in strategy work as a result of all routes being buttressed by strong fundamentals and solid preparation. That means engaging in a perpetual process of planning out your steps, both short- and long-term: Building "goal maps," if you will—defined, calculated, time-specific actions to take en route to your destination. Wherever that ends up being.

Over the near stretch, the moves have a routine, everyday sort of flavor to them; yet the immediacy with which they can be tallied off provides an always-satisfying quick win. (Plus the most reliable kind of progress is the gradual variety). What big industry event, conference, or schmooze-fest is coming up, for example, and which trade organization or consortium is playing host? Are you a member, and can you pass any of your costs on to the firm? Which training classes are on the radar screen, and what kind of issues should your business cases address to best tap your budget? What's the hot book or emerging area to read up on next? Which rumor-mill projects should you already be inquiring about and lobbying for? Where are the holes in your network, and which contacts are going to help you plug up the gaps? Do you call her or wait?

These day-in, day-out questions, in turn, are supplemented by your long-haul milestones, which have a much more encompassing and personal impact. Again, we'll pick these topics apart next chapter, but they surround concerns like your readiness to take that next step toward your passion—both professionally and psychologically—and the proper timing with which to do so; what that passion has even evolved to look like, and what kinds of skills and experiences are going to get you as marketable and well-prepared as possible; the specific contacts and inroads that must be gained and forged prior to your forthcoming move, and so on.

And while the process of uncovering your calling isn't necessarily one of penmanship, the course of planning your way there and tracking your progress is. Among the most effective ways to record and evaluate your goal maps, in fact, is by creating lists: simple or detailed, structured or stream-of-consciousness, wherever and however you feel comfortable making them. No matter the residence or inscription process, when you live by your lists you're never at a loss for what quick-snapped or drawn-out step is next.

Richard Branson, flamboyant founder of the aforementioned Virgin brand, created an empire this way, as he describes in his immensely enjoyable autobiography, *Losing My Virginity*: "I have always lived my life by making lists—lists of people to call, lists of ideas, lists of companies to set up, lists of people who can make things happen." Never without a cheap, standard-sized school notebook to jot down his goldmine of thoughts, Branson has filled an entire bookcase of scribble pads as he's built business after business based on this simple technique. "Each day I work through these lists," he explains, "and that sequence of calls propels me forward." That, and his fleet of commercial jetliners.

It speaks to the value of also committing your more far-reaching, grandiose career dreams to paper: Just seeing things laid out in front of you can itself allay a surprising amount of uncertainty, and the writing process gives your visions a reality, tangibility, and organization that they never quite possess as ethereal images bouncing carelessly about your head. Plus they're easier to file.

Especially with others. Your cadre of trusted advisors can't do their job of keeping you focused and motivated if they don't know what, in fact, to keep you focused on and motivated about. Importantly, none of this says the goals can't shift, or that you allow yourself to continue down a misguided path out of guilt or embarrassment or not having an eraser; your happiness ought to be everyone's main concern—however you record it and wherever it ends up going. Even back-and-forth.

Actually, it's not a bad idea to let the rest of the world in on your broader, less intimate aspirations. You obviously don't want to rattle off your proprietary business concepts to others who may try to move on them, but at the same time you need to put the feelers out on the range of fellow professionals you come into contact with. It's amazing how interconnected we all are, and how often somebody knows somebody who knows somebody in the business. And even if you can't make a direct inlet, most people are usually good for at least one piece of unpredictably fine advice if you give them the chance to dig it up. With the exception, naturally, of Fortune 500 managers.

10

zigzag careers

chutes and broken ladders

Back in 1999, I did some consulting work for a major Midwest manufacturing concern, and was absolutely floored to meet people who'd been with the organization for something like 25 or 30 years. Many had inched their way up through the ranks; still more were essentially doing the same job they took right out of high school. All with thick, sedimentary layers of dust on the desk and on the brains, these "cradle-to-grave" workers represent the last crumbling remnants of an almost-dead breed.

Historically, though, this has been the culturally accepted norm: to make that long, brutish climb up the rigid corporate ladder—drudging through a long-ago mastered position with sedating patience, waiting for the godly hand of some shirt-stained firm administrator to yank you up to the next rung. Which generally isn't all too better a place to hang around until the charitable appendage emerges again, doubtfully endowing you with your heavy new responsibilities.

It's the only instance I can think of where the national divorce rate of 50-plus percent would, in fact, be too low. Indeed, while the intolerant, self-serving tendencies of this country's wedded don't do much to uphold the strength of the highest institution, they do, however, nicely underpin the millennial career path. Decidedly non-linear nor snugly time allotted, this next-generation professional track is much more of a circuitous journey that finds people moving laterally and even backwards from company to company to find the right match. The career, now, is seen as a portfolio of organizations and projects that offer exposure to a range of areas and functions, that engender the development of varied skills and knowledge, and that present the opportunity to work with diverse and intelligent coworkers and superiors. Firms today, moreover, are unapologetically kicked to the curb when they fail in their promises, and once-spoken-for workers are able to stay excited and fulfilled by a steady diet of changes, challenges, and colleagues.

Which naturally follows from recognizing "the probability that the first choice you make is right is roughly one in a million," as warns the Yoda of Management, Peter Drucker. "If you decide your first choice is the right one, chances are you are just plain lazy." Plain words, too, from this markedly less green and much taller modern legend, supporting the mob of research out there showing that the people who are most satisfied with their careers are doing something today that they never planned on earlier in their lives. As discussed, passion can be an incredibly elusive partner—a tease, really—and sometimes the most effective way to capture it is by leaving it no place else to turn. Just as one of the best operating procedures is "management by exception," there's equally profession by exception: determining where you fit by first figuring out where you don't. Besides, your values are going to need some time and variety to gel anyway, requiring a certain baseline level of work experience to let you know exactly how you feel about what.

It's a methodology, in fact, that Harvard has put their name on. "During one's 20s and 30s, the only way to assess oneself is to take different jobs in different companies to find out what kind of work one does best, enjoys most, and finds most meaningful," says that peach of an *HBR* study, "Must Success Cost So Much?" Failure to fully engage in this search, authors Bartolomé and Evans continue, can prove to be disappointing, delimiting, and ultimately destructive for career freshmen: "Our research indicates that foreclosing this phase of exploration too quickly may have negative consequences later in one's career," they conclude. Like, say, staying in the same HEPA-filter-needing cubicle for a couple of decades.

And, as is regrettably the case with so many real-world facts, university greenbeans once again have the wrong idea. Recent surveys conducted by the National Association of Colleges and Employers (NACE) show that almost 60 percent of new college graduates expect to stay in their first job at least two to three years, and that over a quarter plan to hang on past the five-year mark. What's more, upwards of one-third of working newbies identify "stability" (i.e., providing a secure future) as an attribute they look for in their first employers, and more than half of those asked cite "opportunity for advancement" as the most important aspect of an initial job.

The truth of the matter, conversely, is that today's average school departee can expect to change jobs up to 10 or 12 times throughout their life, and to swap careers—new positions in completely new industries—in as many as six or seven of those instances. Moreover, a good number of these switch-ups are typically made before one's early to mid-30s. (You know, NACE and Harvard should really use their free weekend minutes and start talking to each other). Regardless, that's a whole lot of personal progression for twentysomethings, nixing the notion of sitting on the hands for 2-to-5 of hard time. Also poking back the tongue-in-cheek promise of corporate safety, for that matter, which isn't to say that there's even going to be the opportunity to hang around that long.

What Color is Your Parachute? author Richard Nelson Bolles captures the idea well in his benchmark book, calling on employees to consider each position as impermanent and short-lived: "I am essentially a 'temp' worker, hunting for a job that is basically a temporary job, whose length I do not know," he recommends thinking while on the prowl. "I'm going to have to be mentally prepared to start job-hunting again, at any time." Thus the parachute metaphor. (Although the color at issue is most usually green; at least for the people doing the pushing out of the plane).

Nonetheless, it's a mindset that meshes perfectly with the advice of Carol Bartz, chairman and chief executive of the world's largest CAD software-maker, Autodesk. "I think people really need to build their career like a pyramid, not like a ladder," she explains, hacksawing in half the rickety and splintered thinking of more than half a century ago. "I think too often they go for the almighty promotion, and as a result stay in a very narrow field...the safest, surest way to the top is to have a strong, broad base of experience." (And she knows one or two things about constructing stuff).

Remember, even if the next move is to a completely different field or out of the corporate realm altogether, it's amazing how transferable is a person's experience, perspective, and understanding about the ways things in general work. There's nothing out there, as you know, that isn't a business; so it's essential to view your early years as an opportunity to acquaint yourself with the overarching set of rules, customs, and best practices risk-free—however much gruntwork and kowtowing that may take. More fundamentally, though, it requires an acceptance of your career not as a fixed-route, premeditated destination, but rather an openly walked, uncontrived path. Rather than a deliberate trip up the dowels, it's instead a wonderfully unpredictable, zigzagging journey in which you both evolve in tandem. We'll spend the rest of the chapter talking about the types of, reasons for, and timings surrounding your moves, but everything presupposes one core philosophy:

> Your résumé is an explanation of your experience,
> not a reason for it.

Far too many laborers manage their occupational course to the implications it might have on their namesake paper, restricting their environments and experiences to satisfy some stand-in body snatcher holding out for the "proper" firms to show up. Not only running squarely counter to the broader considerations of professional development and personal happiness, this cart-before-the-horse practice harnesses a person's career to the wagon-wheel priorities of Wall Street—spinning round and round as does the market turn.

The whirls of your work track, by divergent contrast, should never be an arbitrary or economy-driven collection of brand-name hops and jumps, but instead a calculated and carefully timed series of values-based steps and leaps—each one bringing you that much closer to the life you envision. (And that much further away from some headhunter's commission). After all, there's no individuality, no discovery, no *meaning* in merely doing what you're told; the distinctiveness, strength, and purpose of a career, rather, come from doing what you love. And if the right-named companies aren't interested in what your heart independently guided you to do, then how well do you think you might fare anyway with the compost heap they'd have you shoveling away at?

across, down, and learning all around

Still, the knee-deep waste pile has a mighty powerful draw—as with flies, one might compare—and the Egyptian-architected foundation of experience Ms. Bartz describes can be too much heavy lifting for career freshmen unwilling to put the proper pieces in place: "But to get to that strong base," she continues, "you may have to take lateral promotions, or maybe even take a step backward in your career." I suppose they don't call the Great Pyramid a "Wonder of the World" for nothing.

Thankfully, though, putting together this kind of structure doesn't involve living at the worksite or dragging blocks around the desert with a couple thousand smelly colleagues. Yet you do have to learn from them. In fact, it takes chiseling free every last pebble of knowledge you possibly can from your company, shifting into whatever capacity or onto whatever work team required to do so. You're in a symbiotic relationship with your employer, remember, meaning that in return for your animal toil, your position should supply the mix of experiences and information that's going to best lay the brickwork for your vision. (And, perhaps, afford for the occasional long-distance phone call). So you can't reflexively snub a trip that doesn't go straight up.

Looking at what the market has generally done to the shape of organizations since the 1980s, you see that they've gotten "flatter" (i.e., less tiered and layered), and certainly much thinner with regard to personnel. The money just isn't around anymore to support that tubby style of business operations (nor the music to justify the hairdos), and the rampant cost-cutting has required workers to de-specialize to an extent—to become more expense-conscious generalists who can wear any number of hats when called upon.

This, in turn, means that horizontal and slightly reverse movements don't necessarily represent what they might appear to. In fact, organizations regularly shuffle the deck these days to expose workers to different areas of the business, watching for which transfers take hold. (Also for how many it takes to completely burn them out). You see it all the time with executives, who commonly bounce between divisions to impose efficiencies and drive revenue; as that goes, even summer internship programs are increasingly being built to rotate. Plus not only will a sideways step—at the same company or another—often also compensate with more responsibility and better work, it'll help to make your background a little more round. The slide might even be more, perish the thought, fun.

No, don't kill the idea. Considering that career freshmen typically master the basics of their job in anywhere from three weeks to several months, all-consuming boredom, restlessness, and frustration can take hold in less than half a calendar year. So even if it's just the opportunity to dip into a different strain of stupidity within the firm, it at least gives you a fresh way to get used up all over again. Given also that even the tallest entry level post still more or less rests on the ground floor, there's really not very far to fall as a result of a hierarchically insensitive jump. Never, in fact, will any career move you make have relatively less impact than as a young professional, so now is the time to welcomingly hit the working canvas with a triumphant thump if that's where your path leads you.

Especially if it means joining up with smarter people. Intelligent, well-educated colleagues raise the level of play in a company, driving you to ambitiously match and outmatch their performance—which itself makes the game more fun and rewarding. Going to a place where you'll get this kind of rich and effortless learning environment—no matter where it sits in the grander corporate landscape or where you sit within there—will help to fully exploit your growth opportunities, as well as introduce you to a collection of individuals who can help inform your moves for years to come.

"I've always based my career decisions on the quality of people I'd be working with," reveals Fay Vincent, who among other titles was the eighth commissioner of Major League Baseball. Never unwilling to step outside of his comfort zone and tackle new obstacles, Vincent jumped from the Big Leagues to the Big Screen when he recognized how much he stood to learn from the high-caliber individuals he'd be working with. "At the age of 40, I was offered the job of president and CEO of Columbia Pictures...I knew nothing about business, disliked the movies, and occasionally wore brown shoes with a blue suit...How could I say no?"

Saying no, however, is one of the hardest utterances a professional can make in the face of a lucrative, if not so stimulating position. And unfortunately the choice between dollars and development all too often comes out as, "Yes, please, oh absolutely, and can you refer me to a local real estate agent?" Still, Bob Cohn, former CEO of both Lucent and Octel Communications, helps to rationalize the right choice, pointing again to people: "Even though you might be offered a good position," he explains, "if it's for a bunch of loose cannons who don't know what they're doing, you will make a lot of mistakes and won't learn much from them." Hand-in-hand with superstar engineer Peter Olsen, Mr. Cohn found his way into voicemail technology through an industry contact, and together they created one of the most successful, widely used systems around. "If you work for the right people, however, they will teach you well, and you'll be able to visualize how these people solve problems," Cohn continues. "You'll then have the right values and skill sets." It's something even Andy Grove, paranoid Intel Corporation cofounder, understood from the very start, tacitly following Gordon Moore (as in Moore's Law) to go do this wacky microprocessor thing.

Again, it doesn't matter what direction the move you make is in so long as it's done according to your priorities and in the name of development. You can always explain to your next prospective employer the expertise you acquired, regardless of the job title; yet you'll obviously never be able to use the talents you didn't cultivate, no matter how pretty the ring of your position name. To worry about sitting high enough on some org chart before coming away with tangible learnings, you might as well run for political office.

temper and forebear

Helping the nomadic cause is the fact that once-checkered backgrounds are widely seen as strengths nowadays, with a broadened acceptance of sector-hopping among corporations, nonprofits, and government agencies. In fact, the really wised-up employers shop actively for this sprawling pyramid-base of experience, recognizing that workers with years in different disciplines bring to the table new and important perspectives and strengths, and can see how to integrate traditional methodologies in more holistic, valuable ways.

But the stigma still lingers for short job tenures—particularly those lasting less than a year. However mobile the slippery new economy might be, companies still aren't very comfortable with laborers who can't stick it out for at least a full fiscal four; and not necessarily without cause. After subtracting out the initial months required to properly settle in and ramp up—adjusting for those additional weeks chewed up by seasonal rushes and slumps—and figuring in any internal restructuring efforts or uncharacteristic market spikes and dips, there may only be a pocketful of time left in the employment year for a new worker to finally catch their breath and make a fair assessment of what's going on. So the picture taken away from, say, any three to nine months at an organization can be highly skewed and misleading.

It can also be torturously long. Underused entry levelers are highly susceptible to a kind of "second quarter itch," where the job pool starts to look a whole lot more inviting once things begin to level out after the first 90 days. Part of it, of course, is attributable to the expected greener-grass and novelty-wear effects; but there's often a sizeable lump of legitimacy involved, and sometimes with dicey consequences—including anxiety, depression, and too many two-hour lunches.

The inclination to turn tail, however, is frequently one more of basic frustration, resentment, and impatience than anything with truly serious implications. Plus skipping town forestalls all of the unique learning and growth events that come with hanging on to a job through a tough stretch. And the résumé gets dinged to boot. So it all comes down to a careful self-evaluation about where you are professionally and psychologically: If the sum of your experiences with a company is telling you that staying there is going to strip you of your sanity, then the decision to move on is a no-brainer—regardless of how few months you've been at it. But if the ennui is attributable to more benign origins, then even if the work is without destination, you'd still do well to put the brakes on your next one.

Not only for impression's sake either. To best leverage your current position to earn the next, you've got to look at everything this firm has to show you before you go. When walking away from a company, the feeling should be that you didn't leave any knowledge on the table—that you captured all of the information and experience that the people and projects at this place were going to yield. And that can be a fuzzy determination sometimes, giving rise to the question, "Where am I more likely to find Cheese—here or in the Maze?"

At least that's how Dr. Spencer Johnson phrases it in his cross-category bestseller, *Who Moved My Cheese?* Once they've taken it back or after it's slowly been eaten away, Johnson explains, "Yesterday's Cheese" (i.e., the tasty stuff about a job) is never going to be put in place again by an organization. So the question becomes when does the value of Today's Cheese fall below the value of going back out into the Maze (i.e., the labor market) and taking that next step toward your passion.

When things start to stink, Spencer says. "Smell the Cheese often so you know when it's getting old," he advises, taking special notice of the slight changes along the way. This will alert you to spoiling cheddar long before it becomes inedible (as well as prepare you for the extended metaphors in Johnson's next book). Deteriorating relations with colleagues, big slowdowns in business, lower personal working standards, later arrivals at and earlier departures from the office, use of more and more sick-days: all are telltale signs that the learning curve is flattening out and that the time to go is probably nearing. Again, if it's not going to leave grave, unfixable scars, try to stick things out until your evacuation is cosmetically palatable. Just don't get ill on the fumes.

right back at ya!

The slickness of the new economy is proving to be especially worrisome for big corporations, whose primary adhesive to date, *loyalty*, has begun to lose its stick in a big way. Like an old Post-It note on some unwiped middle-aged Midwesterner's desk, employees are refusing to stay put and taking their insights with them.

And why shouldn't they? The company's not running the business for its laborers, but rather its investors—a point they're completely candid about (even Enron was). In fact, I'd hazard to say there's an annual report out there where the CEO doesn't articulate the core objective of "maximizing shareholder value" somewhere in his introductory pitch. As he well should: those are the owners, and the business will rightly be operated in their best interests—just as you would direct your own firm to look out for yours. Workers are little more than a means to an end.

Just don't tell *them* that. Corporations figured out a long time ago that if they could get their hired help to feel warm and fuzzy about the place, they'd hang around through thick and thin. Well, thick mostly; thin has all those layoffs. Whatever, healthy attrition numbers translate into bottom-line savings, and that makes for happy equity carriers. Beginning back in the day, then, firms promised to protect their employees' futures and offer safe, 30-year trips up the soaring ladder. Some of them, in their callowness, even meant it.

All they asked for in exchange was a fair commitment to the goals of the organization: Put in a solid 9-to-5, hop on a plane every now and again, occasionally open up the briefcase on weekends, don't quit, and that'll pretty much do it. So companies got reliable and predictable employees, and workers, in turn, got jobs that had many of the same perks. Ergo, tract homes in the suburbs, newfangled kitchen appliances, and *Leave It to Beaver*. Say what you will, it was certainly an easier way to live—provided you could deal with the homogeneous colleagues, antiseptic neighborhoods, clunky cars, and general golly-gosh-gee-whiz of everything.

Fast-forward 40 or so years, however, and that upstanding social compact is lining the bird's cage. Loyalty, it turns out, can be a bother-some way to do business, and especially if you can do business overseas for cheaper. Plus it doesn't bode well for national pride when you're getting beaten at your own game: As the economy began to globalize and markets started seriously tightening during the early to mid-1990s, Corporate America discovered that their mawkish "company pater-nalism" ideology—the one that created those pudgy rolls of middle management fat up through the '80s—was making them slow and unresponsive. Meanwhile, the fit and trim workforces of Japan and Germany were poking fun and selling boatloads of their stuff.

So with Richard Simmons-like zest and panache (if more modestly hemmed shorts), U.S. Big Business unapologetically sweated their way through the cellulite, crunching and jogging away whole depart-ments at a time: Sears Roebuck, for beginners, shed 50,000 employees; AT&T cut 40,000; IBM let go a staggering 63,000 souls. And these were supposedly the "best places to work," Joanne Ciulla points out in *The Working Life*. With sobriety she explains how the loss of their jobs led to the loss of so much more for these displaced devotees, including their friends, their reputations, and sometimes even their families.

"One of the great ironies of the 1990s," Ciulla continues, "was that business books and business rhetoric focused on 'commitment,' 'loyalty,' and 'trust,' while at the same time business practices stressed downsizing." The lesson here, she concludes, is that there's no quick fix for the loss of goodwill that comes from firms viewing their staff as disposable. Still, macroeconomists will tell you that the slashing and burning was good for the long-term viability of this country's com-merce; and I'll actually be the first one in line to agree. Just don't expect me to blow up the balloon animals at the next company picnic.

As the most highly educated generation of Americans in history, today's career freshmen are a little too smart and a little too jaded to buy into the corporate family charade sold to their parents—in spite of the "lifestyle" resurgence led by those trendy (and transparent) corporate campuses. Particularly as a result of the Internet bubble, early-stagers have seen the dramatic impact that the younger set can make on a company, and it's inspired a brazenly free-agent, what-about-me mindset. Maybe that's also what's finally forced the Fortune 500 to start cozying up to tech-savvy entry levelers, who they're finding can actually contribute to an organization outside of the supply room.

Regardless, Corporate America is far from disabused of their prejudices and predispositions. And so long as they continue to put the economic interests of their shareholders first—which, if forecasts and leading indicators are right, looks to be, oh, roughly forever—it really doesn't matter how well they eventually end up regarding their college-bred pups. Employee loyalty is, and will remain, a cleverly orchestrated farce, calling on you the laborer to ensure that the receipts you earn in exchange for your services continue to be equitable.

It's a tit-for-tat game: once your compensations of information, experience, skills, and contacts dry up, you go find a new well. (Before you're thirsty, actually). Remember, the value you add to the company and all of the braggables you create along the way—contributing to projects, developing internal processes, spearheading initiatives, making customers happy—help to generate strong returns for the firm. Whatever's good for you is *great* for them, and the inherent imbalance of power remains an attractive deal only so long as the organization keeps putting out. Coldly, allegiance attached anywhere but to your own knowledgebase is mournfully misplaced.

And if you insist on feeling bad about it, you can go talk to "Larry," a top-ten MBA marketing manager I used to work with. In addition to being a superstar at his job and all-around good guy, he was also an incredible husband—who was overjoyed to learn that he would now get the chance to be an equally wonderful father to a new baby girl. Throughout his wife's second and third trimesters, in fact, Larry never shined brighter, seeming to be just where everyone in his professional and personal lives needed him, just when they needed him there.

After his daughter's birth, the firm showed their gratitude by throwing him a congratulatory celebration, lauding his efforts on both the working and home fronts. Nowhere, however, was their appreciation better felt than a few weeks later, when a company director asked Larry into a small, undecorated conference room to inform him that he would now have to finance his expanded family with unemployment checks. You see, the downturn in the economy just couldn't substantiate his position any longer—marketing *is* pure overhead, after all—and the firm, regrettably, would have to let him go.

But wait a minute. Isn't this the same Larry who consistently returned to the office at nights to finish up what the pregnancy preempted? Isn't this the same Larry who still took those weeklong business trips, sometimes foregoing his role as Lamaze coach? Isn't this the same Larry who just a few short days ago was heralded as a "leading light" in the company newsletter? Isn't this the same Larry who the firm knows has a tiny, fragile new mouth to feed? One and the same. Oh, and good luck with that, hey.

Make no mistake, the new economy street still very much runs two ways: As ready as people are to company-hop, firms are equally willing—if not more so—to employee-toss. And they're a little more ungiven to sentiment about it: "The worst kind of mistake I made was misjudging people, trusting people I shouldn't have trusted," reveals ex-Apple Computer CEO John Sculley about his employment past, illustrating that even the top aren't insulated from betrayal. "And then, after trusting them and being loyal to them, having them turn around and stab me in the back."

What's happening today as a result of this prolonged, fulsome deception is a kind of "20-year-long boomerang effect," as Monster.com chief executive Jeff Taylor puts it: The millennial generation of workers—only too aware of what happened to their folks—is now ducking the back-numbered scam, letting the results hit the Fortune 500 right in their specious heads on the return. And while the trend may be late in coming, the poetic justice of it all, you have to admit, is really just too sweet.

But, hey—"It's nothing personal," like AT&T Comcast chairman

Mike Armstrong says when he's at the chopping block. Yet he also adds, "And I'll do it, even if you're my best friend." That's probably a little further than most career freshmen would go to revel in the reckoning. Although Armstrong, something tells me, won't ever run into that situation to begin with.

who's winning?

later, son, later

During my last exit interview prior to starting Career Freshman Co., my reporting manager, whom I'll call JW, was trying to express his thoughts on my decision to pursue writing and career counseling full-time. An everyman's kind of laidback boss, he nonetheless had a cautious reticence about him—which made it agreeably unexpected and out-of-character when he decided to share a story about his father to capture his point. And with this last-minute outbreak of candor, he proceeded to compensate for months worth of general caginess, moving me such that I'm now passing his narrative on to you to introduce this chapter.

For years, JW's father was a highflying lawyer in Seattle—top of the trade, pulling in nearly half a million a year, and twice that much during the good ones. A student of his work (more on the order of a monk or disciple, really), the man devoted the better part of his life to mastering the U.S. legal system: canoodling with contracts, tucking into torts, and all but losing himself in case law. He could cite precedents almost biblically, as if by chapter and verse. And during those noteworthy occasions when his nose wasn't buried in some leather-bound legal volume or yawning LexisNexis database, it was generally poking out of one of his Porsches or sailboats. At one point he had three of each. (After, of course, getting rid of his Ferraris; he couldn't have the boys in Stuttgart know he was seeing an Italian, you realize).

Twilight was gently easing its way over the counselor's storybook career when he became preoccupied with disentangling himself from a soured business partnership—the timing of which, fatefully, coincided both with JW's entry into high school, as well as the teenager's realization that he really only knew his father by his job. Although, granted, there wasn't much else to know: When they talked, it was typical dad – son stuff, not venturing far from cars and sports (and not nearly far enough from law), and whatever activities they did together tended to be distanced and stuffy—attending the theater, for instance—or tasked and impersonal, like racing the boats or one of their horses. I'm sure you can relate.

JW needed an attentive male figure more than ever during this rocky adolescent stretch, and created as much noise in his life as he could to finally make himself visible to this blinkered breadwinner; he even garnered the attention of local authorities on more than one occasion. The attorney, however, was ultimately more interested in his cases' development than his son's—particularly this personal venture gone bad—and JW could only press his face up against the hard, streaked glass as he had done for so many years.

But he couldn't possibly have known the trouble he was looking at. Dad was taking some aggressive tax positions prior to dissolving the fractured union (to inch closer to that "magic number" he'd feel comfortable retiring on, however much that was), and had worked his estranged partner over pretty handily in the separation. Armed with the books, the aggrieved associate then turned whistleblower, signaling the IRS to come take a closer look at what JW's pop had been paying in. So instead of being able to begin winding down his practice and start doing all of those things he'd thought about over the years—like maybe having a relationship with his son—he was now locked in a battle with the federal government.

It's funny how life only lets us get away with something for so long. And when we've really earned it, the payback usually finds a way to be richly ironic. Ever the deserving candidate, this father of one (read: none) ended up losing his freedom by applying that which he used all his freedom to develop: It turns out the arcane legal loopholes he threaded—which only an individual of his practice could have uncovered—weren't wide enough to hold up in court.

So after three and a half long and draining years of tussling, he found himself charged with multiple counts of tax evasion, earning him a 42-month trip to the pokey. And after attorneys' fees (yet another irony) and massive fines and penalties, he donned that orange jumpsuit without a single home, boat, or car to his name. Most painful by far, however, was the fact that that name would never again be recognized by the American Bar Association—his church of 25 years.

Yet he somehow managed to keep his son, as both entered their respective four-year institutions. Still not giving up on the man who had spent his emotional life miles away, JW spent his Sundays at the lockup instead of the library, just a few miles from his carefully chosen university campus. With nowhere to look now but face-to-face, JW finally developed that long-yearned-for bond with his dad over the course of his undergraduate studies. Plus the time in the pen, in turn, gave the ex-defender the most serious kind of pause to reflect on the decisions that he had made with his life. And let's just leave it at saying he did a lot of quiet sobbing at nights.

When JW's old man stepped out of prison a college career later, now in his late 50s, he rededicated himself to his family, and has since rebuilt a very comfortable living. Today he's happier and more fulfilled than he has ever been—with far less money than he's ever had—and hugs onto an appreciation for life that he'd never embraced before; the arms, for that matter, get thrown around his adult child more often, too. Indeed, it took him three-quarters of a lifetime (and several years of jail time) to understand the real cost of his fortune, and the only regret he goes to sleep with at night is that he never really watched his son grow up.

"So," JW tells me, "go write this book, go start this company. Take the risk that you may not get published; take the risk that things may never get off the ground; take the risk that you might run into financial hardship. The money will never make you happy, and the greatest risk is having regrets when it's too late to do anything about them."

on the treadmill

The National Association of Colleges and Employers also interviewed graduating seniors to gauge the leading jobs for the Class of 2002. Rounding out the top five, in order, were accounting, engineering, education, rental services, and petroleum products manufacturing. Reading this list, I'm dumbfounded.

Having been a fairly observant—even nosy—student during my undergrad years, I know that most of the subjects I saw people really excited about couldn't have had anything less to do with general ledgers or general dynamics. Tell me, how is it that accounting can occupy the top overall slot when most students favor the "last in, first out" inventory method to guide their very own trips to lecture? (Plus try to recall the last campus rally you saw organized to protest a new FASB standard). And fuel stuffs? Most collegians can't even tell you how gas makes their car go.

Once again, don't get me wrong; I debited and credited my way right into the Big Five—I'm as guilty as anyone. The point is that students usually take these kinds of classes only as a "backup," or because mom and dad threaten to forget to pay their tuition if they don't. So it's striking to see how many actually follow through and decide to devote the first years of their professional lives to it. Truthfully, I always thought I was in the minority when chasing after hardcore business work, believing that others were pursuing far more fascinating and significant careers. I mean, if they were going to all the trouble of starting clubs and making signs and stuff, it made sense that they'd also look for jobs in those fields. But cultural dance and promoting dolphin-safe tuna, I suppose, don't pay the bills very well, and that's what new graduates are most concerned with. At least that's what their parents tell them.

Yet the result is a "cognitive dissonance" that arises from abandoning those passions—which is just a fancy psych way of saying that when our actions don't fit our beliefs, we get all knotted up inside. To cope, we generally try to change one of the two to match, usually whichever is easiest. Something, though, about the clash between dollars and values (its centrality to modern life and the meaning of our existences, I'm guessing) isn't letting us reason this one away very easily. And, just as with finding a work – life balance, the thrust-and-parry feud endures long after the entry level drops its stick.

Another illuminating *Fast Company* survey recently revealed that most corporateers feel money is the most powerful factor in their success, in their satisfaction, and in their ability to determine the structure and substance of their lives. Yet the editor tells us that, at the same time, people "are not altogether comfortable with the habits of acquisitiveness and consumerism—or even the drive to make more money." Fellow publisher of the now-defunct *Spy* magazine, Kurt Andersen, in looking at the conflict pulls a page out of the Taoist bible, attributing the brawl to an inherent cultural tug-of-war: "Moneygrubbing and idealism are the yin and yang of the American soul," he says, "perpetually coexisting." But the whole idea of yin and yang is balance, which this country is decidedly out of. It's not that we allow the warm, pure *chi* to flush us naturally of our covetous energies; we just keep soullessly spending and getting all mopey about it.

Everyone's doing it, though, and that's just one of those parentally admonished, jumping-off-a-bridge-too kind of things we can't seem to help ourselves from. So people are scrambling faster than ever to keep up with the Joneses, buying not for their own pleasure but to outdo the neighbors. It's a wearying and financially burdensome proposition (except for the brass over at MasterCard and Best Buy), and the phenomenon feeds an endless hunger: Enough is only enough until the next thing comes along. A growing tenet of the new "hypermaterialism" it seems to be, where we're much more interested in shopping for goods than actually putting them to use. How often, after all, does the average SUV see a patch of that "No Boundaries" dirt, or the average wardrobe of workout clothes see the outside of the closet?

The upshot of all of this, says Daniel Kahneman, Princeton University professor and Nobel Prize recipient for his work to bridge the fields of psychology and economics, is that we're taking a nowhere run on the so-called satisfaction treadmill. "People find that their demands from life keep pace with their increases in income," he explains, meaning that as we get more money, we want more fulfillment from the world. And when we mysteriously don't find it (in our purchases or elsewhere), we grow disillusioned and unhappy. Even good-ol' Siggy Freud saw this coming way back when, writing in *Civilization and Its Discontents* (1929): "It is impossible to escape the impression that people commonly use false standards of measurement—that they seek power, success, and wealth for themselves and admire them in others, and that they underestimate what is of true value in life."

Actually, an old Grecian beat everyone to the punch again. Aristotle recognized the pattern in B.C. times, noting that those who organize their lives around hoarding and rationing money are "intent on living only, and not upon living well." Nothing is valued for itself, but is instead a means to more possessions. Which, as we know, there'll never be enough of. Importantly, modern research chimes in here with the addendum that this M.O. is equally true of the rich as it is of the middle class as it is of the poor. So not only will ultra-affluent lawyers never have enough roadsters and yachts, but everyday laborers won't ever have fancy enough barbeque grills and bowling balls. Or the underclass enough education and breakfast.

And all of this may be more deeply alienating than we realize. There are upwards of 3,500,000 households in the United States boasting a net worth of or above $1 million, with more threshold-breakers under the age of 50 than over it—a first in this land's history. Another record is the number of Americans who've been diagnosed with depression, as the National Institute for Health Care Management Foundation now clocks antidepressants as the most commonly purchased prescription drug—above ulcer, asthma, and even cholesterol pills. One could argue, of course, that the correlation is a quirk or that our drug-happy doctors are overprescribing. But then they'd also have to explain why WebMD reports that financial issues have been found to help bring on the clinical doldrums, and why this country is footing an estimated $43 billion a year in absenteeism, reduced productivity, and medical bills as a result. Flipping through the history books, people as a whole have been poor throughout most of civilization (and especially before that), so why should it be weighing so heavily now?

Because an extra zero on some watermarked paper has eclipsed values-guided work, and it's leaving people directionless, unfilled, and clutching for whatever they can afford. When dreams of music production or political activism, for instance, are bitterly exchanged for computer programming and asset leasing, people spend to make up for it. They use "stuff" as a distracter: occupied with material things, they don't have to spend time thinking about how unrewarding their professional lives are. But the diversion only holds for so long, and the goods only do so good a job. The greatest obstacle to true happiness, in fact, may very well be that healthy paycheck.

When you do the work you value, money comes; but when you do it just for the money, all that comes is more work. "Don't think that your only goal is to make $100,000 a year, because you'll make $100,000 probably quicker than you think," cautions Charles Wang, retired founder of Computer Associates (the world's third-largest indy software company after Microsoft and Oracle). "Is your life over once you've made $100,000? No. You have to be pointed in the right direction. You're building a career. You're doing something you really enjoy." Because if you measure it by the heft of your bank account or the make of your car, then not only are you forever beholden to your finances for your distorted sense of pleasure and self-worth, but you also drive the most risky course of all: Anything at any time, remember, can be taken away from you. Just ask JW's family.

the two questions

who's to say?

Can the world go without another consultant or investment banker or middle manager? That's a judgment call, obviously, and a moot issue when the person has a true passion for consulting or investment banking or, well, middle managing. But we do already have hundreds of thousands of these folks (a quarter-million PowerPoint-pushing consultants alone), and a regrettably large swath of them are in it just for the hundreds of thousands of dollars. Plus one's not terribly distinguished from the other.

Even the fast-tracker who makes it to partner or vice president by his early 30s and does a record amount of business over the next 20 years—he's still basically spent his life selling stuff, just like the guy down the street. Everybody's selling something, of course, and the question of whether petroleum products or rental cars, say, are more important than professional services in my opinion isn't the right one; it all depends on whether or not the peddler finds it meaningful. The point is that the entire scope of value here for most people has taxes withheld from it.

Now can the world go without another teacher or social worker or urban planner? Again, this is a matter of opinion, and really for no one to say when an individual finds a calling in one of these venues. But when looking at the markedly fewer inhabitants of these industries…you actually want to keep looking: A nice, roomy percentage of them—the ample majority by any count—report feelings of fulfillment and reward with regard to their jobs, empowered by their ability to make a real difference in people's lives. Notably, as a group they tend to make significantly less than the marketers of the more traditional ilk; and as a group, just as notably, they also tend to care a hell of a lot less.

To live and die the corporate life is really a foregone conclusion for a great many Americans, and not always the wrong one. Certain people fit the mold better than others, plenty content just to do work that provides for their material comforts; obviously not everyone is suited for that riskier, more independent line of work. And others still were practically punched from the pattern curve-for-curve, many of whom eventually join the top ranks. This kind of natural-born businessman is quite at home bending clients and competitors to the will of his organization, casually fingering the hopes and dreams of employees, and rendering make-or-break decisions before lunch. Which, in addition to other ways, usually renders him filthy rich.

The go – no-go decision for most people, however, is much softer around the edges. Their skills, interests, and aspirations commonly reach out far enough to accommodate both the Fortune 500 route and the more unconventional one that might be blazed by their own hearts—and not that those two courses diverge by definition. But for many ideal-driven young professionals, the tracks do part company, and early on, which is something we'll talk about next chapter to end the book; at issue here is what those winning executives have actually won. The love affair that people seem to have with them pushed aside, two questions emerge for every prospective career freshman standing in their footsteps: So what, and at what cost?

so what?

For starters, what difference do their lives make to their communities or to society? What kind of mark will they leave? Have they done anything important enough such that I should care or even know about them? To qualify the idea, you can pick up the *Wall Street Journal* most any day of the week and read about big company heads combining businesses, spinning them off, taking them over, slimming them down, screwing them up, covering it over, and so on. As the case has it, I do pick that paper up most days and usually enjoy the stories thoroughly; but, as our existence goes, are they *meaningful*?

At the time of this book, for example, Hewlett-Packard chief Carly Fiorina was trying desperately to cinch the biggest tech merger ever and get her company hooked up with Compaq Computer Corp., facing a dissident group led by cofounder son Walter Hewlett. Her job on the line, the deal ended up going through by a 2000-presidential-election margin, speaking to the internal fissures, integration issues, and host of other challenges she faces in making the new $80 billion company successful. Now, whether or not things end up working out, when you think about it, is really more a matter for the annals of business history than anything else. It definitely makes for good journalism—and unquestionably affects her laborers and stakeholders and computer shoppers at large—but is what she's doing all that significant? Does it count in a meaning-of-life sort of way?

MBA maharishi Mark Albion effectively put that same question to the once-CEO of Gap Inc., Millard "Mickey" Drexler, during their first phone conversation. "Mr. Drexler," he asked, "what if the Gap disappeared tomorrow? Who other than your employees would really care? I mean, why is the Gap important? What does it *really* stand for?" They haven't spoken since. Yet while that sort of roughshod, smack-you-with-a-smile approach clearly isn't going to soften many people up to what you have to say, the message has a sting all of its own.

A couple of decades from now, is anything that Ms. Fiorina or Mr. Drexler did with their companies going to seriously matter to the world? Well, Mickey is going to hang it up without any foreseeable household-name legacy (regardless of what he's done to dress the American workplace down into khakis). And Carly's story, in spite of its girth, doesn't look to be one that John Q. Public is going to hand down through the generations either. So the answer, it appears, is that it's going to matter only if it mattered to them.

Outside of the Gandhis and Martin Luther Kings who come along every few generations and genuinely shape humanity, value remains a relative phenomenon. To you and I, Drexler's and Fiorina's accolades are probably going to be little more than clever nibblets of corporate trivia, maybe useful once or twice at an industry mixer or snooty cocktail party. And still more to the point, better than 99 percent of all corporate wheels—including directors of this and VPs of that—won't ever get their name in the headlines, meaning that if they aren't finding what they're doing particularly relevant, nobody else is going to have the chance to do it for them. (Plus even the *Journal* gets thrown out at the end of the day).

Although they *are* loaded. Proclaimed or not, top company officers can pull down incomes well into the seven- and eight-figure range after bonuses, and that's hard to overlook. Cash-poor entry levelers, in particular, can hardly keep their tongues in their mouths. But, again, you have to ask what that cash means in the long run—in terms of the impact it has on the consequence of a person's life. So it's instructive, I think, to look at the chance recipients of hulking inheritances and overflowing trust funds, pulling free what their hereditary prosperity in fact represents. Here in its most passive form, what does money really suggest about a person?

Does their wealth say anything about the timely relatives as individuals? Does it offer any insight into the non-numeric worth of their existences? Certainly of their grandparents' or parents', but to them it speaks only of a serendipitous bloodline, a windfall birthright. Yet when reporting for 2002 on the people in America most rolling in it, *Forbes* magazine lionized page after page of these hand-me-down rich without any special asterisks or dividers or subcategories. For reasons technical or political or whatever, they saw fit to enter them right alongside the people whose vision, courage, and talent have transformed entire economic markets. And it leaves one asking: are they really members, or just footnotes?

Not that the next-of-kin have had their fingers up their noses either, but you get the idea. The merit isn't in the owning; it's in the *doing*. For the legal tender to bear any real significance, it should be the product of something worthwhile—to which mere custody has no claim to advance. In the same way, the multi-comma compensation of Corporate America's elite carries only as much weight as the job does purpose for its earner.

So if an executive works without love, then his stock awards are in fact a penalty; if he doesn't find value in his labor, then his incentive plan just pushes him away from his truth; if his job leaves him empty, then so will be his slot on any list of comparative belongings. Just like the also-named heirs. As Aristotle says (and what doesn't he?), "Dignity does not consist in possessing honors, but in deserving them."

Now does this mean you can say that an abused-youth counselor making $30,000 a year is leading a more commendable life than one of Sam Walton's five offspring, each of whom is sitting on about $20 billion because pop had a knockout idea with Wal-Mart? No. But I'd be curious to see how well you can inherit passion.

at what cost?

Second, what's the price of these trumpeted leaders' fortunes? What kind of husbands and wives are they to their partners, or fathers and mothers to their children? How often do these people laugh, or exercise, or visit with good friends, or breathe unrefrigerated air? How much time do they spend on their personal interests? Have they figured out what those might be?

Typically not, as the "successful" Big Business administrator in America today is most often a stranger to his family and a servant to his work, living the bulk of his days in an office or on an airplane—usually in a semiconscious funk of gnawing headaches, dangerous food, and still more treacherous people. And, no matter where he goes, it's always under the oppressive thumb of the organization. I can recall housesitting, in fact, for one of the managing partners at yet another Big Four firm (Six at the time) I worked for during yet another college internship. This plump and pleasant enough man—who I'd met only hours before he invited me to have free run of his abode—was going on vacation with his wife and two girls for a couple of weeks. How nice, I thought. It wasn't until he got back that I found out he hadn't seen them for three straight months due to an extended overseas business trip.

Nobody on record has ever died wishing they'd spent more time at work, yet this seems to be the anointed path of the "societally correct" wage earner. Corporateers these days are more than ready to marginalize their friendships and neglect their loves, opting instead to invest their lucid hours scrutinizing reams of abstruse financial statements or babying a roster of wet-bottomed clients. Seemingly without thought or recess do they devote themselves to individuals whom they barely know and hardly care about, endure a lifestyle imposed by an organization whose values they don't even endorse, and allow the only real people in their lives to slowly atrophy. Their cubicles become a cell without bars, and their offices a purgatory with fluorescent lighting. But damned if they aren't putting away nine grand a month!

And the irony in all this (which, again, we're seldom without) is that most of them claim to be doing it *for* their dependents. As honorable, stable providers—properly concerned about their children's futures and their spouse's interior decorations—it's up to them to make sure the bacon stays sizzling; even though the rest of the house may be chilly and echoing. It's a powerful and upsetting trend, and begs the question of just how much money families need to be comfortable. While NACE never posed the question, it's undeniably on the minds of forward-thinking career freshmen—and, once more, males in particular. Why else would European-backpacking, apartment-swapping, pub-crawling, relationship-leaping young professionals be so interested in jobs with "stability?" (Plus I asked enough entry levelers myself to get a sense of things—some even at pubs in Europe).

To follow decades of research on child development, little ones need little more than attention, love, encouragement, and lots of protein to grow up big and strong and well adjusted. When kids can return to a warm, comforting home everyday, they usually get over pretty easily whatever material things their parents can't supply that home with. (Case in point, as adults we can recall when our father didn't make it to our baseball game or music recital, but can't summon up the concessionary toy he bought us to make up for it). Financial aid and on-campus jobs and stolen food from dorm cafeterias, later on, also help to get the flesh-and-blood through college just fine, and typically with no ill will toward mom and dad—at least none more than usual—if they know that they always did their best. And even sometimes didn't.

Healthy families find a way to make it through tough times, and especially when they're guided by people who love what they're doing; full hearts can almost always compensate for empty purses. But it's never the other way around, illustrating that the truest disservice a head-of-household can do to their brood—where they genuinely fail to provide—is when their work leaves them vacant, hostile, and unable to give of themselves. (Especially when it does so from another continent for a quarter-year). That makes for a distant, unreceptive parent and partner, doing nobody this person touches—or doesn't, as it were—much good. And, not inconsequentially, it also makes for a whole bunch less fun around the house, which itself is pretty hard to valuate and measure.

Not coming from a lot of money personally, growing up I remember doing things like filming wobbly homemade lip-synch videos, bodysurfing at Venice Beach, and playing board games with family on the back patio in the cool nighttime summer air. What great times those were, and what does it mean today that I didn't go to school in the right zip code? Would I have been happier if I slept in a bigger room or had gone on better vacations? That point could be debated, I suppose, but what does it really matter if a person can look back and smile? From a twice-broken home, I was nonetheless raised by people who did the kind of work that made them emotionally available to me, and that's what makes a childhood. Mine, at least.

It's relatively easy to keep life upholstered; the question is where to sit. To be clear, the money itself isn't the problem: we all need it, more is frequently better than less, and each person deserves as much as they can honestly and passionately make. The fault rests in the reasons for which it's acquired, the costs that are borne to do it, and the ignorance with which everything is veiled. If someone wants to eschew their babies or jeopardize their health for a fatter paystub or faster promotion, for instance, then that's their prerogative; just as long as they do it with a full appreciation of what they stand to gain *and* lose (including, one day, their jobs).

But what's unacceptable is when families are riven in the name of their own salvation, as if caught up in some Joseph Hellerish Catch-22. What doesn't sit is when workers are made to believe there's no alternative to indentured servitude and frequent-flyer programs. And what's especially intolerable is when it causes career freshmen to start thinking down that unlit executive alleyway, right when they should be roaming about the lush, rolling possibilities of their dreams. Of all people, droning rock icon Bob Dylan may have actually summed it up best: "Money doesn't talk—it swears."

when all's said and done

Richard Leider, a 30-year career counselor and author of several books, has spent a good portion of his professional time hanging out with the geriatric clique, interviewing over 1,000 senior citizens. So what do 70-plus centuries of combined experience and rumination and early-bird specials have to say about making the days count? "Remarkably," Leider says, "I hear the same answer: The good life means living in the place where you belong, being with the people you love, doing the right work—on purpose."

On balance, our elders wish they would have taken more risks, pursued their true fulfillment, and been more reflective during their lives: not to have played it so safe, not to have worried so much about financial success, and not to have wrapped themselves up in the "doing" so much that they lost sight of the meaning. Just being busy from business made them numb; they instead felt alive only when they were learning and growing and stretching. Business, apparently, made them forgetful, as well: lost from their memories are the habitual, addicted days at the office, as if deleted from time altogether.

The moments in seniors' lives that can be conjured up with any clarity or emotion, rather, are generally those spent with loved ones—talking, traveling, trysting, and simply being. Entire decades, amazingly, have been filtered down into just a brief montage of events and conversations, making quite the case for opening up wider, reaching deeper, loving harder, and also playing more hooky. Especially because most 65-plusers report that everything moves faster in the second half of life, viewing time as the rich currency it is looks to be something best done while there's still plenty of it to spend.

Thanks to modern medicine, that work-in-progress, we've been able to give the clock an extra few turns back and add increasingly more years to life. But we still haven't figured out how to add more life to our years, and the good people in lab coats over at Merck and Pfizer probably won't ever have a wonderdrug in the pipeline to fix that. As an entry leveler, then, with more than two-thirds of your days still in front of you—and with the sound advice of folks who've already got more than two-thirds of theirs behind them—you're in a position of unparalleled opportunity and nearly limitless potential.

If you decide to use it. Enough dead politicians and poets have reminded us about history and its repetitiveness, and it's not like our predecessors were doomed to do-over without the warnings of their own. So instead of reiterating the reiterated, I'll take a more direct (if grim) route and point out here that the elderly are highly fortunate to have survived to the point they have: Life plays all manner of jokes, and perhaps none meaner than on the worker who passes an entire career with hopes only to retire from it…and who passes on just afterward. The so-called golden years, for which people regularly mortgage away a lifetime of professional fulfillment and personal happiness, can sometimes be preciously brief and scarcely worth the price.

It's macabre, but none of us really know the expiration date on our packages; the horrific terrorist attacks of September 11th, to be sure, drove that point home for a lot of people. Yet it did so for many in a wonderfully empowering and positive way: Enlistment inquiries at the U.S. Marine Corps, for instance, soared more than 400 percent; the American Red Cross, in just a half-month, fielded in excess of 160,000 hits to the employment section of its Web site; applications at fire departments across the country were filed at unprecedented rates. And some kids finally grew up to be firemen.

Of course everything is more pronounced in the aftermath of a tragedy, but that's sometimes what it takes to ignite the powder keg of passion resting dormant inside of so many bellies. And not that these are the "right" ways to help humanity—even for the people who ended up doing so—and not that every life, or even most, is best fitted to be looking out for all of the other ones. Rather, it's the acknowledgement that their existences are about more than what they were being put to use doing. (Humanity, for its sake, would do well just to see more people happy with themselves).

More commonly, it's a battle with a major illness—personal or otherwise—or some kind of mortality-scraping accident that gets people to sit up and really take stock. Whatever and however difficult the impetus, so long as it gives rise to the thought about what you want to look back on your life and see when you're old and gray and gumming your food, then it's a blessing. Whether or not you ultimately get to that rocking chair, of course, is God's will; but it's by your own force that you create the medley of memories each day that you'd most like to keep you company.

As Ferris Bueller reminded us, if you don't stop and look around at life once in a while, you could miss it. (If only the world were more like John Hughes films). The reality, however, is that it takes untold amounts of strength and conviction to make sure you're with the right people and doing the right kind of work as the years go by. The cash and the prestige and all that "stuff"—it's so hollow and so very, very expensive. You only get so much time, after all, to create your life's meaning. And you only get so many days off.

on rock stars & lemmings

the rock star

A couple of years ago, I got a call at work from my old dorm roommate, Raymond Muñoz. Unshakably my closest friend (and I've tried), every three or four conversations he finds a way to get us reminiscing about some obscure episode or person from however many years back that he's managed to remember. We were well overdue at the time—and I certainly wasn't much interested in wiping the client's nose anymore that day—so I was glad to welcome in his nonchalant mention of an old mutual friend of ours named Brad.

Brad was one of those now-and-again type of college buddies who you'd only run into once or twice a term, but would always get a kick out of seeing. He was forever involved in putting together some sort of event, promoting his band, performing at a local club, or even doing work on a music video shoot or movie set. The guy had a quiet energy to him that you just wanted to be around, so no story really came as a surprise; although it never did seem to stop me from imposing the customary song and dance about him landing a good corporate gig.

You see, Brad wasn't just connected, but *smart*—which isn't exactly a prerequisite in the entertainment industry. To my way of thinking, he was grossly misspending his generous brainpower with all of that underpaying noise, foregoing what was sure to be a brilliant career in Big Business. It was only too obvious I was wasting my breath (I still have an entrepreneurship book on my shelf, for instance, that he "loaned" me), but I felt compelled to put the idea out there regardless, as if I were somehow doing my part. In the end, though, Brad was just one of those people who was going to handle things his way, and you actually felt a little lucky to peer into his world when he drew the curtain back far enough.

So after Ray and I had a good laugh about this character from our past, he tells me to go get the most recent issue of *Rolling Stone*; apparently there was an article in there that I might be interested in. Since he refused to provide me with any further detail and I naturally refused to humor him, the subject was forgotten until I passed a newsstand later on that week. My curiosity getting the better of me, I begrudgingly picked up the magazine and easily thumbed through it, half-preparing one of my customary sarcasms for Ray the next time we spoke. Finding nothing especially remarkable, I was about to put the copy back down when something caught my eye. And then, after a cartoon-like double take, I nearly fell over.

Could it be? Could that possibly be him? Wait, let me check the caption…it is him! Once a big-haired, droopy-panted UCLA undergrad, there was a clean-headed, full-bearded Brad Delson alongside his band—a young, pierced-and-tattooed bunch called "Linkin Park." My first thought: I *knew* I should've stayed in touch!

While the unexpectedness of finding my old acquaintance in print was certainly jolting, I can't say it was altogether surprising. He was bound to do something like this; I'm sure he knew it all along, and I certainly would've guessed as much. And as I eyed over the piece, I found myself feeling oddly proud of the guy (to whom I'm just another face in the crowd today), and pretty fortunate to have known him when I did. In truth, I was also humbly gratified to see that he had continued to ignore people like me, who would've stamped out his life with a cookie-cutter. Now I can't be sure, but it's probably safe to say my advice back then wouldn't have sold over eight million records or earned a Grammy.

It's something that gets you thinking. In fact, I couldn't stop for weeks. The traditional path was about as ill fitting for Brad as his trousers, so what was I really hoping to accomplish with all my talk of conventionality and predictability and not wearing oversized headphones to work? How was it that I couldn't at least appreciate the same value and purpose that he saw in his pursuits, much as they quarreled with mine? En route, I also began to reflect on the other "Brads" that swept in and out of my life during those exploratory times. There were so many unique perspectives, talents, and gifts out there, and I wondered how many of them were eventually sold into the very story I was so staunchly advertising to this lead guitarist at heart. What about all the career freshmen who must've wearily succumbed to the pressure, and ended up at some technology company or professional services firm because it's what "made sense?" Even though it didn't.

And while I was reproachfully asking myself what kind of arrogant, self-indulgent mouthpiece I thought I was to be peddling a message that could potentially sabotage a person's dreams, I was all at once struck with an even more unsettling question: Who fed it to *me*?

the lemmings

I didn't even know what the Big Four (again, Six at the time) was until I met a girl named Kelly midway through my sophomore year of college. As is the impulse for many—arguably most—things men will do, I was trying earnestly to impress a date out of her, and unexpectedly found myself in competition with her ex. You see, *he* had an internship with Deloitte & Touche, and *they* pay in the 30s when you graduate (good at the time), and what are *your* plans?

Well, I was a psych major looking for an advanced degree, which meant that my near future was going to revolve pretty closely around dingy university laboratories, rats and mazes, preserved brains, and abject poverty. So, uh, can I call you?

Uh, no. But, too late, the wheels were already spinning: Within a week's time, I had picked up a specialization in business administration, and was slated to enroll in introductory accounting the very next quarter. Women.

My stroke of ego turned out to be a stroke of luck, however, as bean counting (taught by the masterful and widely-feared David Ravetch) is what ignited my love for commerce. And though passions have a tendency to sneak up on you in this way, my motivation for starting where I did couldn't have been more tainted and fouled: While I clearly didn't have any lasting affection for the intrigues of perception and cognition, I believe I would've followed the money—or very seriously considered it—even if I saw a real future for myself in psychology. Even if my heart leapt at the thought of schizophrenia and bipolar disorder. Even if I could've been a technical advisor for the therapy scenes on *The Sopranos*.

But as a college student, it can feel like there are only two roads to choose from: A straight and smooth footpath lined with a comforting throng of coeds and cash, or a winding and rocky backwoods trail dotted with "Beware of Poorness" signs and the occasional unshaven Greenpeace member. With only a pre-entry level perspective, however, it's difficult to see that the paved route eventually grows rough and snaking, and that the weaving course quietly uncurls, becoming even and level. The companionship there gets better and more hygienic, too, while the swarm of graduates grows frustrated and cramped, wishing they had read more M. Scott Peck.

It's probably why fewer than 5 percent of late twentysomethings report having found their calling—even after earning that supposedly rescuing MBA (a track boasting plenty of flat driveway asphalt itself). In fact, the percentage doesn't climb much higher as you ask people in their 30s and even their 40s, who are now so thick in the foot that turning around feels even heavier than holding the deceitful line. Which they don't realize has one last twist around the bend: dropping off one abrupt morning.

There's an old expression that says if everyone's headed in one direction, it's probably wrong. Nowhere is that principle better exemplified than here, with its followers most constructively (and amusingly) thought of as *lemmings*—you know, those miniature purple creatures all blindly following each other around, walking off of cliffs and going splat and whatnot. Everyone's under the impression that the guy in front of them knows where he's marching, so they just sort of amble along without any real questioning of the direction of things. (What the wee animal who actually tumbles off the ledge first is thinking, I still haven't quite figured out). To be a lemming, though, requires little contemplation and less courage, which helps explain the allure of the option: It's always plain who's in front of you, who's behind you, and where the whole line of you is pointed... Down.

With such a steady and mindless plodding forward, however, there's tremendous pressure to maintain a place in line. Should a lemming break rank—even for just a moment—they stand to lose their spot. That's a frightening prospect in this controlled little world, as everybody knows that the only thing worse than being a lemming is being a lemming who's been sent to the back of the line. So they relent, accept, and simply keep up.

Which is also why you can find big violet and green heaps of them at the bottoms of canyons and gulches. But they don't know that until they've actually plunged, in the meantime recruiting, recruiting, recruiting in order to validate their forfeited individuality and forsaken dreams. Or else whom would they trudge along in file with? That means too many freshly minted bachelor degrees get put to use "properly," as nascent lemmings scurry off to go join their respective queues, dumbly following whatever carrot is being dangled in front of them. And to be clear again, the problem isn't the carrot; it's that nobody turns around to see who's holding the stick.

the cliffs

As a career freshman, chances are you don't drive a luxury automobile, can't claim to own a home or a company, any real amounts of capital either, and don't even enjoy very good prospects for getting much of it anytime soon. And thank God.

They don't call them *trappings* of success without cause, and it's equally uncoincidental that Corporate America wags them so vigorously in front of their young employees. As Big Business anglers baited with clout, they cast their perceptions of the "right" car, the "right" house, the "right" clothes—and all of it right now. Since the work obviously isn't going to reel entry levelers back into the office every morning, companies hook them instead with these unending, supposedly sine qua non financial commitments. Break the contract and bear the financial and social penalties.

It's virtually unthinkable for the mass of older lemmings, who've wedged themselves nice and tight into that swarming pack over the years. No trotting away at this point, even if they wanted to (and that's not to say they'd even know how). Mark Albion ever-appropriately calls it "keeping your walking costs low," where you position yourself to drop most of whatever you've got when your passion leads you in a different—and probably less lucrative—direction. If you've got a host of monetary burdens, he explains, you aren't very nimble; you're tied down to the lifestyle you've bought into.

And as a young professional, there shouldn't be that much to let go of. The crux of the matter, really, is *accountability*, and right now the only person you're accountable to at the end of the day is you. After you get married, say, and have kids, buy a piece of property, open up a business, or fumble your way into any of life's other wheedling but worthwhile milestones, your interests are no longer separable from those whom you're committed to. Want to go get a doctorate in political science, for instance, and become a professor? So long as junior gets his braces. Cultivated a love for French cuisine and hunger for an apprenticeship in Paris? If you can close escrow, sell off your partnership interests, and persuade the spouse to take up a foreign language, bathe less, and start being sneeringly existential, then *bonne chance*!

One of the most under-regarded aspects of being a young worker, in fact, is its impermanence, its mobility. There are so many geographies, environments, lifestyles, and careers still to explore, to try out, to give a whirl, to dip your pinky toe into. With that much personal and professional change on deck, it's entirely impractical and self-defeating to sink your roots too deep. Otherwise, goals and dreams that were once within arm's reach suddenly become farflung, pie-in-the-sky sort of aspirations; a 30-year mortgage and a box of Pampers can roil even the narrowest of amendments to the plan, to be sure. Yet the beautiful freedom and simplicity in the temporary—one of college's informally taught lessons—is regrettably forgotten by grads almost as quickly as what it's like to go to the beach in the middle of a Wednesday afternoon.

Although they do seem to glom onto the concept amazingly well when trying to justify putting their passions on the backburner in favor of corporate lemminghood. You see, this is just something that they have to do "for now"—only until they can get enough money to do what they really want to. By then society won't be able to furrow their brow at them, because they'll have played the game long enough to amass all of the things that they're supposed to have, must own, simply can't live without.

Never mind that if they ever wriggle free, they'll have handed decades over to a work that's left them unfulfilled and aching for purpose. And never mind that by then their reserves of energy and ambition are going to be just about tapped out, as probably will their savings account. And definitely never mind the harrowing reception it's going to elicit from family, associates, and a cross-eyed society at large. Nope, at the tender age of 47 it's time to start living! As Berkshire Hathaway CEO and "Sage of Omaha" Warren Buffett remarks, "I always worry about people who say, 'I'm going to do this for ten years; I really don't like it very well. And then I'll do this...' That's a little like saving up sex for your old age." Everything's an investment when you think about it.

Musicians seem to instinctively know that. And while the rock and rap sort do have a reputation for abusing most of the people and things in their lives (including themselves), you've still got to give them credit for the astonishingly limited amount of BS they put up with. Sure, they may not much care for sleeping on tour buses or horse-trading with their record label, but there's scarcely one out there that's not living their dream in writing, recording, and performing their songs—which is what they spend most of their working time doing (next to the stuff that lands them on *Behind the Music*). And as far as the integrity of their craft is concerned, a true artist would never willingly put out an album he or she didn't believe in, whatever the payday.

So maybe there are two roads: to be a lemming or a Rock Star. It's an oversimplification, obviously, yet the most straightforward approaches do tend to work the best. And not that any of us will ever see heavy rotation on MTV or a heavy statuette on our mantle, but most true-to-life callings don't look like that anyway. Still, the young professional's mindset measures up against the Rock Star's unpredictably well; and when used as inspiration, can produce results unpredictably good. Results like, well, Brad.

making your music

Creating your harmony at the entry level, then, is made up of three basic chords:

- Play the first note.
- Keep writing your songs.
- Perform even when they don't cheer.

play the first note

Leaving the hard sciences to the harder-headed, I partially ducked my college general education requirements with a course colloquially known as "Physics for Poets"—probably the only such class since Newton got his noggin rattled by a Red Delicious to offer take-home exams. So isn't it interesting that I'm now drawing from there to discuss the greatest force acting against career freshmen, *inertia*, and quoting Shakespeare to introduce it.

"To climb steep hills requires a slow pace at first," muses Stratford-upon-Avon's hometown-boy-made-good (and probably with some indecorous double-entendre). Nonetheless, it's advice well taken for anyone facing a long journey: to favor a deliberate and measured pace over the quick dash – early flameout approach. But for young professionals, to whom the trek for passion can feel more like a Sisyphean game of push-the-stone, it doesn't seem to matter how careful the trip up is; eventually they're chasing the thing back down again. So many choose simply to avoid the mound altogether, opting to get tuckered-out like everyone else—on the couch.

And safe as that may sound, there's more going on under those cushions than loose change and dirty magazines. It's a very dangerous thing, understand, to casually get good at a job you don't like, as the success that follows will keep you fastened to it (saying nothing of the sticky accouterments). How many people out there, after all, just sort of "fell into" their line of work, and now can't get up? You'll begin to earn the necessary know-how to do whatever it is you want to do, instead, only as soon as you actually start doing it, making the entry level (with semantic curiosity) the ideal entry point. All it takes is that one person at that one company on that one day to let you in. And not throw you right back out.

Something inertia is also dead-set against. Movement at the start is most often goadingly gradual, progressing just scant feet at the time in certain spots. Lengthy hours of research and investigation can commonly turn up few leads and fewer hairs on your head. Plus the initial chances that do present themselves may be no great shakes, or dead-end after only a short time, meaning that the trawling has to continue for better exposure. And after getting that closer look, you may yet decide that the field really isn't for you, sending the boulder rolling right back down to the foot of the mountain. Which, of course, can be blamed on physics.

But this is how dreams usually translate into reality: a lot of exploration and heartache and shoving rocks around until things get going. In the interim, however, you do an incredible amount of growing and learning, gaining a better sense of who you are and what you want to get out of your career. Opportunities, in retrospect, are always perfectly timed to match your professional and personal circumstances—including those that involve an off-brand company, a pay cut, a lateral or downward move, or any of those other nervous strides. So long as you keep pushing, fighting, and climbing, *momentum* builds, and that's what's going to carry you forward; inertia only likes to hang out with those blubbery bodies staying at rest.

And no one becomes a Rock Star overnight. Even the best have to earn their following gig-by-gig, initially performing at tiny venues for next to no money, just waiting for the right face in the crowd to discover them. For many, it takes some lean, hard years. Yet it's also the only way to make yourself known, to get people excited, to really reach your fans—when chances to play bigger and better spots start to open up all by themselves. Plus one night that right face pops up, too. But everything begins with getting up on stage and playing the first note, sacrificing the security of the sofa, following your heart step after arduous step.

It's not a life of guarantee (although ask a "downsized" corporateer, and they'll probably tell you the same thing about the Fortune 500 trail), and not every story is one of blinding success. Still, there's not a single life in the lot either that's haunted by the thought of what could have been. And all along the way, Rock Stars get to do something they love, define the rules, leave their mark. Even if it never does lead to a life of glamour and excess, is that really such a bad way to spend your numbered days here? Personally, I know I'd rather be poor doing my own thing than rich doing somebody else's. And that's probably not a tradeoff I'll ever have to make. Nor you.

keep writing your songs

Estimates are that by your early 20s, you will have heard the word "can't" 25,000 times. Unluckily, whereas the majority of input will pass unmolested from one ear to the other with kids and teenagers, this is one that seems to stick. Maybe because youth centers so closely on being told what to do—and especially what not to—that it almost becomes second nature. Or maybe as children, we buy into the idea that because the adults in our lives haven't pulled it off, it's not possible. Or maybe we just want to keep an updated tally of all the stuff that's going to give the old man an ulcer.

Whatever the case, it's a message most career freshmen *can't* seem to get past. Should the door be slammed on their dreams even once, they're generally all too ready to concede it as deadbolted, sullenly turning around to the steadiest paycheck. When looking at the figures, though, even the hulky corporations to which they then relegate themselves only make a sale to about a quarter of the customers they pitch—and that's during a good season. So if firms wrote-off a top target client after only one declination, we'd probably be talking about the Fortune 15 and the Big One. (And maybe I should've tried harder with Kelly)?

There certainly wouldn't be a Starbucks. "In the course of the year I spent trying to raise money, I spoke to 242 people," recalls founder Howard Schultz, who was trying to capture the Seattle java shop and grow his little Il Giornale coffeehouse into the brewing behemoth it is today, "and 217 of them said 'no.' Try to imagine how disheartening it can be to hear that many times why your idea is not worth investing in." (And try to imagine the bruises they've since inflicted on themselves).

There wouldn't be a Pure Play Press either. Starting a publishing house, in truth, wasn't exactly my first idea; really, it came to me only after the first 27 major publishers passed on this book. Considering that there are roughly, oh, 27 major publishers who print this kind of material—or, rather, don't—I decided that a couple dozen editors-on-high in New York weren't going to be the final arbiters of my passion. And as a result, I'm now not only a grateful independent author who's kept full creative control over his work (and substantially more than a 10 or 15 percent royalty), but one positioned to bring other fresh and important voices to market. Maybe one of the 32 literary agents who also turned me down might even want to submit a manuscript.

But achievement doesn't come in spite of disappointments; it happens *because* of them. When properly leveraged, a letdown offers a stronger sense of how to better approach the next time, and that's one less potential mistake and heartbreak. Loving your work, too, also means loving the daily drudgery and setbacks that tangle it up at the ankles—as most wins are small and most lurches backward. Even the profession that stirs you up from the inside is going to tear you to pieces at times; it's the knowledge you're pursuing your truth that ultimately holds you together.

Plus it only hurts for so long. "The pain is temporary. It may last a minute, or an hour, or a day, or a year, but eventually it subsides," promises cancer survivor and repeated Tour de France champion Lance Armstrong. "And when it does, something else takes its place, and that thing might be called a greater space for happiness." Yet an inordinate number of young professionals are stifling their dreams for fear of falling, or getting their egos slapped around, or having their confidence mugged. They're abandoning the strength and assurance that come from bleeding and mending, but in favor of the easy protection of the corporate security blanket. And they're doing it when all their passion really wants is a little backbone and some staying power.

The situation almost mirrors the life of a stonecutter (a man Sisyphus could've used), who hammers away at a rock maybe 100 times without even a crack forming. To the untutored onlooker, the exercise seems futile and dusty besides. But on the 101st blow, sure enough that oversized mineral splits in two. Then the dirt doesn't taste so bad. Importantly, the final strike is no more valuable than the hundred others that come before it; in fact, there would be no final strike at all without its predecessors. Each one plays an equally significant part in the process, amalgamating to loosen things up until the circumstances can finally be broken open.

And sometimes the stone is an unpredictably hard one, taking perhaps twice as many whacks as expected to get it in half. What your obstinate persistence does here is hedge against the elements of timing and luck you can't control for—making sure your chipping cycle eventually moves you through whatever seemingly impenetrable igneous thing you've hunkered down on. Thomas Jefferson, in fact, was a great believer in luck, noting, "I find that the harder I work, the more I have of it." Indeed, chance tends to favor the pushy and the busy, which means being a whole lot of both at the entry level.

Because the people who find their calling in this world aren't necessarily the ones with the most talent or experience (which they'll usually be the first to admit), but rather those who refuse to stop working until they get what they're after. Your dream may not have a job description, for example, or the market may not understand it yet, or you may be looking at more professional or personal growth before moving forward, or whatever. There's almost sure to be some sort of hindrance. But when things are left to their own devices to open up, they generally just end up wasting their time with that bad influence inertia.

Passionate career freshmen, instead, hunt down a position that satisfies as many elements of their vision as possible, and then work from there to fully build it into reality. Perhaps they try to develop their idea from within a company (so-called corporate entrepreneurship), or they use their job experience and network of contacts to guide their outside endeavors, or maybe they even go back to school first to get the right skills and credentials. However it plays out, the point is that the dream leads the way, that a flexible plan is in force to bring it to fruition, and that the state of affairs is relentlessly challenged to ensure that it gets there.

Fulfillment, after all, doesn't just happen. Unlike "faith, wisdom, and romance" which "sometimes lie in wait for us," as genius humorist P.J. O'Rourke considers, "...happiness is the TV remote, the car key, the other earring of life." It takes some looking around, and in places you might not think of straight off. Those consigned to lemminghood, instead—waiting to providentially march across their joy one day— usually end up hoping all the way to the bottom.

And in this country, a place that's formally in pursuit of the stuff, it's inexcusable not to be digging on all fours. Most of us take for granted that, as U.S. citizens, we're pretty well free to shake the Invisible Hand without fear of being arbitrarily shot, jailed, or starved by our government—a luxury not widely enjoyed around the globe. In fact, (so long as we pay up every mid-April) Washington even pledges not to whimsically take our stuff away or unduly inhibit trade, safeguarding any commercial enterprise we might decide to undertake. Perhaps more than any other human beings on the planet, Americans have the greatest chance to find their bliss. How do we justify, then, handing all of this liberty and justice and self-determination back over to some overpaid, overfed, over-aged chief executive? They call that, in other nations, something else.

And even Rock Stars are under the gun over there. So, for all of its woes, the Entry Level of the United States is as good as it gets for self-styled career freshmen trying to break onto the scene. Which also means it's the place to keep pushing and fighting; it means practicing into the morning hours, playing with gashed and aching fingers; it means shoving that demo into every industry face you can find your way in front of; it means doing whatever it takes, as many times as it takes. I doubt even Brad's band earned their fateful appearance at the Whisky without some of that.

perform even when they don't cheer

Renowned philosopher Georg Hegel pronounced, "To be independent of public opinion is the first formal condition of achieving anything great." Although he also said, "What is rational is real and what is real is rational," so you can see how it might have been useful to disclaim his fellow Germans circling their index fingers around their temples.

Still, he was on to something. Just as college had its "proper" majors, so it is with careers, but more so. The idea of financial underabundance—even when begotten from a profession broadly regarded as important and meaningful—just doesn't digest with society. The satire, of course, is that if teaching, say, paid like venture capital, we'd have a run on textbooks and credential exams and, um, literacy. But it's much easier to be rich than righteous. (It's even easier to spell).

So the less remunerative pursuits of graduates continue to earn a collective group frown, and none more puckered than from the folks. Naturally, mom and dad want to see their children follow their hearts; they recoil, however, at the idea of them being marginalized by the public. Of course they want to watch their pride-and-joy's dreams come to life—but they also want them to stop asking for money. In a way you've got to sympathize.

Yet not with the result, which is a twist that parents put on their expectations for the offspring's happiness: Make it *their* version of happy. This time around it's got the baby-boomer bent, as they frantically try to impart their mid-20th-century dogma of stability, conservatism, and professional safety on the kids. When predictably unsuccessful, these former hippies and flower children then forgetfully accuse the fruit-of-the-loin of having grown up "impractical" and "dreamy" through the comforts of their childhood. Which, if I'm not mistaken, is exactly what they set out to provide them with.

Nonetheless, studies have it that the millennial generation is looking to their upbringers for support and approval more than any other in recent history. So when career freshmen call up father-dearest for encouragement to chase their passion, they're more likely instead to get an earful of hackneyed oratory about endurance, dependability, responsibility, or any of those other things he didn't have much of until his late 30s. "If I ran around following my *passion*," it goes, "you wouldn't have had food on the table or a roof over your head." And for about half it continues, "Plus your mother and I probably would've separated much sooner than we did."

Yet it does work out that supervisory part of their job is more or less over at the entry level; the folks, rather, become much more like consultants. And the great thing about consultants (other than seeing them head off to the airport) is that you can take or leave their advice—nothing's binding. It may be an expensive opinion, sure, but really just one among many. Plus it usually makes the least sense out of all of them.

Of course the yearning for parental approval is one that follows most people throughout life (usually undeservedly), and the tendency to placate the folks' wishes can be particularly strong should they still hold the purse strings. But you're also in a position now to legitimately assert a certain autonomy, whatever the situation; your age, diploma, and professional prospects command it (as does the measured play on the empty nest syndrome, and maybe an offhand comment here and there about their relationships with their own parents). Besides, if they've managed to get that whole unconditional love thing down, you could probably screw around for the next 10 years like Kurt Vonnegut says and have them ultimately be okay with the deal.

As we grow older, though, we come to believe the irrationality of our dreams, whatever the caregivers have to say. We find ourselves subscribing to those neatly defined societal boxes and categories, looking back on our childhood imaginings with blushed cheeks and weathered words. Yes, how silly to have wanted to be an actor or a dancer or a writer; it's not like you see any of those around. Playing out their fantasies. Living rewarding, worthwhile lives. On their terms. Damn shame.

And this rolling-over we all obediently practice doesn't even have clear origins—as if some permeating, Seinfeldian "they" have been around since antiquity telling people what to do. Certainly the names and faces have had pretty clear definition at times; but it's always been at the fore of a quieter, much more powerful groundswell of neighborly pressure. Perhaps Jerry was asking a better question than assumed when he quipped, "Who *are* these people?"

But then look at whom we give awards to and reflect upon in our chronicles—certainly not business analysts or brokers or lemmings of that stripe. No, we celebrate and remember human rights advocates and artists and the Rock Stars who break the rules to make our lives richer and more worthwhile. They sneeze defiantly on the mandate, and we offer them a tissue. Perhaps it's that we're all nonconformists deep down, looking to vicariously strike out through whomever will allow us to. Yet how is it that a go-between should end up living anyone's passion for them? Since when does the courage to find life's calling require an agent? After all, they're just out making their own way in the world—and really don't care, quite frankly, what you think about it.

As Nietzsche said, "Those who have a *why* can endure any *how*." That's where the strength comes from. That's how you survive through the early years of frustration, struggle, and derision. That's what brings you a lifetime of fulfillment, success, and respect. That's why they'll cheer for you when it's your turn.

But you don't get on stage for anyone's admiration: You're a Rock

Star, and you're going to do it your way no matter who's watching. They don't applaud because you need them to; they applaud because you give them no choice. Now go make your music.

inde

a

index

f

index

h

Hall, Anthony Michael, 77
Hambrecht and Quist (J.P. Morgan
    H&Q), 210
Handspring, Inc., 121
Handy, Charles, 199
happiness:
    Americans' opportunity for, 261–262
    as a graduated adult, 41
    decisions and, 28
    from fighting through pain, 260
    passionate work and, 198
    persistence required to find, 261–262
    through learning, 97
Harlem Renaissance, 93
Harvard Business Review, 43, 173, 218
Harvard Business School, 90, 197, 219
Harvard University, 43, 61, 198, 218
headhunters, *see* recruiters
Hegel, Georg Wilhelm Friedrich, 262
Heller, Joseph, 244
Herman Miller, Inc., 133
Hewlett, Walter, 239
Hewlett-Packard Company, 146, 239
hiring practices, 20, 45, 46–47, 51, 54,
    55, 58–59, 83, 135–136, 171
Holmes, Oliver Wendell, 206
Honeywell International, Inc., 61, 83
How They Achieved (Watson), 8, 90
Hughes, John, 247
humility:
    development of, 60–63
    during performance reviews, 163–164
    effects of, 62, 87

in executives, 61–62, 121
Hungry Spirit, The (Handy), 199
Hurston, Zora Neale, 93, 98
"hypermaterialism," 235

i

IBM (International Business Machines
    Corporation), 146, 227
idealism, 19–20, 178, 235, 239
identity (personal), 39–41, 43, 182
impression management, 149, 162, *see
    also* accountability
individuality, 84, 253
inheritors, 241
initiatives:
    acceptance by management of, 161,
        162
    benefits of, 156
    business cases and, 157–159
    impact of, 163
    in teams, 85–86
    limits to, 156–157
    priorities and, 156
    purpose of, 161–162
    selection of, 101–102, 144, 155–156,
        160
    spurning by management of, 160–161
    theft of, 161, 162
Intel Corporation, 223
interests (personal):
    effects of lacking, 177, 184
    importance of, 183, 184
    surrendering of, 174
internships, 42, 45, 53, 62, 83, 128,

index

index

index

y

z